Child Care and Public Policy

Child Care and Public Policy

Studies of the Economic Issues

Edited by

Philip K. Robins
Samuel Weiner
SRI International

Lexington Books
D.C. Heath and Company
Lexington, Massachusetts
Toronto

Library of Congress Cataloging in Publication Data
Main entry under title:

Child care and public policy.

Includes index.
1. Day care centers—United States—Economic aspects—Case studies.
2. United States—Social policy. I. Robins, Philip K. II. Weiner, Samuel,
1932—
HV854.C44   362.7'1   77-17724
ISBN 0-669-02088-5

Published simultaneously in Canada.

Printed in the United States of America.

International Standard Book Number: 0-669-02088-5

Library of Congress Catalog Card Number: 77-17724

Contents

Foreword

As chairman of the Senate Subcommittee on Child and Human Development, I welcome this volume and its attempt to present some of the economic and public policy issues related to child care. *Child Care and Public Policy: Studies of the Economic Issues* provides data and analysis for a number of questions that have been too long ignored in the child care debate.

Although direct and indirect funding by the federal government for child care amounted to about $2.5 billion dollars during the last fiscal year, many parents who need child care cannot find it at a price they can afford or cannot find adequate care at all; child care providers have long waiting lists but are unable to expand their programs because of a lack of available funds; and those trying to start new programs are often confronted with a bureaucratic maze that would defy the skill of any navigator.

It is clear that we need to re-examine closely the role of the federal government in child care and determine what changes should be made to make the current federal involvement more responsive to the needs of families who require child care services. I expect that the material collected here will be a valuable resource in this endeavor. The authors have brought an economic and historical perspective to many of the important questions that will confront legislators and other policy makers in the years ahead as they assess the need and consider alternative designs for future legislation involving child care.

March 1978

Senator Alan Cranston
Chairman
U.S. Senate Subcommittee on
Child and Human Development

Preface

The studies presented in this book represent recent research undertaken on several important economic and policy-related issues of child care. Most of the work was performed by economists using, not unexpectedly, an economic perspective. Up to the present, only a small proportion of the literature on child care has been written from an economic perspective. We hope, therefore, that this book will contribute to a broader understanding of the issues that need to be considered in any discussion of proposed changes in the size and composition of the child care sector.

In a field that has historically been the preserve of educators, psychologists, sociologists, and social workers, economists would be prudent to enter and tread carefully. This can be done, in part, by a clear understanding and acknowledgment of the relative importance of the sociopsychological aspects of child care. However, it is critical that the importance of those aspects does not lead one to neglect the economic considerations. By presenting these research findings, concerned primarily with the economics of child care, we hope to help promote a balanced view of the issues surrounding child care.

The studies reported on in this book involved the efforts of many people other than the individual authors. Most of the research was supported by contracts with agencies of the federal government. The research reported in Chapters 3, 4, 7, and 8 was performed pursuant to contracts with the states of Washington and Colorado, prime contractors for the Department of Health, Education and Welfare (HEW), Washington, D.C., under SRI Project URD-8750/1190. The opinions expressed in those chapters are those of the authors and should not be construed as representing the opinions or policies of the states of Washington or Colorado or any agency of the federal government.

We wish to express a special debt of gratitude to Robert G. Spiegelman, who reviewed most of the research undertaken for this book, and to Marcellus L. Henderson, who was instrumental in getting us to coordinate these chapters into a single book. The authors of Chapter 2 are grateful to Sheldon Bloom, Jane Gold, Gertrude Hoffman, and Lyn Wolff of HEW for their critical review of an earlier version. The authors of chapters 3, 7, and 8 are indebted to Gail Inderfurth, Lois Blanchard, Janey Elliott, and Tony Muller of Mathematica Policy Research, who helped prepare the interviews and collect data; Christine Decker and Barbara Ferber, who monitored the survey operation; and David Grembowski and Jarvis Rich, who provided invaluable computational assistance. The authors of Chapter 4 acknowledge the computational assistance of Steven Spickard and helpful comments by Michael Keeley, Mordecai Kurz, Terry Johnson, and Richard West.

Child Care and Public Policy

1

An Introduction to the Economic and Policy Issues of Child Care
Philip K. Robins and *Samuel Weiner*

Many groups support a large-scale expansion of the child care sector,* along with a sharp increase in federal involvement in that sector. Others are opposed to any expansion of the child care sector and argue that child care should be kept within the family if at all possible. Between those who favor a rapidly expanded, universally available, system of child care and those who want child care to be a system of last resort are those who feel that adequate child care should be available in whatever form it is desired by users, and that government should not dictate through fiscal policies the particular modes to be used, nor should the government attempt to foster comprehensive development programs.

The arguments for and against each of these positions are often based on research and analysis concerned with the effect of extra family child care on the child's emotional, physical, and cognitive development. This book, however, attempts to present research and analysis of the economic and public-policy issues that should also be considered in any discussion of the role of child care. Heretofore research and analysis related to economic issues have been grossly neglected. In the first section of this chapter we briefly review research that has been concerned with the child's emotional, cognitive, and physical development; the second section is devoted to a discussion of the economic issues of child care; the third section summarizes the remaining chapters in this book; and the final section presents conclusions and a prognosis.

Research Concerned with Emotional, Cognitive, and Physical Development

Professionalization of child care, which received its first big push after World War I when social workers became involved in that field, spurred research in child care. In the early period that research focused on the "maladjusted" families that provided, it was assumed, the bulk of child care users.[1] The basis of the maladjustment was usually thought to be the absence of a father or economic or emotional difficulties that prevented full-time care from being provided to the child by its parents. Research resulting from this view emphasized

---

*Throughout this book the terms *child care* and *day care* are used interchangeably.

1

family adjustment to adverse social and economic conditions and the role of child care in the adjustment process. The research undertaken was generally anecdotal or based on case workers' records.

However, another line of research carried on by psychologists during, and since, that period was more scientifically structured.[2] Most prominent of these researchers were Jean Piaget, Jerome Bruner, and J. McViker Hunt. They were instrumental in showing the importance of cognitive development in the first five years of a child's life. These research findings have been, and are still, used to support the need for developmental child care programs during the preschool years.[3]

Similarly, others in the field of human development have investigated the causes and effects of being raised in a socioeconomically disadvantaged environment. On the basis of their research, they have consistently promoted programs that would compensate children for what was lacking in their home environments, with day care becoming an increasingly attractive framework within which such compensatory developmental stimulation can be promoted.

What we find is that up to the present, the need for day care based on adverse economic and social conditions within which the family operates has continued to be of prime importance. Furthermore, over time research concerning the effect of these conditions has shifted to include a wider representation from educators, psychologists, and sociologists. It has been due to the influx of researchers in these fields that the orientation regarding day care as a factor in ameliorating the "maladjusted" family condition has been pushed. Increasingly, they have stressed the need for developmental, mental as well as physical, care to compensate for the deficiencies found in a deprived family environment.[4]

More recently, some opposition to the preceding view on cultural deprivation and its implication for early childhood programs has surfaced. In general this opposition has disputed the need and/or desirability of an expansion of so-called high quality day care center operations, which are supported largely by federal funds.[5] However, the bulk of the research to date still supports the need for developmental programs in day care settings. Moreover, a distinguished advisory committee on child development recently presented an agenda for public policies for children. Among the recommendations offered were two for day care, which, if implemented, would have a major economic impact. Their first recommendation was that alternative forms of day care should be available for all those who need and/or desire such care, and that those services should be free of cost to users. Their other day care recommendation was that whatever care is promoted by the government should meet minimum standards, and these standards should be based on what researchers have found to be needed for high-quality care.[6]

What comes through clearly from this brief review of the research and writing to date on day care is that it has been concerned almost exclusively with developmental issues—cognitive, emotional, and physical. What has been most conspicuously missing is comparable research and analysis of the economic issues involved.[7] At best, what is normally found are estimates of the costs of various types of day care services. This is not to say that costs are not relevant or important, nor that economic issues are of paramount importance in the controversy over the place of day care in public policies. The effect of day care upon the family and the child are clearly the primary concerns. But if a significant change in public responsibility for financing the day care sector, either through direct subsidies or indirect tax schemes, is envisioned, we need to pay more attention to the economic implications of that choice.

Economic Justification of Government Intervention

From an economic point of view, government intervention is justified if the private market does not fully take account of private *and* social benefits or costs; that is, in many instances the production or consumption of a good or service affects others than those directly involved in the transaction. This generates externalities, i.e., benefits or costs that are external to the parties involved in the transaction and not paid for in a market. In the case of social benefits, where the private market does not compensate those producing the external effects, the absence of government intervention would mean that the commodity in question is not optimally produced or consumed. In general, if there are external benefits, then output should be increased beyond what it would be simply in response to market demand; whereas in the presence of external costs, output, from the social viewpoint, should be reduced. Intervention would then be justified on the basis of economic efficiency.

Education has typically been viewed as a good with significant externalities. Many benefits accrue to society because of the existence of an educated populace. It has been shown that education benefits the individual receiving it, both as an investment as well as a consumption good. Consequently, it is possible to price educational services on the basis of the private benefits received. However, there are other social benefits in terms of reduced crime, increased productivity from other than the individual involved, or other factors such as health that are correlated with increased education. Therefore, governments are justified in subsidizing the service in order to reap these social benefits. This argument is being used for expanding the role of government in financing child care. If the argument for day care presented in the preceding section is correct, i.e., that child care can be a compensating factor for disadvantaged children, then the externalities inherent in the provision of child care justifies governmental support. Moreover, if developmental care generates the educational benefits suggested above, then the social benefits from this source reinforces the justification for governmental support of developmental child care in order to increase output.

Whatever the justification, if governmental support of child care is warranted, an understanding of the economic implications of that support is needed. Knowledge of the demand as well as the supply characteristics of the child care market will enable policymakers to allocate funds into that sector more efficiently.

Considerations Relevant to the Economics of Child Care

Although there is no unique, formal theoretical model available for understanding the economics of child care, child care can be viewed from an economic perspective as an industry consisting of a large number of sellers of a differentiated product, whether that differentiation is due to location or actual service differences. Using that perspective, we can examine the supply and demand relationships existing in that industry, and we can discuss price, quantity, and quality adjustments found in the market for child care services.[8] However, such a view is likely to elicit howls of pain from child care advocates and cries of outrage from child development experts. In many ways that pain and those cries would certainly be justified; for although we can in many ways view child care as an industry, it has some very unique characteristics. Those unique characteristics make it necessary to emphasize the fact that the economics of child care is only a partial, very limited view of that activity.

Although it is only one of the relevant components to consider, the economics of child care should not be neglected, nor relegated to a secondary role. This section presents some of the relevant considerations. Of prime importance are the price elasticities of supply and demand, which indicate how supply and demand respond to changes in the price of child care services. Other considerations include defining what is meant by a unit of child care services, as well as conditions of entry and pricing policy. One important consideration is that providers, especially in-home and family day care home (FDCH) but also center staff, often care for their own children or children of close relatives at the same time that they provide paid care for nonrelated children. This means that the operator is providing a joint product, consisting of paid care for nonrelatives and unpaid care for their own children.[9] There is clearly some value to be attributed to the care provided for their own children.[10] Since no money is exchanged, this value is often ignored. However, the total revenue of such a provider should be increased to take account of the nonmonetized value of services provided to their children. If that were done, we could easily imagine an acceptable long-run adjustment where many providers were not covering (monetized) marginal costs.[11]

The idea of joint products has another dimension that is brought about because child care services consist of custodial and educational-developmental components provided at the same time. In any market adjustment process we would have to decompose price, quantity, and quality effects into those two components of child care. Over the long run, adjustments to changes in price, quantity, and quality may be quite different for providers whose cost functions are heavily weighted with an educational-developmental component.

Another important factor is that child care costs, if they fall on someone using the service in order to work, would reduce the user's net wage, which is a critical variable in the labor-force participation decision. A public subsidy of child care would, therefore, counteract the negative effect resulting from this reduction in the net wage.

Public subsidies can also affect the price of the service being subsidized. Knowledge of the price elasticity of the supply of child care would help to determine the extent to which a public subsidy would, given the change in demand, result in simple price adjustments or lead to an actual change in quantity or quality. Therefore, whatever information we can obtain regarding the price elasticity of supply would be very useful. One way of getting that information is to obtain reliable estimates of the cost functions for child care services. In order to obtain these cost functions, we would have to determine all costs of production. This includes not only the current labor or equipment and supply costs, but also properly apportioned capital costs. It also means that the imputed monetary value of donated time or supplies and equipment would be required. This is especially relevant for FDCH operators who often perform market and nonmarket activities at the same time; that is, while they care for their own children, for which no client money payment is made, they also provide paid child care for other children in their home. This creates the need to value both market and nonmarket activities, as was pointed out previously.

Since labor is the primary cost in all child care operations, the manner in which the market wage imputation problem is handled will have an important effect on the perceived economic viability of child care operations, especially noncenter operations. For example, it appears that FDCH operators, because of their low gross receipts, seem to be subsidizing child care users. It may be true that FDCH providers subsidize buyers of their service, in the sense that providers are not covering their total cost. However, it might also be true that an incorrect valuation of the services provided their own children means we have failed to add an indirect benefit to the wages received; that is, the nonmonetized benefits are not properly accounted for.

Another aspect of imputed costs concerns the voluntary services supplied, especially for centers, as well as the use of their own home for FDCH operators. In general, the value of volunteer services is simply the expected earnings that could be obtained by that individual if the time were spent in paid market activities. However, if the volunteer's child is enrolled in the center, as is often the case, an adjustment to the market wage will be needed to subtract the value of free child care time. The imputed cost of that volunteer labor would then be the expected earnings net of the adjustment.

Along with those costs, we must also face the issue of what appropriate measure of output to use in estimating cost equations. This is related to the activity mix provided children. At a minimum, the activities must be dichotomized into custodial and educational-developmental care. For each of these types of care, it would be useful to measure variations in the quality of services. This can be accomplished by fixing the quantity of services at some predetermined level in calculating total costs.

Related to the price elasticity of supply previously mentioned is the corresponding price elasticity of demand for child care services. Knowledge of that elasticity, determined by the demand for and price of child care services, helps us to estimate the effect of subsidies on demand for child care. Estimates of the supply *and* demand elasticities also help to determine equilibrium in the child care industry.

Another relevant area of concern in the economics of child care is entry barriers and the utilization of capacity within each sector of the industry. The issue of entry barriers is related to licensing requirements, zoning restrictions, and capital needs. If there were high barriers to entry, the industry would be less competitive and therefore less efficient in resource allocation. The utilization of capacity tells us something about the structure of the child care market, with less-competitive markets having a lower level of capacity utilization. *Capacity* here usually refers to the licensed upper limit on the number of children that can be cared for. However, *capacity* may also be defined to encompass consideration of the quality of service. For example, different child/staff ratios may reflect differences in quality rather than in capacity utilization.

Pricing policy is yet another important issue in the economics of the child care industry. It includes not only the fee charged per unit of service offered but also takes into consideration the quality of services provided. Related to the issue of price is the question of the relationship between prices charged and subsidies received. Furthermore, an adequate review of pricing practices would give us some insight into the extent of price competition in the day care industry.

Since we do not have a developed theoretical model applicable to the child care industry, we have reviewed issues of importance in the economics of child care. These are clearly not the only relevant considerations, but they are probably the most important. The studies examined in this book provide some understanding and analysis of these issues. To clarify our approach, as well as to provide a path through this book, the next section presents a summary of the remaining chapters.

Summary of the Studies in this Book

In Chapter 2, James Marver and Meredith Larson provide an overview of the types of child care services available to working parents and trace the historical development of federal child care policies in America. Recognizing the multi-faceted nature of the term *child care,* the authors review several approaches to defining child care. They argue that subjective approaches, which define child care in terms of provider intentions (e.g., distinguishing between custodial care and developmental care), are inherently ambiguous and considerably less appealing than objective approaches, which define child care in terms of the institutional setting in which care is provided. The authors define a continuum of child care types that range from full-time public preschools and intensive day care centers, which have large enrollments, to child care by a family member, which usually involves only one or two children. This approach to defining child care is useful from both a research and policy perspective and is adopted by several of the other authors of this book.

Having defined child care, Marver and Larson present some statistics on utilization rates of the various types of child care. Like others, they find that the majority of children of working parents are cared for at home by a member of the family. This type of care, in-home, is used by more than 80 percent of the families with working parents. Day care centers, which are often the focus of public-policy discussions, are used by less than 2 percent of the families.

Marver and Larson then discuss current federal involvement in child care, which is of two types—direct and indirect subsidization. Direct subsidization consists primarily of federal funds (e.g., Title XX monies) distributed to states on various matching bases, with the funds being used to directly support child care programs. Indirect subsidization occurs through work-expense provisions of the positive income tax system and various public transfer programs, such as Aid to Families with Dependent Children (AFDC), Food Stamps, and Public Housing. Under these programs, subsidization occurs because child care expenses are reimbursed or taxes are lowered for users who generally have the option of selecting the type of child care desired. Most programs only partially reimburse child care expenses, although some (such as AFDC) provide full reimbursement. Most paid forms of child care are eligible for indirect subsidization.

Federal involvement in child care did not occur suddenly; indeed it dates back to the Civil War. Since that time there have been frequent changes in public attitudes toward child care. These changes have followed a predictable pattern. During wartime periods, child care is highly regarded, primarily because full employment of the labor force is viewed as essential. During postwar periods and periods of economic prosperity, child care is viewed as a social stigma and women are encouraged to stay in the home. During periods of economic hardship, federal expenditures on child care are used to stimulate employment. It is clear from Marver and Larson's description that child care represents not only an end in itself, but also is a tool for other economic, political, or social ends.

The authors conclude their survey by outlining possible courses of action for the federal government. First, the government can move toward greater direct support and sponsorship of day care facilities. Second, a universal system of indirect subsidies through, say, a voucher system can be instituted. Third, a mixed system, similar to what exists today, can be maintained and expanded. The authors emphasize that in any case, the current ad hoc policymaking process needs better information and analysis regarding market structure, consumer preferences, quality of care, and the interrelations with other social and economic policies.

In Chapter 3, Samuel Weiner presents an economic analysis of the supply of child care services in two major Western cities of the United States: Seattle, Washington and Denver, Colorado. Based on a survey of child care providers taken during 1974 in conjunction with the Seattle and Denver Income Maintenance Experiments (SIME/DIME),[12] Weiner studies the structure of the child care markets in the two cities. For purposes of analysis, he divides the child care market into two sectors: a formal sector consisting of day care centers and licensed family day care homes and an informal sector consisting of unlicensed family day care homes and in-home providers.

Several interesting conclusions emerge from Weiner's study. First, there do not appear to be substantial barriers to entry into the child care markets of Seattle and Denver. Day care centers, and perhaps family day care homes, require capital investment, but the amount is probably less than that required of most small businesses. Moreover, the licensing and zoning requirements for formal sector providers are not particularly onerous. Second, the supply of informal child care services appears to be price elastic. Virtually all the input costs to the informal sector are labor costs, and there is considerable empirical evidence that the supply of female labor is wage elastic. Third, there is some evidence that the child care markets in Seattle and Denver operate with excess capacity, despite the existence of waiting lists at many facilities. Fourth, between 10 and 20 percent of total child care time in the informal sector is spent in educational-developmental (as opposed to custodial) activities, while in the formal sector almost one-third of the time is spent in such activities. While this would appear to imply that the "quality" of child care is greater in the formal sector, intersectoral comparisons of quality are difficult to make because (1) differences in the characteristics of the providers (i.e., education, wage rate, age, etc.) may lead to differences in the quality of educational-developmental care between sectors, and (2) differences in staff/child ratios may lead to differences in the quality of custodial care between sectors. Fifth, and perhaps the most important finding of Weiner's study, direct subsidization of child care does not appear to lead to a reduction in the cost of child care to the user. Although Weiner acknowledges the possibility that the subsidies are used to upgrade the quality of child care provided, as a means of reducing the cost of child care to the user, direct subsidization does not appear to be economically efficient. Indirect subsidies, combined with greater regulation or stricter enforcement of existing regulations, would probably be more efficient.

In Chapter 4, Philip Robins and Robert Spiegelman specify an econometric model of the demand for child care in which the choice of child care mode depends on price, income, and other socioeconomic characteristics of the family and its members. In the empirical analysis, three modes of child care are distinguished: formal market care, informal market care, and nonmarket care. As previously mentioned, formal market care includes day care centers and licensed family day care homes, while informal market care includes all other paid forms of child care. Nonmarket care includes all nonpaid forms of child care. The authors assume a competitive child care market and measure variation in prices in a cross section by differences in subsidy rates available to families.

The authors obtain several interesting results from their empirical analysis. First, the demand for market forms of child care is estimated to be price elastic: formal market care has a greater price elasticity than informal market care. Second, the demand for market care increases with the wage rate of the mother. As in the case of price, the estimated wage elasticity is greater for formal market care. Third, the demand for market child care varies systematically with family structure. In families with only younger children (under 5 years of age), the utilization rate of market care is estimated to be about 70 percent. In families with only older children (between the ages of 6 and 12), the utilization rate is estimated to be about 50 percent. If a teenager or other adult is present in the household, the estimated utilization rate of market care drops to 20 percent.

One of the most elusive concepts in research on child care is *quality*. Not only is quality difficult to define (the definition has changed considerably since World War II), it is also difficult to measure. In "Quality of Child Care: Can It Be Measured?" Jane Stallings and Mary Wilcox describe the use of new observation instruments they and their colleagues have developed to determine the quality of child care. To motivate their research, Stallings and Wilcox present a brief summary of the shift in public opinion that has occurred since World War II regarding "quality" child care. Prior to and just after World War II, quality child care was equated with nurturing programs that usually did not include an educational-development component. Institutional care (the day care center) was viewed as leading to social and emotional ills, as well as alienation from parents. During the 1960s, the concern was for the cognitive development of children and programs such as Head Start were initiated. However, several studies undertaken during the 1970s suggested that cognitive development for young children does not seem to have any lasting educational value. The concept of quality was consequently expanded to encompass social, emotional, and physical growth aspects of children's lives, as well as the cognitive aspects.

The actual quality of care provided children, however, remained an elusive concept. The difficulty of obtaining a measure of that concept was, as pointed out in Chapter 5, that no one was able to capture how care givers actually interact with children. Stallings and Wilcox describe four newly developed observation instruments that can systematically record provider/child interactions. The ability of these instruments to measure child care quality is being tested in a national sample of day care centers and family day care homes.

There is considerable debate among policymakers regarding the appropriate mechanism for subsidizing the delivery of child care services. Some favor direct methods of subsidization, while others favor indirect methods. One of the more attractive indirect methods of subsidization is a voucher system. In Chapter 6, Susan Stoddard describes a pilot study conducted in Santa Clara County, California between July 1975 and July 1977 that tested a voucher system for child care. In its purest form, a voucher system gives the consumer complete freedom of choice in purchasing a particular commodity. In the Santa Clara County Child Care Pilot Study, however, only licensed forms of child care were eligible to be subsidized. Nevertheless, the Santa Clara project, which was the first of its kind in the nation, has provided policymakers and child care researchers with a wealth of data on child care use and preferences.

Like most voucher schemes, the Santa Clara County project scaled the subsidy with family income. The subsidy rate ranged from 100 percent for families with low incomes to 20 percent for families with high incomes. The subsidies were subject to a maximum allowable amount, and eligibility for the subsidies was not limited by income. For the first year, subsidy recipients were selected on a random basis. After the first year, all eligible applicants were accepted into the program. Thus, all residents of Santa Clara County with at least one child under 15 years of age were eligible to apply and receive a minimum subsidy of 20 percent of their child care costs.

The Santa Clara County Child Care Pilot Study distributed approximately $2.1 million in subsidies during its two years of operation. Approximately 75 percent of the providers were family day care homes. About one-fifth of the total licensed day care slots and one-tenth of the total licensed and unlicensed day care slots in Santa Clara County were subsidized in part by the program. Stoddard reports that during the time the program was in operation there was little change in the number of day care centers in the county, but that the number of licensed family day care homes rose dramatically (by about 35 percent). However, because unlicensed homes were ineligible for the subsidies, Stoddard points out that the total supply of day care slots may not have increased. Unlicensed homes, not eligible for the subsidies, may have become licensed in order to be eligible for the subsidies.

The pilot study appears to have fulfilled its overall objective of demonstrating the feasibility of an alternative method of subsidizing child care. However, while the study apparently induced additional licensing of family day care homes and reduced the costs of child care to the consumer, it is not clear that either the quantity or quality of child care services in Santa Clara County was affected.

In Chapter 7, Arden Hall investigates the effects of child care quality on child care costs. The methodology developed by Hall enables him to identify separately the custodial and educational-developmental components of child care costs.

The total cost of child care depends on both the quantity *and* quality. To remove the effects of quantity on cost, Hall calculates a charge for each child for a standard 40-hour week of service. All remaining variation in cost is therefore attributable to variation in quality.

Hall identifies two groups of attributes that define quality. The first group refers to the interaction between the provider and the child. In this dimension, high-quality care is equated with a "warm nurturing" atmosphere, and with a provider who is attentive and takes an affirmative and encouraging attitude toward the child. To measure this dimension empirically, Hall uses the staff/ child ratio and characteristics of the provider, such as race, education, and work experience. The second group of attributes refers to the various activities of the child care facility that are designed to affect child development. Hall includes a variable in his model that denotes the percentage of time spent in such activities at a particular child care facility. Additional services that affect quality but are not developmental in nature, such as the provision of meals, laundering, and overnight services, are also assumed to affect the cost of child care.

Using regression analysis, Hall estimates cost equations for child care providers. His sample consists of day care centers, family day care homes, and in-home providers in the cities of Seattle and Denver. The sample is the same as the one analyzed in Chapters 3 and 8. Separate cost equations are estimated for combined in-home providers and family day care homes, as well as for day care centers. Some of the more interesting results obtained for the combined in-home–family day care home sample indicate that costs are positively associated with education of the provider and negatively associated with the average capacity utilization rate.[13] There are also differences in cost among the various types of providers. In both Seattle and Denver, in-home providers have the highest cost, while licensed family day care homes have the lowest cost, although the differences in cost between licensed and unlicensed family day care homes are small. In the day care center sample, Hall finds that cost is positively associated with the average level of education of staff members. For each additional year of education, the cost per child increases by almost two dollars per week. Hall also finds that day care centers operating for profit have a significantly higher cost than private, nonprofit centers, holding constant all other characteristics of the centers. In neither of the samples is there a significant relationship between cost and the percentage of time spent in developmental activities.

Hall demonstrates how his cost equations can be used to derive an estimate of the custodial component of child care costs. By substituting into the equations values of the independent variables that are appropriate for custodial care, an estimate of the custodial component of child care cost can be made. Because quality is being held constant, it is possible to compare custodial costs between day care centers and family day care homes. Hall finds that the cost of custodial care is lower in day care centers.

The last chapter, by Samuel Weiner, shows how survey data can be used to aid policymakers in answering specific questions regarding child care legislation. Using data from the previously mentioned 1974 survey of child care providers, estimates are made of the cost to the day care industry of meeting federal standards for the provision of licensed child care services. Estimates are provided separately for day care centers and family care homes.

Weiner considers two cases: the cost of compliance to federal standards put into effect in October 1975 and the cost of compliance to meeting the more stringent requirements proposed for later implementation. Weiner compares actual child/staff ratios from the surveys with the child/staff ratios required in the legislation to derive the cost estimates.

The findings indicate that the cost of compliance would be greatest for private, profit-making day care centers, ranging from 5 to 27 percent, depending on the city or case under consideration. Between 43 and 59 percent of the profit-making day care centers in the sample are not in compliance with the federal standards.

For private, nonprofit day care centers, the cost of compliance ranges from 2 to 13 percent, with between 15 and 55 percent of those centers not in compliance. For public day care centers, the cost of compliance is about 8 percent; and between 10 and 38 percent of those centers are not in compliance. For family day care homes, Weiner estimates the cost of compliance in terms of the number of additional family day care homes needed to serve the same amount of children while complying with the newly legislated child/staff standards. In Seattle, an increase in supply of about 8 percent is required; in Denver an increase in supply of 6 percent is required. A significant proportion of licensed family day care homes in Seattle and Denver are not in compliance with existing and proposed standards.

Weiner extrapolates his Seattle-Denver results to the nation as a whole. He finds that under one set of assumptions the cost of compliance is between $31 million and $51 million. Under another set of assumptions, the cost of compliance ranges from between $79 million and $110 million.

Conclusions and Prognosis

Recent trends in American society have signaled major changes in the status of women, particularly with regard to labor-force participation. It therefore becomes imperative that policymakers comprehend the complex economic issues involved in extra family child care. These policymakers will be making decisions that may commit billions of dollars of public funds to the establishment of major child care programs. The chapters in this volume represent an attempt to study some of these economic issues.

From an economic perspective, there are two separate but interrelated issues that must be considered in formulating child care policy. First, it must be determined whether large-scale government subsidization is at all warranted. As described earlier, the usual rationale for government intervention is the notion that the private sector cannot optimally (in the sense of both quantity *and* quality) provide enough child care services because the amount of external, or social, benefits produced by the industry greatly outweighs the private benefits. It is not at all obvious, however, that a massive child care program would produce large social benefits. For example, preschool learning may not ensure that a child would achieve greater academic success in later years than he or she would achieve in the absence of such a program. Furthermore, large-scale subsidization of child care may not lead to an increase in either the quantity or quality of child care services. Before committing public funds to the establishment of such programs, definitive answers to questions raised by these and other issues are needed. Research on the economics of child care can help to provide some of those answers.

Second, given that subsidization is warranted, policymakers must determine which method of subsidization is best. Should child care subsidies be distributed directly or indirectly? Evidence presented in this book suggests that indirect methods, such as a voucher scheme, may be economically more efficient. Should subsidies be restricted to particular types of child care arrangements? Evidence presented in this book suggests that very few families prefer formal types of child care arrangements for their children while they work. Thus, programs aimed at subsidizing day care centers may not be an economically efficient way of allocating resources toward the preferred choices of consumers.

The purpose of this book is not to provide definitive answers to these complex economic questions. Rather, it is our intent to demonstrate the feasibility of using an economic approach to studying issues related to child care policy. While we have not dealt with all the major issues relevant to the economics of child care, several conclusions emerge from the studies that have important policy implications. For example, a national program of child care subsidies, such as that available under the federal income tax system, has two important economic effects that are relevant to public policy. First, a child care subsidy program is likely to increase the labor force participation rates of adult men and women, because a program that reduces the price of child care is similar to a program that increases the net wage rate. Second, because only paid forms of child care are eligible for subsidization under existing and proposed programs, the utilization rate of paid forms (relative to unpaid forms) is likely to increase when the price of child care is reduced. In Chapter 4, Robins and Spiegelman show that programs which either reduce the price of child care or increase the wage rate of the mother would lead to considerable increases in the utilization rates of market forms of child care. Because of its greater sensitivity to price and wage rate changes, formal market care would exhibit relatively greater increases in use. The authors' analysis also suggests that in making projections of the demand for market forms of child care under a national program of subsidies it does not suffice to merely count up the number of children in households with working parents. The age structure of family members is an important determinant of demand that must be taken into account.

The economic approach to child care cannot be considered in isolation. It must be combined with the approaches of sociologists, psychologists, social workers, and educators if it is to be an effective force in influencing child care policies in the future. It is hoped that the studies in this book will serve to stimulate additional research on the economics of child care and foster a balanced view toward the potential repercussions of any major national child care policy.

Notes

1. See Margaret O'Brien Steinfels, *Who's Minding the Children: The History and Politics of Day Care in America,* New York: Simon & Schuster, 1973, for a lucid and comprehensive review of day care in America.

2. *Ibid.,* Chapter 1.

3. These findings have been especially important in promoting programs to compensate for disadvantaged environments. The major development in that area was initiation of the Head Start Program in 1965.

4. This orientation was a main support for the Comprehensive Child Development Act of 1971, introduced by (then) Senator Walter Mondale and Congressman John Brandemas. That bill was passed by the Congress and vetoed by President Nixon.

5. See, for example, Suzanne H. Woolsey, "Pied-Piper Politics and the Child Care Debate," *Daedalus* (Spring 1977): 127-145; and B. Bruce-Briggs, "'Child Care': The Fiscal Time Bomb," *The Public Interest* (Fall 1977): 87-102.

6. *Toward a National Policy for Children and Families,* Advisory Committee on Child Development, Assembly of Behavioral and Social Sciences, National Research Council, Washington, D.C., National Academy of Science, 1976. In an appendix to that report, Urie Bronfenbrenner summarizes a number of published and unpublished research efforts that were concerned with the effect of day care on child development. These studies cover research on intellectual development, emotional attachment, motivation, and social behavior. For a more comprehensive overview of how educators and psychologists view the state of and need for early childhood education, see *As the Twig Is Bent: Readings in Early Childhood Education,* R. H. Anderson and H. G. Shane, eds., Boston: Houghton Mifflin, 1971. See also, *Day Care: Resources for Decisions,* Edith H. Grotberg, ed., Office of Economic Opportunity, 1971.

7. For an excellent review of some notable exceptions, see C. Russell Hill, "The Child Care Market: A Review of the Evidence and Implications for Federal Policy," a report presented to HEW, OS/ASPE/SSHD, January 1977.

8. The total cost of child care can be divided into three components: the price per unit of child care services (or the quality adjusted price), the quality of child care (or child care services provided per hour of care), and the quantity of child care (or the number of hours of child care provided). The economics of child care involves understanding how public policy affects each of these three components.

9. In fact, day care is one of the few activities in which home production and market production are carried out at the same time.

10. In economic terms, the value of unpaid or nonmarket care is called the shadow price of nonmarket care.

11. In a competitive industry, the marginal cost curve is the industry's supply curve.

12. SIME/DIME is a social experiment in negative income taxation that began in 1971 and is currently in progress. For a description of SIME/DIME, see Mordecai Kurz and Robert G. Spiegelman, "The Design of the Seattle and Denver Income Maintenance Experiments," Research Memorandum 18, Center for the Study of Welfare Policy, Stanford Research Institute, May 1972.

13. Since cost is measured on a full-time equivalent basis, the negative relationship between the average utilization rate and cost suggests that there are economies of scale in the provision of these types of child care services.

2

Public Policy Toward Child Care in America: A Historical Perspective

James D. Marver and Meredith A. Larson

For a variety of reasons, the popularity of day care has increased steadily over the last several years: women are entering the work force at a rapid rate; many women are demanding relief from sole child rearing responsibility; and welfare critics are pressing for reduced welfare rolls. In response, Congress has considered dozens of bills to promote some type of federal involvement in the care of children. Today countless federal programs have child care components, and federal direct and indirect support of day care has climbed into the millions of dollars. But despite all the interest, most people know very little about day care—who uses it, how much it costs, or what role the federal government plays in it. The purpose of this chapter is to provide an overview of the types of child care and of the historical development of child care policies so that the issues raised in succeeding chapters can be seen in perspective.

Defining Child Care

As used here, *child care* (and *day care*) may be thought of as any kind of regular supervision of a child when he is not in school that is provided by anyone other than the child's parents. Thus it could include children at home with a neighbor, in nursery schools, or in play groups, and the supervision provided by organized sports teams and clubs. This definition is useful regardless of whether or not the service is bought in the marketplace. In other words, it does not matter that no explicit price tag is attached to the service.[1]

The distinction commonly used in the past is the distinction between custodial and developmental care. In common usage, *custodial care* meant supervision with acceptable levels of safety and health, while *developmental care* also provided for the child's social, emotional, and educational growth.[2] This form of classification is of greater rhetorical than practical value, however, since almost every day care situation serves some measure of both custodial and developmental functions. More important, if one is concerned with policy, such a distinction confuses inputs and outputs as regards what happens to children.

Another familiar distinction is between day care that has been prefaced in discussions by *work-related* (or sometimes *training-related*) child care and day care that is *early childhood education*. In this case, the intent is to distinguish between day care that principally benefits parents who now can join the labor force and day care provided for the short-term (recreational) or long-term (educational) benefit of the child. This distinction is of equally little practical value, since any given day care arrangement is likely to include the children of both working and nonworking mothers, providing a broad mix of benefits to both parents and the children. In fact, this contrast is simply a variation on the first: work-related child care is presumed to be custodial, while early childhood education is, by definition, developmental. Finally, *work-related* day care is sometimes contrasted with *welfare-related* day care. In theory, this distinguishes among the intended effects of day care; in practice, it distinguishes among its participants and, in so doing, affects federal funding and eligibility.

It is more useful to think about the objectives of a child care facility and to consider the characteristics that may be related to child outcomes. In any event, characteristics such as child/staff ratios, day care classroom processes, program costs, group size, and staff professionalism are more helpful in thinking about different types of day care.[3] One useful classification scheme is based on the setting in which day care is provided. This classification scheme reduces the problem of circularity inherent in classifications that depend upon what the staff *intends* to do, and it seems to correspond quite well to the way in which families think about child care. As Figure 2–1 suggests, day care settings may be represented on a continuum of complexity and staff professionalization, both of which are related to enrollment size.[4]

When the mother, or sole parent, is employed, the simplest arrangement is that of using a relative to care for the child in his own home. When nonrelatives provide care in a child's home, that person may have only child care responsibilities (i.e., a babysitter) or may also have other household duties (usually as a housekeeper).

Another arrangement is to have the child cared for in a home not his own. Usually such care is provided by another mother who cares for her own and neighborhood children in her home (often called *family day care*). Such family day care centers may or may not be registered through a local agency; the care-giver is ordinarily not a certified professional or a trained paraprofessional. Again, some training may be given to the care-giver to upgrade the quality of health, cognitive development, or child protection that the visiting child receives, but the care remains essentially nonprofessional.

Next in order of complexity are small child-care centers providing for as many as perhaps 20 children. Although a few such centers operate in private homes (where several rooms have been set aside), most are set in separate facilities. They are often sponsored by community organizations or are tangential services of churches, universities, or fraternal organizations. Sometimes the sponsor provides a small subsidy in the form of rent-free facilities. In general, there is more than one care-giver, at least one of whom is a certified professional or paraprofessional.

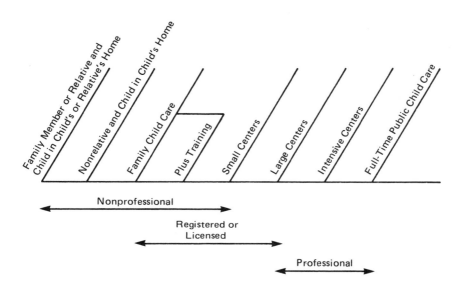

Figure 2-1. Optional Settings for Child Care Services by Complexity and Staff Type.

As the enrollment increases in these small child-care centers, so does the tendency to use professional, certified personnel, such as nurses or teachers. The largest centers may care for up to 200 children, using diversified professional staffs. Centers enrolling 50 or more children are often under government sponsorship at local, state, or federal levels. Any program receiving federal subsidies must satisfy staffing and child/staff ratio requirements for type of care and age of child.[5]

In a few instances, day care may be provided through all-day, formal, preschool programs operating either privately or, more commonly, through some special state program of the public schools. Ordinarily only certified personnel are used in such programs. Having defined a number of types of day care, we can now ask who uses which types.

Who Uses What Kind of Child Care?

No data should ever be accepted uncritically, for the vagaries of collecting that data often are known only to their collectors. What's more, the rapid growth of the women's labor force, combined with the repeated changes of federal and state policy, raise the strong possibility that any data more than five years old may not accurately represent the current day care market. Moreover, even when current data are available, their interpretation is problematic, for authors writing on day care frequently have employed questionable methodology.[6] Yet one must make do with available information, and fortunately, the Census Bureau recently (in October 1974 and February 1975) conducted a study that indicates the types of day care arrangements employed mothers are making for their children.[7] (In interpreting the tables, the reader should consider that many families use multiple child care arrangements.)[8]

Table 2-1 indicates that the majority of children are cared for by their own parents at home. (Although the proportion of children receiving parent care is reduced when mothers are employed full time, about half these children are usually cared for by one of their parents.)[9] Parent care is more likely to be given to children of grade school age (7 to 13 years old) than those of pre-school age.

Table 2-1
Percent Distribution of Arrangements for Daytime
Care of Children Ages 3-13 of Employed Mothers

	Child 3-6	Child 7-13	Child 3-13
Care in Own Home			
Child's Parent	54.0	64.0	61.1
Child Cares for Self	0.4	13.8	9.9
Other Relative	7.4	10.2	9.4
Nonrelative	3.2	2.7	2.9
Subtotal	65.0	90.7	83.3
Care in Someone Else's Home			
Relative	12.2	3.2	5.8
Nonrelative	16.6	3.5	7.3
Subtotal	28.8	6.7	13.1
Other Arrangements			
Day Care Center	4.1	0.8	1.7
Other	0.0	0.6	0.4
Not Reported	2.1	1.3	1.5
Subtotal	6.2	2.7	3.6
Total[a]	100%	100%	100%

Source: U.S. Bureau of the Census, *Current Population Reports,* Series P-20, No. 298, "Daytime Care of Children: October 1974 and February 1975," U.S. Government Printing Office, Washington, D.C., 1976, p. 6.

[a]Totals may not sum to 100 percent because of rounding.

Approximately 14 percent of the older children care for themselves, and this percentage increases to 18 when the mother works full time. It is reported that rarely are younger children left to care for themselves; instead they are supervised by a relative about as often (19.6 percent) as by an unrelated person (19.8 percent) excluding center care. Noncenter care for these younger children is more likely to take place in someone else's home (28.8 percent) than at their own home (10.6 percent). When the mother is employed full time, the frequency of care of preschool age children in someone else's home increases to 36 percent.[10] Day care centers are used by working mothers infrequently. Approximately 4 percent of their children three to six years old and less than 1 percent of the older children receive center care.

As Table 2-2 demonstrates, the type of care provided for grade-school age children of employed mothers does not vary by race, with the exception that somewhat more white parents supervise their children in contrast to having

Table 2-2
Percent Distribution of Arrangements for Daytime Care of Children Ages 7-13 of Employed Mothers by Race

	White	Black
Care in Own Home		
Child's Parents	65.7	55.9
Child Cares for Self	13.2	14.9
Other Relative	8.8	17.1
Nonrelative	2.8	2.8
Subtotal	90.5	90.7
Care in Someone Else's Home		
Relative	3.0	4.6
Nonrelative	3.7	2.2
Subtotal	6.7	6.8
Other Arrangements		
Day Care Center	.8	.6
Other	.6	.7
Not Reported	1.3	1.3
Subtotal	2.7	2.6
Total[a]	100%	100%

Source: U.S. Bureau of the Census, *Current Population Reports,* Series P-20, No. 298, "Daytime Care of Children: October 1974 and February 1975," U.S. Government Printing Office, Washington, D.C., 1976, p. 13.

[a]Totals may not sum to 100 percent because of rounding.

other relatives care for them than do their black counterparts. For working mothers of younger children, however, the differences are greater, as shown in Table 2-3. For these children, two patterns are apparent. One is that black fathers are about twice as likely as white fathers to care for their children. (If one looks only at families where the mother is in the labor force and the father is present, the greater likelihood is three times.)[11] The second is that a black child is more likely to be cared for by someone to whom he is related (81 percent versus 72 percent).

Shortlidge also found that blacks depended on siblings and relatives for day care more often than did whites.[12] He accounts for this by reasoning that relatives are more likely to live in the households of blacks than whites and older black siblings may be more available for child care because of their higher incidence of unemployment.

According to the Census Bureau report, the type of care provided for grade-school age children of mothers in the labor force varies only slightly with family

Table 2-3
Percent Distribution of Arrangements for Daytime Care of Children Ages 3-6 of Employed Mothers by Race

	White	Black
Care in Own Home		
Child's Mother	49.6	37.7
Child's Father	5.7	11.9
Other Relative	6.2	12.4
Nonrelative	3.8	0.5
Subtotal	65.3	62.5
Care in Someone Else's Home		
Relative	10.6	19.0
Nonrelative	17.9	12.8
Subtotal	28.5	31.8
Other Arrangements		
Day Care Center	4.2	2.8
Not Reported	1.9	2.9
Subtotal	6.1	5.7
Total[a]	100%	100%

Source: U.S. Bureau of the Census, *Current Population Reports,* Series P-20, No. 298, "Daytime Care of Children: October 1974 and February 1975," U.S. Government Printing Office, Washington, D.C., 1976, p. 7.

[a]Totals may not sum to 100 percent because of rounding.

income level. And this is only somewhat less true for children aged 7 to 13 years. For these children, there are a few differences that are statistically significant (e.g., a larger proportion of children from relatively low- than from high-income families are cared for by relatives) but they appear to be very small.[13]

These findings are supported by the work of Duncan and Hill[14] and also Kurz, Robins, and Spiegelman.[15] Both studies conclude that a family's choice of a type of child care is not affected by family income, other things being equal. However, the working woman's wage is a significant predictor of day care mode: in two-parent households, the likelihood of the family using informal market care increases with the wife's wage rate. Duncan and Hill found the same thing for one parent families, whereas Kurz et al. found no effect insofar as wage rates were concerned. Both studies found that other family income does not appear to affect the type of child care chosen, but Love and Angrist concluded otherwise.[16]

Several studies, including those by Shortlidge, Unco, Duncan and Hill, and Kurz et al., have found that a family's choice of child care is affected by the family's size and age composition. According to Hill, "the lack of teenage siblings or other adults, or a one-parent family, sharply increases the probability of the family using an extrafamily mode of child care for its preschoolers."[17] There have not been any formal investigations of how different family environments might affect child care choices in different income groups.[18]

Users of various types of child care cannot be studied in a vacuum. The role of the federal government is not so invisible as to be ignored. Let us now consider some aspects of the federal government's involvement in the delivery of day care services.

Current Federal Involvement

It is useful to classify federal involvement in the provision of work-related day care into two major types: direct subsidization and indirect subsidization. We will now describe the most important current programs in each category.

Direct Subsidization

Both municipal governments (through the Human Resources Departments) and state governments (through matching funds, especially) provide a substantial amount of day care funds. The overwhelming majority of support, however, is the product of direct federal subsidization of child care services. Many federal programs in a variety of agencies have subsidized day care components, but most federal funding is concentrated within a small number of programs—Title XX of the Social Services Amendments of 1974 and Titles IVA, IVB, and IVC of the 1967 Amendments to the Social Security Act.

Title XX. Title XX, the Social Services Amendments of 1974 to the Social Security Act (Public Law 93-647), became effective on October 1, 1975. Under its provisions, $2.5 billion is allocated to states, based on population, to provide social services, including "child care services, protective services for children, services for children in foster care, services related to the management and maintenance of the home, and appropriate combinations of services designed to meet the special needs of children."[19] The federal government pays for 75 percent of the costs, and states must contribute 25 percent in matching funds, except for family planning, which is 90/10. The federal contribution for day care for children is estimated to be approximately $600 million for FY1977.

Services funded by Title XX are available to people whose family gross income is not greater than 115 percent of the median income for a family of four in that state, adjusted for family size. People with incomes greater than 115 percent of the median income are ineligible for Title XX matching funds, except for certain services provided without regard to income—namely, Information and Referral, Protective Services for Children and Adults, and Family Planning. People whose family gross income is between 80 and 115 percent of the median income must pay a fee for services, and states may set fees below 80 percent median income if they choose. States can provide any service described in its Title XX plan without regard to income in documented cases of abuse, neglect, or exploitation. This includes day care for children.

In 1976 Public Law 94-401 was enacted to amend certain sections of Title XX. The law waived the Federal Interagency Day Care Requirements (FIDCR) for another year, provided a $240 million transitional quarter and FY1977 appropriation for child care to be distributed to states on the basis of their populations, and permitted the use of group eligibility for services. Group eligibility is permitted for all services except day care for children, and day care for migrant children is exempt from the exception. For a state to use group eligibility, it must be able to show that 75 percent of the group falls below 90 percent median income adjusted for family size. PL 94-401 also provided a tax incentive for the hiring of welfare mothers in day care centers.

There is no "maintenance of effort" provision in PL 94-401. Therefore, the money can be used to replace current matched Title XX day care funds. In addition, PL 94-401 is 100 percent federal money and requires no match. States receive their PL 94-401 monies up to the maximum based on their expenditures for day care for children. For example, if a state's PL 94-401 allotment is $2 million and it spends $1.5 million on day care for children, it can receive only $1.5 million of its $2 million PL 94-401 allotment. However, if the state so chooses, it can match its PL 94-401 funds at 75/25 and draw down its full allotment regardless of the level of day care expenditures.

The FIDCR waiver provisions of PL 94-401 have been extended through FY1978, and Congress is also planning to extend the $200 million supplement for another year.

1967 Amendments to the Social Security Act. Since 1962 the Social Security Act has included day care for children of welfare recipients, but the 1967 amendments broadened its authorization significantly. The two most important programs are the Work Incentive Program and Child Welfare Services.

Work Incentive (WIN) Program (Titles IVA and IVC). Enacted in 1967, WIN actually began operation in 1969.[20] Through its provisions, poor families involved in training or employment were entitled to child care services in keeping with the requirement that states actively try to place all suitable adult welfare recipients in jobs or in job training. On the basis of the 1971 Talmadge Amendments (which took effect in FY1972), all adult recipients must register for WIN as a condition of eligibility for AFDC benefits, unless they are in school (up to age twenty-one); are mothers with children under the age of six; are ill, disabled, or aged; or live too far from a WIN project.[21] The other exemption is for a woman with an adult male in the family group who is registered for WIN.[22] State and local welfare departments receive funds from HEW and may use these to operate their own child care programs, to contract for services with other agencies or organizations, or to provide direct assistance to individuals for privately arranged services.[23]

Employment and training funds are provided for under Title IVC, and WIN receives funds for child care and other services necessary for training or employment under IVA as a separate appropriation. The federal/state contribution ratio is 90/10, with the federal government providing $55 million to $60 million for child care in FY1976. (Roughly 30 percent of that amount offsets staff costs for administering the program.)

Child Welfare Services (Title IVB, 422(a)). Title IVB authorized the federal government to provide matching grants to state welfare agencies for child welfare services, including child care. The federal/state reimbursable match is not uniform among states; instead it varies according to the under-21 population and the average per capita income. It appears that as a child welfare service, priority is given to day care for protective services; in other words, day care that will help protect children from abuse and neglect and day care for handicapped children. In effect, the funds are likely to go to families that are ineligible for Title XX child care monies. It is estimated that the federal child care contribution in Title IVB for FY1977 will be $4.7 million.[24]

Other Programs for Directly Subsidized Child Care. The aforementioned programs are the vehicles supplying most federal funds for child care services. In addition to these, there are numerous federal programs that have child care components and accordingly provide at least some resources for day care program operations, staffing, facilities, and nutrition.[25] We make no attempt to be comprehensive in this section, both because there are virtually dozens of programs with at least minor child care components and because it is not unlikely that many of these current programs will have disappeared within a few years.[26] Instead, we describe briefly a few programs of this genre.

CETA. The Department of Labor's Employment and Training Administration is responsible for the Comprehensive Employment and Training Act (CETA), which seeks to increase the employability of low-income people. It also provides funds to create jobs in the public and private sectors with the objective of transition to unsubsidized jobs. Each prospective prime sponsor's proposal includes a Comprehensive Manpower Plan, which may have a day care component as a supportive service. The significant segments of the population to be served (female heads of households, for example) may warrant a significant portion of CETA funds for authorized day care activity.

Federal Employment Assistance Program. Run by the Bureau of Indian Affairs in the Department of the Interior, the Federal Employment Assistance Program has two primary purposes. It endeavors to help its Indian target population gain job skills through enrollment at trade schools and junior colleges. It also helps find jobs for people who have gone through these educational programs. The day care funds are to facilitate the student's education. Consequently, the funds are predominantly for single parents who are in a trade school or junior college. Typically, the student chooses someone to care for his children, and the Bureau of Indian Affairs then makes direct payments to the designated care provider.

Community Services Administration (CSA). Among the prime sponsors receiving Title XX day care monies are local community action agencies (CAA). Because the CSA helps pay for the administrative superstructure of CAAs (accountants, finance officers, and other administrative personnel), the CSA may be considered a direct subsidizer of day care.

Head Start. Child care services are provided to a great many preschool children through such programs as Head Start and, to a lesser degree, Home Start and Parent-Child Centers. However, because these programs combine elements of day care and preschool education, and because these components cannot be separated, we do not address Head Start and its variants here.

Indirect Subsidization

Two principal mechanisms are used by the federal government to subsidize indirectly the provision of day care services—income tax and the AFDC work-expense credit. To a lesser extent, day care services are also supported indirectly through public housing and food stamp provisions.

Income Tax. The provisions of the Tax Reform Act of 1976 have not yet been fully interpreted. However, the general outlines appear to be as follows: a credit against income liability is permitted to taxpayers for 20 percent of qualified child care expenses. Qualified expenses may not exceed $2000 for one dependent (child) and $4000 for two or more. Eligibility for the credit is not limited by family income or by type of child care arrangements and payments. The taxpayer's relatives also qualify for this credit, except when the relative is the taxpayer's dependent or when the wages are not subject to social security tax.

In the case of dual worker families filing a joint return, both spouses do not have to work full time in order to qualify, but the allowable expenses are limited to the earnings of the spouse with the smaller income. The credit is also permitted to full-time students. A divorced or separated parent may claim the credit when he or she supplies more than half the child's support and claims the child as a dependent.

It is estimated that the Tax Reform Act of 1976 will increase from two million to nearly four million the number of tax returns benefitting from provisions in the tax laws related to child care. Projected increases in the indirect subsidization of child care are approximately $346 million in fiscal year 1977, $363 million in fiscal year 1978, and $483 million in fiscal year 1981.[27]

AFDC Work-Expense Credit. The preceding income tax credit assists any parent with an income high enough to be subject to federal income tax. Working parents with earnings below the taxable level also have child care expenses but cannot be assisted through such income tax credits. A similar type of assistance is provided, however, through adjustments to AFDC payments.

In most states, AFDC payments equal the difference between a predetermined need standard and two-thirds of a worker's earnings above $30 per month. Thus, ordinarily, the AFDC payment would be reduced by 66 cents of every additional dollar earned. However, certain work-related expenses, including child care, are fully reimbursed.

This procedure is intended to eliminate any pressure on AFDC parents to provide inadequate child care because they cannot afford better arrangements. The dollar amount of child care expenses that can be reimbursed (deducted from countable income) is limited only by some state regulations and caseworker interpretations.[28]

Public Housing. The Housing Act of 1937 as revised by the Housing and Community Development Act of 1974 provides for, among other things, locally owned, low-income housing projects. Owned by public housing authorities (PHA) under the respective state laws, public housing is available to people whose gross family incomes after appropriate deductions are low enough to qualify. Net family income also determines the rent to be paid to local housing authorities. Since expenses for the "care of children" are an allowable deduction when they are necessary for the employment of the head of household or his spouse, such expenditures reduce the occupant's rent, allowing greater benefits than would be available without the deduction. The amount deducted is limited only to the extent that it cannot exceed the amount received by the family member thus released for employment.[29]

Child care is also subsidized under Section 8 of the Housing Assistance Payments Program. The PHA pays part of a low-income person's rent directly to the owner of the housing. The tenant has a lease directly with the owner and pays not more than 25 percent of his "annual income after allowances," i.e., adjusted gross income, or 15 percent of total income under certain circumstances.[30] As in other public housing programs, day care expenses are deductible in calculating adjusted gross income. Here, though, the children must be under thirteen years of age.

Food Stamps. The U.S. Department of Agriculture's Food Stamp Program provides a further vehicle for indirectly subsidizing day care. In a manner similar to that used for determining public housing eligibility and rents, eligibility for and the cost of food stamps are determined by net income. Several household expenses may be taken as deductions in calculating net income, among them are "the payments necessary for the care of a child or other persons when necessary for a household member to accept or continue employment, or training or education which is preparatory for employment."[31] Households who furnish the attendant or housekeeper the majority of his meals are also entitled to a deduction equal to the one-person monthly coupon allotment.[32] Thus the food stamp recipient receives a greater amount of food stamps when he takes a child care expense deduction than when he does not, all other things being equal.

From one perspective, the federal involvement in child care is quite small, for much child care is paid for by private individuals, charitable organizations, or is provided without money transfer. Most observers would argue, however, that the federal government has a disproportionately large influence over day care and the choices that families have available to them. There are few forms of child care that are beyond the scope of federal impact. Moreover, since child care is linked to economic, social and political objectives beyond the care of children, many other aspects of American life are affected by child care policies. How, we may ask, did federal involvement and influence get so large?

A Brief History of Child Care in America

Tracing the history of child care in America allows one to see a number of recurring and converging rationales for its emergence and development. Day care allows mothers to enter the work force in times of war, unemployment, and feminist discontent. Children may be socialized into the American middle-class culture with the hope that ultimately they will become self-sustaining citizens. Moreover, it is a means to teach similarly middle-class values and practices to the poor and/or immigrants by letting child care children act as teachers. Finally, some care is seen as a means for helping children develop to their full potential educationally and socioemotionally.

Throughout American history, most children have been cared for by their own mothers, domestics, neighbors, or relatives, whether or not their parents were employed. But formal day care seems not to have been introduced in the United States until early in the nineteenth century. The Boston Infant School, established in 1828, was intended to provide services both to employed parents and to their children by providing what might now be called a "learning environment."[33] Another day nursery was opened in Boston in 1838 to care for the children of seamen's wives and widows,[34] and in 1854 two New York hospitals established similar nurseries.[35] These and the few other nurseries established during this period prior to the Civil War were all under private sponsorship.

The federal government did not become a sponsor of day care until the Civil War, when in 1863 a day nursery, modeled on the Paris *crèche,* was established in Philadelphia to care for the children of women who worked in wartime clothing factories and hospitals. When the war ended, the Philadelphia day nursery continued to receive federal funds to take care of the children of war widows seeking work.[36]

Thus from as far back as the early nineteenth century the primary justification for formal child care was providing a service to parents who must work outside the home. But even at this early date, other purposes were expressed as well. Many of the Utopian communities instituted varieties of formal child care and even residential nurseries. These were considered valuable for teaching children to give their primary loyalties to the community rather than to the "selfish" interests of the family.

During the latter part of the nineteenth century, interest in day nurseries for the poor was tied to concern over immigration from Northern Europe and Ireland. The influx of immigrants into the Northeastern cities further unsettled more traditional economic and social patterns already disrupted by the Civil War and the second Industrial Revolution. One organization that emerged to cope with these conditions was the "charity society," which viewed daytime child care, aside from easing the burden of working mothers, as an excellent vehicle for assimilating this "dangerous class" of the children of the foreign poor.[37] Anyone familiar with some of the early rhetoric of Head Start will recognize this familiar rationale: the child as teacher to his parents. Moreover, it was hoped that with proper socialization, day nursery children would not continue to depend on charity as they grew older.[38]

Usually housed in converted houses or brownstones, these nurseries focused on the needs of the working mother.[39] She was considered an unfortunate soul and, unless widowed, the victim of an irresponsible, lazy, or criminal husband.

Unless she could obtain employment, the family would be permanently separated. Thus, in addition to supplying her with daytime child care, the day nursery acted as a type of employment agency, assisting the mothers to find work as laundresses or domestics, often for the same group of middle- and upper-class families who operated the nurseries.[40]

The federal government showed little, if any, interest in these nineteenth-century developments; as charity, the day nurseries were the province of philanthropists. Accordingly, an undercurrent of bad feeling accompanied the use of the day nursery. Its users were faulted for being in a position of need. As the twentieth century began, however, these feelings subsided somewhat; charity organizations, while still the principal backers of day nurseries, lost some influence to the emerging day nursery establishment itself.

A Turn-of-the-Century Concern for Quality

As the twentieth century began, day nurseries began to change in response to a variety of changing social attitudes. During the first decade, the first generation of college-educated women began to seek careers, often strongly influenced by the new feminist movement and its concern for improving the human condition in general and women's lot in particular. The day nursery and after-school programs of the settlement houses were, in part, an effort by early feminists to improve women's conditions by working together.[41]

The ethic of collective improvement can also be seen in the formation, at the turn of the century, of associations of private day nurseries. These associations, together with individual day nurseries and local government agencies, helped to focus attention on the quality of child care services.[42] Civil authorities also took an interest in the "quality" of nurseries, though in a more narrow sense. Abuses in other types of institutions (e.g., foster homes, orphan asylums) led to the enactment of some state laws giving Boards of Charities licensing responsibility for child care facilities.[43] In 1910 the New York City Board of Health and Fire Department began to inspect local day nurseries; in 1917 California enacted a law governing day nurseries; and in 1918 a city ordinance regulated day nurseries in Cleveland.[44] Such measures were rarely backed up by adequate enforcement.[45] Nevertheless, this period does mark the entry of local government into the regulatory role.

World War I and the Professionalization of Day Care

World War I increased the demand for child care, as large numbers of women went to work in the factories supplying the front. These child care needs seem generally to have been met through the auspices of local government and through an expansion of the existing private facilities. No federal action was taken. Nevertheless, the war focused national attention on child care issues indirectly because of the common belief that early childhood problems were responsible for the high rate of physical and mental deficiencies that disqualified men for military service.[46]

After the war, however, day nurseries fared less well than before as a result of four developments. As Steinfels writes,

First, the reform spirit of the progressive period was dealt a fatal blow by the war, and the day nursery, as other innovative ideas, suffered a decline in interest and popularity. Second, wide-scale immigration stopped in 1921 with the passage of legislation restricting immigrants. . . . Third, the collapse of militant feminism after the passage of the Nineteenth Amendment giving women the right to vote probably removed the counterbalance to the widespread opinion that the mother's place was in the home. And the passage of widow's pensions in many states allowed a large group of mothers to stay home and raise their children in genteel poverty. Fourth, after a mild business recession the decade took on [a] . . . spirit of affluence and economic expansion which . . . did not actually get rid of slums or poverty, but in flush times there seemed to be less reasons to notice that not everyone's street was paved with gold. If men were working they could support their families, and that made the day nursery seem less of a necessity.[47]

The Depression: Enter the Federal Government

Not until the depression of the 1930s did the federal government demonstrate serious interest in day care. In 1933 the Federal Emergency Relief Act was passed as part of Roosevelt's New Deal. The bill provided jobs for the unemployed and emergency nursery schools for "children of needy, unemployed families or neglected or underprivileged homes where preschool age children [would] benefit from the program offered."[48] All the personnel, including teachers, nurses, social workers, nutritionists, janitors, cooks, and clerical workers, were to come from the relief rolls. There were funds for in-service and pre-service training for staff and parent education; and although technically a "welfare" program, funds were administered through state departments of education and local school boards, perhaps because the aims of the program were primarily educational.

In a separate though related development, Title V of the original Social Security Act of 1935 was enacted to provide grants-in-aid for child welfare services, child care included, and grants for child care research.[49] In 1936 Congress provided another $6 million for nurseries under the Works Progress Administration.[50] Additional day care programs were run by the Farm Security and Federal Housing Administration. At its peak, New Deal programs were funding 1900 child care centers serving 75,000 children.[51] The common theme among all these programs was the use of child care facilities as a vehicle for public employment and for stimulating the economy.

As employment increased at the end of the 1930s, child care centers were no longer needed as a source of jobs and quickly disappeared when federal funding was withdrawn. However, center care had been given an official seal of approval that would stand it in good stead for several decades, and it had acquired a new rationale: day care centers as a last resort for hiring the unemployed. In addition, the channeling of day care funds through educational agencies and school boards established a connection with the public school network, a linkage that teacher unions today are trying to reforge.

World War II: Another Emergency Measure

The federal government again entered the day care business in response to the labor demands of World War II. Funds for day care services became available in 1942, when a ruling specified that child care centers in war-impacted areas could be considered public works so that they would qualify for monies authorized by the Community Facilities Act (The Lanham Act). By the end of the war, $51 million had been spent for the construction and operation of child care centers. At peak use in 1945, 1.6 million children were enrolled in over 3000 centers.[52] Areas not considered war impacted were ineligible for Lanham Act funds, but in some cases state governments provided child care monies.[53] The Lanham Act represented one of the first cooperative arrangements between the federal and state governments in child care, and it did not set a particularly good precedent. The Federal Works Agency (FWA) administered the program, but lines of authority were not always clear. The Lanham Act provided for direct grants to local communities, but the guidelines recommended that funding go to programs approved by the Office of Education or the Children's Bureau, both of which had strong ties to state-level governments. Interagency rivalries for control over the expenditure of funds were prevalent.[54] Unfortunately, these also have become a part of the legacy of day care.

Overall, the FWA was not sympathetic to the use of Lanham Act funds for child care. In 1945 it terminated 2800 centers with very little public outcry. As in the 1920s, postwar economics, values, and simple exhaustion with national causes combined in the affirmation that the proper place for a woman was in the home, and there was no organized constituency to resist the closings.[55]

But despite the propaganda campaign waged in magazine articles exhorting mothers to stay at home, many continued to work, most at blue-collar jobs, but some in the professions. Generally their child care needs were not acknowledged publicly, and most women made child care arrangements in the home of a relative or neighbor. For practical purposes, this was the beginning of the largely unlicensed neighborhood family child care homes that now constitute a major part of the child care market. The small percentage of women who used day care centers were considered pathological or socially deviant, just as had been those women who used organized day nurseries during the post-World War I period.[56]

Opposition to "working women" was so pronounced that mobilization for the Korean War in 1951 did not lead to a renewed interest in child care as a national issue. The 1952 Democratic platform advocated child care for children of women doing defense work, but the end of the war brought an end to child care as an issue. Also contributing to negative public and professional attitudes toward formal child care was the publication in 1951 of Bowlby's *Maternal Care and Mental Health,* which described the "maternal deprivation" syndrome that results from prolonged mother-infant separation.[57] That Bowlby's study focused on infants or children who were living in or had lived in total institutions was less publicized.

Not until 1958 was public child care raised again as an issue in Congress, when Senator Javits proposed the first of a series of "cold war" day care bills to serve the children of working mothers.[58] Then, in the 1960s, day care's image improved again.

Child Care in the 1960s and 1970s

During the last decade and a half, child care has gained considerable prominence as a national political issue, supported by changes in social and academic attitudes that lend greater respectability to the working mother. This progress has been slow but fairly steady.

The Commission on the Status of Women recommended, in its 1963 report, that additional child care facilities for working women of all income levels be established.[59] President Kennedy was receptive and recommended in turn that $4 million be made in grants to states in 1963 to help establish local day care programs, to be increased to $10 million yearly thereafter.[60]

During this period, research findings and opinions were modifying the "maternal deprivation" fears, as researchers such as Milton Willner pointed out that the institutions in Bowlby's studies had little in common with typical day care facilities.[61] Concurrently in the post-Sputnik race for greater brain power, educators and scientists began to look to early childhood as a time of potentially significant intellectual formation.

While these events had no immediate effect on the federal day care role, they set the stage for the Great Society bills of the middle sixties. Aimed primarily at providing educational and economic assistance to low-income families, many of these bills included some form of direct or indirect support for child care. The Economic Opportunity Act (EOA) of 1964, the Housing and Urban Development Act of 1965, and the Model Cities Act of 1966 all provided technical and/or financial assistance to child care services, primarily for the poor. Of these, the most influential was the EOA.

Its subsidiary program, Head Start, was premised on writings such as J. McVickers Hunt's, which drew parallels between the effects of individual maternal deprivation and collective social and cultural deprivation.[62] The remedy for cultural deprivation would be to provide intellectual stimulation through enriched preschool or day care settings. Originally designed as a part-time summer preschool program, Head Start soon expanded into full-day and full-year operations, merging educational and day care characteristics.

Another aspect of mid-sixties legislation was a growing concern for welfare costs and a desire to reduce welfare rolls. This was to be accomplished by providing day care, so that welfare recipients could hold paying jobs. To this end, the 1967 amendments to the Social Security Act provided three-to-one matching grants to states for the purpose of expanding and subsidizing day care for low-income families. For example, prior to being superseded by Title XX, Title IVA (§402(a)14), the AFDC (Aid to Families with Dependent Children) section of the act, allowed state welfare departments to provide day care services to practically all children in low-income families. Neighborhoods with a high rate of former, current, and potential welfare recipients were eligible for child care services, as were all geographic areas meeting the poverty criteria established by the state agency and all areas approved for federally assisted antipoverty projects. Anyone who resided within a qualifying neighborhood, regardless of income, family status, and the like, was eligible for the child care services.[63] Services were provided under a federal/local 75/25 percent reimbursable match; the local share could come from state or local government, donations by private individuals, religious, civic, business, and labor organizations or grants by foundations, national charities (e.g., United Fund), and even other federal programs (e.g., Model Cities). Appropriations were allocated among states on a population-based formula.

Together, the educational and employment-related legislation of the sixties expanded the federal role in child care to one of unprecedented importance in center care for low-income workers. However, despite such events as the National Conference on Day Care Services in 1965 and the Consultation on Working Women and Day Care Needs in 1967, little had been done to assist dual-worker or single-parent families in middle- or upper-income brackets. As rapidly increasing numbers of middle-class women assumed full-time employment during the late sixties and early seventies, they began to form a more vocal constituency for federal assistance.

Several major bills to enlarge, formalize, and extend the federal support of child care centers have been introduced, but none has gained both congressional and presidential approval. Other forms of support have found greater acceptance, however. Most prominently, successive changes in federal income tax regulations have granted, variously, tax credits and deductions for child care as a business expense. The Revenue Act of 1971 greatly liberalized the federal income tax provisions, which since 1954 had permitted taxpayers to deduct child care expenses from gross income. The Tax Reduction of 1975 again increased the number of taxpayers eligible for such deductions. In effect, the deduction relieved parents of the full burden of child care costs by reducing their gross income and thus their federal income tax liability. The recently enacted Tax Reform Act of 1976 liberalizes the income tax provisions even further. In addition to extending benefits to upper-income families, the new regulations are also more helpful to taxpayers in lower brackets because itemized deductions are no longer necessary.

From this survey of federal involvement in child care, some patterns can be discerned. In times of war, child care is usually highly regarded; direct subsidy and control of child care facilities increase, as was the case during both world wars and to some extent during the Vietnam war. In times of postwar prosperity, however, day care is looked down on as a social stigma, and federal support is decreased drastically; severe reduction of federal support during the 1920s and the 1950s follow this pattern. During economic hardship and high unemployment, day care is likely to be used as a direct source of employment and economic stimulation; this has been most evident in the New Deal programs of the thirties, portions of the Economic Opportunity programs during the sixties, and proposals for a national network of child care centers to be established in the public schools during the seventies. Finally, during massive immigration or rapid social change, child care is used as a vehicle of both child and parent socialization; the period of the late 1800s and the 1960s are examples of this. What all these patterns have in common is the use of formal child care not only, or even primarily, as an end in itself, but as a tool for other economic, political, and social ends.

Concluding Remarks

The future federal role in child care is uncertain. Assuming that recent advances in women's employment are not undercut by serious economic reversals, we can expect that demand will continue for government assistance. The form such assistance will take is far less clear.

Child care has come to be seen as the means to a variety of conflicting ends. Some advocates wish to advance child care policy to increase overall women's labor force participation. Some are primarily concerned with reducing welfare rolls. Others are motivated by the goals of protecting children, stimulating their development, and improving their futures. A few are concerned with making child care a paying job for whoever does it, including the child's mother. Child care seems to be an issue that can be attached to multiple objectives and ideologies.

Since the 1960s, child care advocates have become increasingly sophisticated in their efforts to support greater federal involvement. Yet no coalition has formed that can unite child care supporters around a commonly acceptable rationale or remedy. The result is that competition rather than cooperation is the norm among child care advocates as they vie for influence over policy. Users and proponents of center care have formed a strong and vocal lobby that has kept day care an active political issue. However, they have been relatively unsuccessful at expanding the direct federal sponsorship of centers. Users of family group care or care in the child's own home have done little to organize. Nevertheless, they have benefitted substantially from the recent expansion of indirect federal subsidies for child care. The child care constituency is also divided among class and income lines, which may have been strengthened by interest-group rivalry.

The fragmentation of child care interest groups is matched by an equally splintered federal policy. The present collection of programs, subsidies, payments, regulations, and research does not represent a deliberate or unified child care policy. Instead we have a jumble of partial policies, each applying to some special portion of the business or private community, with no unifying premise to explain the diversity.

Federal involvement does appear to be moving toward child care policy that is less class and location bound. More people are viewing child care not as a special obligation to the poor or stricken, but rather as part of the universal entitlement of every citizen to certain social services. At the same time, there is serious concern about the cost and complexity of administering federal day care policies. As programs have multiplied, so has the necessity of strict regulations to ensure that money is used appropriately, that only eligible populations participate, and that services are of at least some minimum quality. Yet the administrative burden of so many programs is overwhelming; state and local agencies and individual users are increasingly annoyed by regulations. From this dilemma, there are only a limited number of ways out.

The federal government may move steadily toward the full assumption of responsibility for day care and for the direct sponsorship of day care facilities. Teachers' unions, of course, urge that federal support be consolidated by locating preschool and child care services in public schools. Our discussions suggest that this would be most likely if unemployment increases or if the nation enters a prolonged war or period of civil unrest.

A second course of action would be to move toward a universal indirect subsidy plan in which neither federal nor state governments directly provided child care but instead "passed through" a subsidy to individual consumers who then made their choices in an entirely private market, say through a voucher plan. In order to approximate some standard of equity, such subsidies would have to be provided according to a graduated scale of income and personal circumstances. This is tantamount to "getting out of the business." The tax credit provisions of the Tax Reform Act of 1976 imply some movement in this direction. However, the history of federal involvement in child care suggests that such a trend is more likely to continue if unemployment declines. But, the declining school-aged population has prompted the American Federation of Teachers to try to co-opt children for the public schools in order to provide jobs for its "excess" teachers.[64]

A third possibility is to try to continue the present mixed system, aimed at various kinds of social and economic engineering, but to do so in a more sophisticated and systematic manner. Because special programs mean special constituencies, and because the Congress does not have to administer what it creates, this course seems the most likely, at least in the short run. It can be successful only if research can provide policymakers with better guidance about such issues as the flexibility of the market; the relationships between setting, staff, cost, and quality; the preferences of selected groups of child care consumers; and the degree to which child care can affect and be affected by other social and economic policies. It is hoped that an understanding of how federal involvement in child care has evolved will facilitate such research and policy efforts.

Notes

1. A price can be given to the in-kind payment that buys the child care; but even if there is no in-kind payment, a shadow price may be calculated for the service.

2. The stereotyped custodial care raised images of children staring at television sets and eating junk food under the nonchalant gaze of a bored housewife. Developmental care was supposed to conjure up images of children playing quietly with Montesorri counting rods under the loving and sensitive eye of a college graduate.

3. The relationships between these characteristics and child outcomes are being studied in the National Day Care Study conducted by Abt Associates, Inc. and SRI International, funded by the U.S. Office of Child Development.

4. This classification scheme may be found in Stanford Research Institute, *Federal Policy for Preschool Services: Assumptions and Evidence,* report prepared for the Office of the Assistant Secretary for Education, Department of Health, Education and Welfare, SRI Project 2158, Menlo Park, CA, Stanford Research Institute, 1975, pp. 11-16.

5. V. Lewis, "Day Care: Needs, Costs, Benefits, Alternatives," in *Issues in the Coordination of Public Welfare Programs,* Paper No. 7, Studies in Public Welfare, pp. 119ff., prepared for the Subcommittee on Fiscal Policy of the Joint Economic Committee, Congress of the United States, Washington, D.C., July 2, 1973; "Federal Interagency Day Care Requirements," *Code of Federal Regulations,* Title 45, Subtitle A.

6. See C. Russell Hill's excellent critique of several analyses of the child care market, *The Child Care Market*, prepared for the Office of the Assistant Secretary for Planning and Evaluation, Department of Health, Education and Welfare, January 1977.

7. U.S. Bureau of the Census, *Current Population Reports*, Series P-20, No. 298, "Daytime Care of Children: October 1974 and February 1975," Washington, D.C., 1976.

8. The National Childcare Consumer Study, prepared by Unco, Inc. for the Office of Child Development, Department of Health, Education and Welfare, 1975, for example, reports that only one-third of the households in its sample relied on a single method of child care. Two-thirds employed at least two types of care.

9. U.S. Bureau of the Census, *Current Population Reports*, p. 1.

10. Ibid., p. 2.

11. Ibid, pp. 3, 9, and 10. "Mothers in the labor force" include those both employed and unemployed (ibid., p. 17).

12. R. L. Shortlidge, "Child Care and the Need for Day Care Centers and Homes in 1971," in *Dual Careers: A Longitudinal Study of the Labor Market Experience of Women*, Volume 3, Columbus, Ohio: Center for Human Resource Research, 1975.

13. U.S. Bureau of the Census, *Current Population Reports*, p. 3.

14. G. J. Duncan and C. R. Hill, "Modal Choice in Child Care Arrangements," in J. N. Morgan, ed., *Five Thousand American Families: Patterns of Economic Progress*, Volume III, Ann Arbor, Michigan: Institute for Social Research, 1975.

15. M. Kurz, P. Robins, and R. Spiegelman, *A Study of the Demand for Child Care by Working Mothers*, Stanford Research Institute, 1975.

16. J. Love and S. Angrist, "Child Care Arrangements of Working Mothers: Social and Economic Aspects," School of Urban and Public Affairs, Carnegie-Mellon University, 1974.

17. Hill, *Child Care Market*, p. 54.

18. Ibid., p. 54.

19. See Section 2002(a) (1).

20. Gilbert Y. Steiner, *The Children's Cause* (Washington, D.C., Brookings Institution, 1976), p. 92.

21. In some states, student status must end at age eighteen.

22. Approximately 25 percent of the registrants are men, and there are a small number of multiple registrants per family. Personal communication from Mr. Sheldon Bloom, Deputy Director, Office of Work Incentive Programs, Department of Health, Education and Welfare, July 18, 1977.

23. Emma Jackson, "The Present System of Publicly Supported Day Care," in *Public Policy for Day Care of Young Children: Organization, Finance and Planning*, Dennis R. Young and Richard R. Nelson, eds. (Lexington, Mass.: Lexington Books, D.C. Heath, 1973), p. 24.

24. Personal communication from Ms. Gertrude Hoffman, specialist on day care services, Public Service Administration, Department of Health, Education and Welfare, July 7, 1977.

25. Appendix B of Unco, Inc., *Day Care for School-Age Children,* prepared for Region X, Department of Health, Education and Welfare under Contract No. OEC-X-72-0055, July 2, 1973, includes descriptive summaries of many programs with child care components as they were in 1972. Some of them, however, no longer have funds available.

26. Our prediction of the dissipation of some currently operating programs should not suggest that we foresee decreasing federal interest in or support of day care. On the contrary, expansion is a more probable eventuality given the apparent policy preferences of President Carter. Our forecast is premised on our observation that many programs do not live forever—a fact that we suspect is largely independent of their day care components, if any. For example, of a dozen or so federal programs listed by Jackson in 1973 as providing funds for child care services or facilities, some have already disappeared (e.g., JOBS funds under the Department of Labor to provide child care for enrollees of these programs; Model Cities funds for child care).

27. U.S. Senate, *Report of the Committee on Finance,* on H.R. 10612, Volume I, p. 135.

28. Lewis, "Day Care," pp. 156-164.

29. Also allowable in this deduction is the care of sick or incapacitated family members (24 CFR, Sec. 860.403(f) (4)). The day care deduction also applies to PHA leased housing (Housing and Community Development Act of 1974, Sec. 23), for which no new funds have been appropriated since January 1973.

30. The 15 percent figure applies to three kinds of families: "very large lower-income families," "large very low-income families," and families with "exceptional medical or other expenses." Even if the 15 percent figure is used, day care is often subsidized because day care expenses are considered in the determination of families with "exceptional medical or other expenses" (24 CFR, Sec. 889.102).

31. 7 CFR, Sec. 271.3(c) (1) (iii) (d).

32. FNS(SF) Instruction 732-1, Sec. 2264.4.

33. Margaret O'Brien Steinfels, *Who's Minding the Children? The History and Politics of Day Care in America* (New York: Simon and Schuster, 1973), p. 36.

34. Ethel S. Beer, *Working Mothers and the Day Nursery* (New York: Whiteside, Inc. and William Morrow, 1957), p. 35.

35. One took care of the children of wet nurses and working mothers; the other cared for the children of employed ex-patients. Steinfels, *Who's Minding the Children?* p. 36; Beer, *Working Mothers,* p. 35; Lewis, "Day Care," p. 109.

36. Irving Lazar and Mae E. Rosenberg, "Day Care in America," in Edith H. Grotberg, ed., *Day Care: Resources for Decisions,* prepared for the Office

of Economic Opportunity, Office of Planning, Research and Evaluation, Washington, D.C., 1972, p. 61.

37. See Charles Loring Brace, *The Dangerous Classes of New York and Twenty Years' Work Among Them* (New York: Wynkoop and Hallenbeck, 1872).

38. Virginia Kerr, "One Step Forward—Two Steps Back: Child Care's Long American History, in *Child Care—Who Cares: Foreign and Domestic Infant and Early Childhood Development Policies,* Student Ed., Pamela Roby, ed. (New York: Basic Books, 1975), p. 87.

39. The nurseries varied considerably in terms of the services offered the children and their families, and this variance could be explained largely by the imagination and energy of the director. Kerr, ibid., p. 86.

40. Sheila Rothman posits that considering the benefits that middle- and upper-class women received from their arrangements, charitable motives may have been, at best, mixed (Sheila M. Rothman, "Other People's Children: The Day Care Experience in America," *The Public Interest* 30 (Winter 1973): 11-27). Yet this was not an objection voiced at the time.

41. June Sochen, *Movers and Shakers: American Women Thinkers and Activists 1900-1970* (New York: Quadrangle, 1973), pp. 31-89.

42. This is not to imply that day nurseries provided educational or developmental services as we know them today, but there seems to have been a definite improvement in the physical, medical, and educational services available to nursery children.

43. Kerr, "One Step Forward," p. 88.

44. Steinfels, *Who's Minding the Children?* pp. 56-57.

45. Shirley Chisholm, "National Day Care Program Introduced," *Congressional Record,* May 18, 1971, extension of remarks, p. 15698. Chisholm's discussion of the early history of day care is taken from Bernice H. Fleiss, "The Relationships of the Mayor's Committee on Wartime Care of Children to Day Care in New York City, 1962," unpublished doctoral dissertation, New York University; and Kerr, "One Step Forward," p. 88.

46. Kerr, "One Step Forward," p. 88.

47. Steinfels, *Who's Minding the Children?* pp. 64-65.

48. Chisholm, "National Day Care," p. E4549; cited in Kerr, "One Step Forward," p. 90.

49. Lewis, "Day Care," p. 109; Kerr, "One Step Forward," p. 90.

50. In 1939 the Works Progress Administration became known as the Works Projects Administration. This name change accounts for the considerable confusion to be found in the writings of others concerned with this era. Critics disagree substantially about the quality and emphasis of the services provided. Compare Rothman, "Other People's Children," p. 20; Kerr, "One Step Forward," p. 90; Steiner, *The Children's Cause,* pp. 15-16.

51. Works Progress Administration, *Final Report on the WPA 1935-43,* Washington, D.C., 1944; cited in Lewis, "Day Care," p. 109.

52. These figures may be found in Lewis, "Day Care," pp. 109-110; Kerr, "One Step Forward," p. 91; and Steinfels, *Who's Minding the Children?* p. 67. Steiner, on the other hand, states that only 105,000 children were served (p. 17). Many WPA nurseries were transferred to community-sponsored, Lanham aided projects. Indeed, by May 1943, 1150 of the former 1700 WPA nurseries or nursery schools were being partly supported by Lanham Act funds. See Kathryn Close, "Day Care Up To Now," *Survey Midmonthly* 79 (July 1943) 195.

53. Steinfels, *Who's Minding the Children?* p. 67, indicates that New York spent $700,000 and Washington spent $500,000. Close puts the New York figure at $2,500,000. Pennsylvania, Connecticut, and Washington also appropriated state funds for community day care programs (p. 197). Employers were also advised to encourage the use of child care; many industries funded and ran their own child care centers; and some companies financially supported community child care facilities and privately operated nursery schools. See "Employment in War Work of Women with Young Children," *Monthly Labor Review* (December 1942): 1184; cited in Kerr, "One Step Forward," p. 91; Lois Meek Stolz, "The Nursery Comes to the Shipyard," *New York Times,* November 7, 1943, pp. 20-39; and Close, "Day Care Up To Now," p. 196.

54. Kerr, "One Step Forward," p. 92. On the conflicting priorities of the cooperating agencies, see William H. Chafe, *The American Women; Her Changing Social, Economic, and Political Roles, 1920-1970* (Oxford: Oxford Univ. Press, 1970), p. 168; cited in Steiner, *The Children's Cause,* p. 17.

55. Only in those states and localities with a previous history of operating day care centers—California, Washington, Massachusetts, Washington, D.C., Hartford, Detroit, New York, and Philadelphia—did Lanham centers remain open on a limited basis, and all but California's centers closed within a few years. The California legislature's support was largely motivated by the desire to preclude welfare dependency. This particular rationale is one of the most frequently voiced today. See Steinfels, *Who's Minding the Children?* p. 70; and Steiner, *The Children's Cause,* pp. 18-20.

56. Steinfels, *Who's Minding the Children?* pp. 70-76.

57. (New York: Schocken Books, 1966). Originally published in the *Bulletin of the World Health Organization* 3 (1951): 355-534.

58. Steiner, *The Children's Cause,* pp. 20-21.

59. *American Women: The Report of the President's Commission on the Status of Women and Other Publications of the Commission* (New York: Scribners, 1965).

60. Sochen, *Movers and Shakers,* p. 233.

61. "Day Care: A Reassessment," *Child Welfare* 44, No. 3 (1965): 125-133.

62. See, for example, J. McVicker Hunt, *Intelligence and Experience* (Ronald Press, 1961). An excellent account of the intellectual development of the Head Start concept and program may be found in Steiner, *The Children's Cause,* pp. 22-35. Additional material on the politics of Project Head Start—and

especially on its evaluation—is in Walter Williams, *Social Policy Research and Analysis* (New York: American Elsevier, 1971).

63. Jackson, "The Present System," pp. 27-28.

64. For a discussion of the child development coalition, see Steiner, *The Children's Cause,* pp. 244-248.

3

The Child Care Market in Seattle and Denver
Samuel Weiner

Introduction

The availability and utilization of child care services for working parents is a critical issue for public policy. It becomes even more important as welfare reform proposals indicate a shift toward realistic work-incentive provisions. Availability of desired child care is an important determinant of the labor force participation decision, especially for mothers. The type and quantity of available child care is also an important element of expenditures for federal, state, and local government. In order to provide a better understanding of child care, a study of the demand for such care was undertaken at SRI International (see Chapter 4). That study emphasized the modal choice decision of child care users. As a complement to that study, a survey of child care providers was also undertaken. This chapter presents the descriptive results of that study by examining the several modes of service offered.

My survey was based on the view that from the supply side at least, there are four main modes of child care service offered: in-home (I-H) care, unlicensed family day care homes (UFDCH), licensed family day care homes (LFDCH), and centers (C). For some analyses, the first two modes, both providing unlicensed care, are viewed as informal care, while the latter two, providing licensed care, are felt to offer formal care. Moreover, for some of our results, the center sector was broken down according to proprietary type: nonprofit public, nonprofit private, and for-profit private. A brief discussion of the four main components of child care will provide a useful background for placing characteristics of the supply of child care services into perspective.

Components of the Day Care Industry

In-home child care vendors provide regular child care for pay in the user's home. This group comes closest to the popular image of the babysitter. They tend to be younger, work fewer hours per week taking care of children for pay, and move in and out of the child care field with greater frequency than do child care providers in other sectors. In general, the in-home sector consists of a large number of highly mobile, atomistic providers.[1]

Family day care home (FDCH) caretakers, whether unlicensed or licensed, provide regular paid child care in the caretaker's own home. Child care is usually for less than 24 hours during any one day; however, a FDCH operator can sometimes take care of children during the entire day. We include in this sector all care given for payment in cash or in kind, but do not include cooperative arrangements. Cooperative FDCHs, unless they are communal types, are usually the weekend or stray-evening variety. This does not mean that cooperative child care arrangements are not in some instances a viable alternative, or may not be more generally in the future. But as an element of the current child care *industry* it appears to have little relevance.[2]

From a purely legalistic point of view, there should be no unlicensed FDCHs as a separate group; that is, in both Seattle and Denver, unlicensed FDCHs are illegal. What this view would imply is that there are only legal and illegal FDCH operations, and that aside from the legality of the operation there is no significant difference between the two in terms of what is offered for sale. One of the important comparisons will be between licensed and unlicensed FDCHs, to determine the differences, if any, between these sectors. My a priori view is that licensing imposes a degree of uniformity and increases stability in licensed facilities. Moreover, the structure of the licensing process may promote a more businesslike attitude on the part of proprietors of licensed facilities.

For centers I attempted to survey the entire population of day care centers in Seattle and Denver.[3] This component of the day care industry is the most structured in terms of child care activities, and probably the most likely to be operated as a business activity. Although it is the least important in terms of the number of child care demanders using the service, of the four major components of the child care industry, it is usually thought of, at least by child care professionals, as the epitome of a child care institution. Formally it is usually defined in terms of the number of children for whom they are licensed to care. Usually centers can care for 7 or more children; although there is a gray area where both centers and FDCHs can have 7 to 11 children. For my purposes, a center was simply defined as a child care facility licensed as a day care center.[4]

Relative Importance of the Four Components

During the past decade several national and regional surveys of child care utilization have been undertaken.[5] From these surveys we can obtain a general view of the relative importance of the different modes of child care services. Of these surveys the most widely quoted, insofar as day care user characteristics are concerned, are the Low-Spindler[6] and the Ruderman[7] studies.

Ruderman takes a sample of working mothers and seeks to determine the arrangements for child care made for children needing such care. She finds that children of working mothers are taken care of in the following ways: (1) child takes care of itself (7 percent), (2) mother takes care of child while working (3 percent), (3) father takes care of the child (23 percent), (4) an older sibling takes care of child (12 percent), (5) child is cared for in home of user by other than parent or sibling (28 percent), (6) child is cared for in the home of child care provider (23 percent), (7) care in center, nursery school, or recreation center (4 percent). The first five categories consist of various forms of care provided within the child's home, whereas the last two are what is usually termed family day care home and center care. What stands out here is the preponderance of care for children of working mothers provided by some relative or by the child itself. Similar results were found in the Westinghouse-Westat survey.[8] In both surveys, almost three-fourths of child care for working mothers was provided by relatives or by self-care.

In most discussions of day care as a business operation, the types of care listed in the preceding categories 1 through 4 is generally not taken into account. Although these forms of child care make up almost half the care provided to the children of working mothers, and although it is substitutable with the other forms of child care listed in 5 through 7, researchers in the child care field consider care provided in categories 1 through 4 as within family transfers. Child care, especially when it is viewed as a business transaction, is concerned with paid for care (in money or in kind) provided in the home of the user, in the home of the provider, or in a specially designated structure devoted to child care.[9] These three sources of care define what we know as in-home, family day care home, and center child care.

In the surveys noted previously, it is clear that the bulk of child care users utilize informal care, whether in their own home or in that of another. Every survey, where the distinction has been employed, has shown that licensed centers and family day care homes provide a small proportion of all child care. However, it is most difficult to get a reliable enumeration of the informal sector. Table 3-1 indicates the estimated importance of the informal sector.

Although the data from the different surveys used in Table 3-1 are not strictly comparable, they are close enough for rough comparisons. Perhaps the most glaring conclusion that comes from Table 3-1 is the small percentage of children who receive child care in formal centers. The significantly higher percentage that I found in the Seattle survey may be due to the attempts being made by state, local, and educational groups to upgrade day care services in Seattle.

The remainder of this chapter sets out the results of my survey of day care vendors in Seattle and Denver. The next section discusses characteristics of the day care providers and the services provided. Following that is a discussion of constraints on the supply of day care activities. That section emphasizes licensing and zoning requirements. Another section looks into the elements of income, including subsidies and fees. The last descriptive section deals with costs; then a section concerned with the implications of my supply survey on public policy concludes the chapter.

Table 3-1
Percent of Day Care Provided within the Three Main Sectors

	Low-Spindler[a]	Ruderman[b]	Westinghouse-Westat[c]	Denver[d]	Seattle[d]
In-Home	57.7%	51.9%	40.6%	25.0 %	37.5%
Unlicensed Family Day Care Home	36.9[e]	42.6[e]	49.2[e]	61.9	35.6
Licensed Family Day Care Home				5.0	9.8
Center	5.4	5.5	10.2	8.1	17.1

[a]See Low and Spindler, "Child Care Arrangements of Working Mothers in the United States," Children's Bureau Publication 461, Department of Health, Education and Welfare, 1968, Tables A-2 and A-3, p. 71.

[b]See Ruderman, *Child Care and Working Mothers: A Survey of Arrangements Made for Daytime Care of Children*, Child Welfare League of America, 1968, Table 49, p. 212.

[c]See Westinghouse Learning Corp. and Westat Res., Inc., *Day Care Survey–1970: Summary Report and Basic Analysis*, April 1971. Tables 4.28 and 4.29, pp. 179–180.

[d]Data collected from the Seattle-Denver Income Maintenance Experiment.

[e]This consists primarily of unlicensed family day care homes.

Child Care Providers and Services Provided

Who are the providers of child care service, and what do they offer to child care users? There is a great deal of data and little disagreement on the characteristics of child care providers reflected in those data. There is perhaps as much data on the services provided, but very little agreement on what is *actually* being provided. In this section I will present characteristics of the provider, as gleaned from my survey results, and relevant characteristics of the services being provided.

Provider Characteristics

Child care is a labor-intensive process. About three-fourths of the input costs for child care services consist of payment to providers. With that level of importance it will be useful to review characteristics of the child care labor inputs. Some characteristics of the providers of child care services are more relevant to service or cost considerations, and these will be discussed in later sections of this chapter. However, there are some general characteristics of the provider, and of the relationship between the provider and the child being cared for, that are relevant to a discussion of the supply of child care services.

In both cities the I-H providers were generally younger than providers in other sectors. Licensed FDCH operators tended to be somewhat older than providers in all other sectors, including centers; while in Seattle the unlicensed FDCH operators and the center staff were approximately the same average age. However, as can be seen from Table 3-2, the distribution of providers by age grouping does not follow the same pattern seen in the averages. For example, although the average age of unlicensed FDCH operators and the staff of for-profit, private centers is about equal, the largest grouping in the center is for twenty- to twenty-nine-year-old staff, while for the unlicensed FDCH operators, the largest proportion is in the nineteen and under and thirty- to forty-nine-year-old group.

Although a larger proportion of the I-H providers in both cities, and of the unlicensed FDCH providers in Seattle, were in the youngest age groups, I still found that a majority of these providers had previously held some full-time paid job other than child care. However, in both cities I found that whereas somewhat over half the unlicensed providers had prior full-time employment, almost all the licensed FDCH operators had previously engaged in full-time work.

Moreover, there is no apparent systematic relationship between the two cities or between licensed and unlicensed sectors, so far as the average number of years that the child care operators had provided child care. Except for the unlicensed FDCH sector, however, the average years providing care was very close when comparing the two cities for each of the other sectors. In each city

Table 3-2
Age and Race of Day Care Providers, and Race of Children (In Percent of Total)

	Seattle						Denver					
	Unlicensed		Licensed				Unlicensed		Licensed			
				Centers						Centers		
	In-Home	Family Day Care Homes	Total	Nonprofit Private	Public	For-Profit Private	In-Home	Family Day Care Homes	Total	Nonprofit Private	Public	For-Profit Private
Racial/Ethnic Group (Providers)												
Black	20.0	22.9	18.5	20.2	26.8	5.0	25.0	42.3	22.1	14.8	35.0	4.9
Chicano	4.0	0	2.2	1.5	5.4	1.7	30.0	26.9	16.3	9.1	26.1	4.9
White	72.0	73.8	74.2	73.2	66.1	85.0	45.0	29.8	58.3	76.1	33.1	87.7
Racial/Ethnic Group (Children)												
Black	23.0	20.7	33.7	35.8	66.6	17.0	20.8	37.7	23.2	26.0	29.2	16.1
Chicano	0	1.5	2.3	2.3	2.7	1.3	33.9	33.2	16.4	9.2	31.9	5.7
White	67.2	70.0	56.5	54.1	23.1	73.9	45.3	24.7	57.9	61.9	36.1	75.4
Age												
50 yrs. & older	8.0	28.4	12.5	12.6	7.1	17.5	15.0	19.3	20.9	21.6	17.8	26.3
30-49 yrs. of age	4.0	48.6	24.8	26.8	34.0	8.8	25.0	27.8	32.9	39.8	35.7	20.0
20-29 yrs. of age	16.0	23.1	50.8	51.0	46.4	54.4	25.0	42.3	38.3	27.2	44.0	38.7
19 yrs. & under	72.0	0	11.9	9.6	12.5	19.3	35.0	10.6	8.0	11.4	2.5	15.0
Average age (years)	23.6	30.2	31.8	32.2	31.3	30.8	31.3	33.3	36.7	38.0	36.3	36.2

Source: The source of all tables in Chapters 2-5 is the survey undertaken by SRI in Seattle and Denver during May 1974, unless otherwise specified.

the average years providing care ran from about two to five with licensed FDCH operators in the high bracket and center staff in the low range. I also found that in the three sectors for which data were available, on the average about 6 to 15 months of care was provided to children receiving care, with the I-H providers in both cities generally caring for the same child the longest period of time.

Another relevant characteristic of providers, so far as the supply of child care services is concerned, is their racial/ethnic composition. It is relevant at least in view of the fact that the racial/ethnic composition of children using child care services is highly correlated to the racial/ethnic composition of providers. In Seattle the percentage of providers who were from minority groups (black or Chicano) was about the same for all sectors other than unlicensed FDCHs, where the percent of minority members involved was much greater. However, in Denver the distinction is between formal and informal sectors, with the former having a significantly lower percentage of providers who were from minority groups. But within the center sector, public centers are comparable insofar as minority member involvement is concerned to the informal sector, while the for-profit, private centers have the lowest minority member participation. Table 3-2 shows that the proportion of child care providers in Seattle who are minority group members is roughly the same in all sectors except for unlicensed FDCHs and the private, for-profit centers, with the percentage much higher in the former and much lower in the latter.

Fairly consistent with what I found for providers with regard to racial/ ethnic groupings was the racial/ethnic breakdown of the children who were being cared for. The percentage of children who were black or Chicano was almost exactly equal to the comparable provider percentages for all except the center sector. In that sector in Seattle I found that a large proportion of the children were from minority groups relative to the providers; this was especially true for the public centers. In Denver the proportion of children from minority groups was also somewhat larger than the proportion of providers from those groups, but only for the private, nonprofit and for-profit centers.

When we look at the percentage of providers who cared for their own children at the same time that they provided care for others, some of whom could have some relationship to the child care vendor, we find a different relationship between sectors and cities. In Seattle none of the I-H providers cared for their own children during the time that other children were being cared for, while about one-quarter of the unlicensed and licensed FDCHs and almost a tenth of all center staff had their own child in attendance when providing child care. In Denver the percentages were comparable for licensed and unlicensed FDCHs, and for centers and I-H providers. So for child care operators providing care while their own children were in attendance, the licensed and unlicensed FDCHs were comparable in and between both cities, while the I-H providers and center staff were reasonably comparable, with the exception of the Seattle I-H providers.

In almost all instances the percentages of providers and children being cared for who were minority group members were larger than the proportions of the total populations of Seattle and Denver who were in those minority groups. In Seattle slightly over 10 percent of the population was black or Chicano (according to 1970 Census figures), while almost 26 percent of the Denver population was in that class. One important reason why the child care sample ratios for minority members are so much greater, in general, than similar ratios for the entire city population is the selection process used in obtaining the sample. My method for selecting I-H and unlicensed FDCH respondents was biased toward lower-income areas in Seattle and Denver because the names of potential respondents were obtained from the SIME/DIME sample, which is biased toward lower-income census tracts. That bias does not hold for the licensed sector, where complete listings of providers were obtained. Consistent with that, I found that the percentages of providers *and* children who were minority group members in centers and licensed FDCHs were almost the same as the proportions of minority group members in the overall city population, except for some sizable discrepancies within the center sector. In Seattle that was especially true for public centers, and in Denver there was a sizable difference for the private, for-profit centers.

I also found that a significant number of children being cared for were related to the providers. These relationships include own child as well as other relationships. In Seattle there is not a great deal of variation, except for black I-H and white unlicensed FDCH providers. In Denver, however, a far larger percentage of the unlicensed sector providers cared for children who were related to them than was found to hold for the licensed FDCH operators. Among Chicanos in Denver, there is a preference, at least as revealed by their actions, for the use of unlicensed providers who are part of the extended family. This seems to be especially true when compared to whites.[10]

Several observations from the data with regard to providers are worth reemphasizing because of their importance in the supply of child care. One such observation is that the majority of formal sector child care providers are probably part of the regular labor force. There are indications that a significant proportion of the providers in the informal sectors may be temporarily out of the regular labor force, primarily because of a desire to stay home to care for their own children or to acquire an education.

The implication of this finding is that there is a fairly elastic supply of labor to the informal sector. Therefore, the supply of informal sector services can expand easily, since the care given is very similar to work generally done by parents staying home to care for their own children. This would not be true if providers had to come from some special group, such as housewives with experience in elementary education. In that case, an expansion of the supply of child care might be limited by a shortage of that type of labor. However, the average level of educational achievement in every sector makes that assumption unlikely, at least as it concerns the majority of providers.

Another important observation is that the proportion of black and Chicano providers in the informal sector in Denver was much greater than in the formal sector. The same finding is true in Seattle, except for I-H providers, where the proportion of providers who are from minority groups is approximately the same as in centers. Moreover, the racial/ethnic composition of day care users was approximately the same as that of providers. However, within the center sector I found that a large percent of the public, nonprofit staff and children were from minority groups, while only a small proportion of users and staff in the private, for-profit centers were black or Chicano. Therefore, except for the profit-oriented centers, I found that there was no apparent restriction on entry into the field of child care by minority group members.

A final observation worth emphasizing is the relationship between providers and users. Providers and users are more likely to be related in Denver than in Seattle. I obtained information on the relationship between users and providers of child care for all but the center sector. For the licensed FDCHs, about one-forth of the children using child care services were related to providers of those services. However, in the informal sectors, there was a much larger percentage of providers who were related to the children for whom they provided care in Denver relative to the percentage in Seattle. For example, almost two-thirds of the unlicensed FDCH operators in Denver were related to the children using their services, whereas in Seattle almost one-third of the unlicensed FDCH operators were related to the children under their care. Furthermore, I found that over four-fifths of the Chicano, unlicensed FDCH operators in Denver provided services for related children. It appears that the more liberal subsidy policy in Denver, whereby related, unlicensed providers can more easily obtain payment for providing day care services relative to Seattle, has resulted in a far greater use of relatives for unlicensed day care.

Service Provided

The type of service provided, and the staff involved in the provision of that service, is closely related to considerations regarding the quality of care. That topic will be dealt with in more detail in Chapter 5. However, in this section, I want to comment on the quality of care as perceived by child care providers— a more subjective measure of quality—as well as discuss some important elements of day care services.

From the survey I was able to obtain a self-structured measure of the percent of total care devoted to educational-developmental activities and to custodial care.[11] For all providers, and for individual center staff members, I asked that they allocate the total number of hours worked last week as a day care vendor into 20 separate activities. These activities were then grouped into custodial care hours, educational-developmental care hours, administrative hours, and other hours. My interest was in the first two types of activities.

The method used in classifying activities into custodial or educational-developmental groups was by a consensus of those involved with the analysis of this study and child care experts. This procedure should not be viewed as providing a rigorous measure of quality. However, the order of magnitude and the relative position of the various sectors appears to provide a useful subjective guide to the type of service provided. In other words, I feel that the data collected are indicative of how respondents perceive and classify the type of care they are providing for children under their care.[12] As perceived by all child care vendors, and using my method for calculating educational-developmental care, I found that the I-H and unlicensed FDCH providers in Seattle said that approximately one-tenth of their time was devoted to such care; while in the licensed FDCHs in Seattle and for all sectors other than centers in Denver, about one-fifth of the time devoted to child care was perceived as being spent in educational-developmental activities. The proportion of the week spent on higher-quality care was somewhat greater for centers—overall, one-third in Seattle and slightly less in Denver. In the latter city there was very little difference in the percent of time devoted to such care between different proprietary types. However, in Seattle the public centers reported spending almost half their time in educational-developmental care, while the other centers showed slightly under a third of their time being used in that type of care.

Within the center sector, there was also a substantial amount of time devoted to "other" activities. A significant part of the "other" activities were administrative tasks.[13] There was a large difference in the percentage of staff time devoted to administrative tasks between the three proprietary types in the Seattle centers. Public, nonprofit centers devoted an average of about 16 percent of their time to such tasks, while the profit-oriented centers spent about 5 percent of their time on administrative matters. In Denver the distribution between proprietary types with regard to the percent of time spent in administrative tasks was fairly uniform, ranging from about 13 percent for private, for-profit centers to a little over 16 percent for the public, nonprofit centers.

The other elements of child care service that I want to mention are health care and sick child care. Both are important considerations for users, and both have an important effect on the cost of the services provided. With regard to health care, I found that public centers are much more likely to provide a full range of such services.[14] But in all cases, less than half both provided and paid for the services given.

In general, where it was provided, an additional charge was assessed against the recipient. Moreover, only 10 to 20 percent of all centers even provided these services, with the exception of immunization. Almost half the centers provided that service in Seattle. Except for dental checkups and psychological testing, the Denver centers appear to provide very few health care services to the children in their care; and when such care is provided, the Denver centers are much less likely to pay for them than are the Seattle centers.

The other element concerned whether or not care was provided to users when the child was ill. I asked whether a child with a minor illness other than a simple cold would, when ill, be taken care of during the hours that the child would normally have been cared for. The I-H providers almost all reported that they would take care of such children (see Table 3-3). The percentage dropped considerably for unlicensed FDCHs in both cities, but there was still about three-fifths in Seattle and over two-fifths in Denver who would provide ill-child care. However, in the licensed FDCH sector, only about one-fourth to one-third of the providers in either city provided such care, while a very small percent of the centers in either city would accept children with a minor illness for care. But for the most prevalent of the minor childhood illness (a simple cold), almost all providers in both cities said that they would accept such children for regular care. For working mothers, being able to leave their children with a child care provider when the child has a minor illness is an important consideration in maintaining a steady work record.

Supply Constraints

In this section, barriers to entry and capacity considerations will be reviewed. Data regarding barriers to entry are mainly concerned with the licensed sector of the child care industry, although the extent to which licensing is enforced, especially with regard to FDCHs, will effectively restrict entry into the unlicensed sector.

Barriers to Entry

Child care licensing requirements are quite similar in Seattle and Denver.[15] The minimum requirements for licensing centers and FDCHs in both cities are concerned with enforcement of fire and health code standards, along with some restriction on staff/child ratios. The latter condition is especially relevant for federally funded centers, but again the regulations are similar in Seattle and Denver. In practice there are probably differences in the way that individual fire or health inspectors view code enforcement. But the within city differences among inspectors may be as great as that between cities. There may also be some variance with regard to caseworker concern and evaluation of the child care providers. However, both cities have a fairly well-educated class of social workers, and my interviews with some of them lead me to the view that there was no systematic difference between the two cities concerning how the caseworkers judge the fitness of day care providers.

In both cities, the licensing regulations for centers and FDCHs are in a state of flux. There is pressure on the one hand to simplify the regulations, while

Table 3-3
Care Provided for Sick Child (In Percent)

	Seattle							Denver						
	Unlicensed		Licensed					Unlicensed		Licensed				
					Centers							Centers		
					Nonprofit							Nonprofit		
	In-Home	Family Day Care Homes	Family Day Care Homes	Total	Private	Public	For-Profit Private	In-Home	Family Day Care Homes	Family Day Care Homes	Total	Private	Public	For-Profit Private
Provides Care for Sick Child during Regular Day of Child Care	88.0	59.3	33.2	7.5	11.4	0	4.8	85.0	43.3	26.4	10.6	15.4	5.9	11.8
Takes Care of Child with Cold for Regular Day of Care	NA	90.9	92.3	90.3	87.1	100.0	90.0	NA	96.6	95.1	76.2	73.7	75.0	80.0

there is opposing pressure from the federal level for more stringent regulations, especially with regard to staffing of centers and child care training for FDCH providers. Moreover, there is a plethora of agencies (health, sanitation, zoning, building, and fire) at state, county, and local levels that are involved in the licensing process. Each brings a sometimes conflicting and sometimes costly view of the minimum licensing standard requirements.

The actual enforcement of child care licensing regulations is a relatively recent phenomenon in both Seattle and Denver. In conjunction with this, inspectors from health or fire departments tend to use standards developed and applied to other types of facilities or institutions when inspecting centers and FDCHs. For example, nursery schools in Denver must be licensed, even though their programs only last three hours during the day.[16] Moreover, these nurseries must have commercial-type dishwashers and cooking facilities if they serve any food.

The licensing staff in both Seattle and Denver feel that from the point of view of the safety and development of the children cared for, the licensing requirements are minimal at best. However, they also feel that regulatory enforcement of the child care industry is relatively new, especially as it pertains to facilities other than federally funded centers. They are also cognizant of the many violations of the rules and the extent of unlicensed FDCHs in operation.[17] The violations, especially in terms of the number of children cared for at any one time, occur in the licensed as well as unlicensed homes. In general, the licensing personnel also feel that they are grossly understaffed, which means that they rarely make the required number of visits to each facility to provide effective monitoring of licensed child care.

Zoning restrictions are particularly burdensome to centers. In Denver, child care is treated as a light industry with regard to zoning. Therefore, it is very difficult to obtain a permit to locate centers in single-family housing areas (R0 and R1). Seattle's zoning laws are far more liberal and flexible, especially as it concerns FDCHs. Seattle recently enacted legislation that allows up to 12 children to be cared for in a FDCH;[18] whereas in Denver the maximum number of children allowed in licensed FDCHs is 4, with a zoning variance needed to raise the allowed number to 6.[19]

Overall licensing standards for FDCHs are not considered too excessive in either Seattle or Denver.[20] Although it is not true that only a "fence and a phone" are needed to obtain a license, it is true that most applicants have little trouble becoming licensed FDCH operators. In Denver less than one-twentieth of all licensed FDCHs needed to make any change in their facility that cost more than $100 in order to meet fire or safety standards.[21] In Seattle almost 14 percent of the FDCH operators had to expend that sum to meet the required standards.

On the average, the waiting time for acquiring a FDCH license is not very long. Almost three-fourths of the operators in both cities waited only two months or less for their license to be approved, with almost three-fifths waiting no more than one month. There were, however, about 6 percent of all licensed FDCH providers who had to wait at least six months for their license. Moreover, there appears to be a considerable amount of turnover among licensed FDCH operators. In Seattle only 13 percent of the FDCH vendors had their current license for five years or more, while slightly over half had it for less than one year. In Denver about 16 percent had their license for at least five years, and almost two-fifths had it for less than one year. This is only partly due to turn-over of existing operators; it is also due to the emphasis on licensing of FDCHs during the past several years, especially in Seattle.

In Denver I also found that over a third of the centers had been licensed for at least five years, while less than one-fourth had been licensed for that long in Seattle. Since the percentage that have been licensed for less than one year is far higher in Seattle than in Denver (one-third versus one-fifth), it appears that the development of centers in Seattle has been a relatively recent occurrence, although there are some that have been in operation for a long period. Moreover, the growth has been most rapid for nonprofit centers in Seattle.

As pointed out earlier, obtaining a zoning variance is more important for centers than for FDCHs. In Denver almost a third of all centers had to obtain a zoning variance, whereas only a fifth of the Seattle centers needed to obtain such a permit. There was also quite a bit of variation within the center sector in Seattle. About a third of the private, for-profit centers in Seattle required a zoning variance, while less than a tenth of the nonprofit, public centers in Seattle needed the variance permit. In Denver about a third of each proprietary type needed a zoning variance.

In Denver new fire standards were also put into effect on January 1, 1973. These standards implied some large expenditures, since they required panic hardware on doors,[22] one-hour fire proof doors, and an outside exit for every room. These new standards forced some of the private, nonprofit centers (mainly church organized) to close down because of lack of the capital required for the changes.

Capital requirements are, of course, another important barrier to entry for centers.[23] My measure of capital cost includes only the current market value of equipment, durables, vehicles, and average cost of structural changes made prior to receiving a license.[24] Unfortunately, because of a lack of reliable facility cost data, or other data with which such costs could be estimated,[25] I was not able to include the most important capital cost component: structure cost. In the private, nonprofit sector I did find that many centers were housed in churches. So the problem of imputing the appropriate facility cost to the child care operations would have been very tenuous, even if overall facility cost data were available. Even with the obvious downward bias resulting from the exclusion of facility costs, I found that the average capital cost, as defined previously, was $11,254, in Seattle and $19,026 in Denver. Although these are not trivial figures, they do not by themselves impose any serious barrier to entering the center sector. The average value of the current market value of equipment and vehicles per currently enrolled child is also a reasonably low absolute amount: $127 for all centers in Seattle and $80 in Denver, with a high of $231 for public centers in Seattle and a high of $111 for private, for-profit centers in Denver (see the section on costs; see also Chapter 7).

In sum, I found that the licensing procedure, although it takes some time, does not seem to be a major barrier to entry into the child care industry. The majority of providers waited less than two months to obtain their licenses, and few family day care homes spent more than $100 complying with licensing requirements. However, there is some indication that the cost of compliance, especially as it concerns the new Title XX child/staff standards, may present a significant financial burden for the private, for-profit centers, if enforced (see Chapter 8). Zoning restrictions may also present something of a barrier to entry for centers. Approximately one-third of the centers in both cities and a smaller proportion of family day care homes had to obtain zoning variances in order to provide child care services. These licensing and zoning requirements did contribute noticeably to the cost of entry into the child care market. However, these are costs which are under the control of the local authorities. Regulations could be simplified and procedures streamlined if the decision was made to increase the availability of child care. For example, in Denver there are a number of different agencies involved in the licensing process, including health, sanitation, zoning, building, and fire. These somewhat overlapping jurisdictions delay the licensing procedure and most certainly impose an additional, if only psychic, cost to the potential entrant into the child care market.

Capacity Considerations

The *capacity* of centers is given by the number of children that the center is licensed to provide care for. That number of children is allowable on the assumption that relevant requirements are met in providing adequate care, such as having the required child/staff ratio. For I-H and FDCH providers, I have constructed my own measure of capacity.[26]

In the discussion to follow, I will use center capacity as measured by the ratio of full-time equivalent enrolled children to licensed capacity rather than using total current enrollment in the numerator. Using that measure, I found that in Seattle the unlicensed FDCHs and the centers as a whole experienced the same level of capacity utilization (about 85 percent), while the I-H sector showed a somewhat higher degree of utilization (93 percent) and the licensed FDCHs a much lower percent of capacity utilized (66 percent). Within the center sector in Seattle, I found the private, for-profit centers showing the same level of utilization as the I-H sector, while the public centers were much closer to the rate found for licensed FDCHs.

In Denver the relationship between sectors with regard to capacity utilization was quite different from that found in Seattle. In Denver licensed and unlicensed FDCHs showed a fairly similar rate of utilization (about 77 percent), while the I-H sector rate was slightly higher (85 percent). Centers in Denver showed a much higher utilization rate (almost 97 percent), both overall and for each of the three proprietary types.

In general there is about a 15 to 20 percent underutilization of measured capacity in the child care industry in Seattle and Denver. Analogous to what has been found in ordinary industrial activities, it may be that child care providers reach an optimum level of efficiency in terms of their interaction with children cared for at about 85 percent utilization of their child caring capacity.

Although the overall average level of capacity utilization is about 85 percent, there are a significant number of child care providers in the different sectors who utilize 100 percent (or more) of their capacity, according to my measure.[27] In the I-H sector, almost half the Denver and three-fourths of the Seattle providers utilize 100 percent of their capacity; in the unlicensed FDCH sector, the percentage with 100 percent utilization is far less, about one-twentieth in Seattle and one-tenth in Denver, while about one-third of the licensed FDCHs in both cities utilize their capacity fully. In the center sector, about half the providers in each proprietary type utilize approximately 100 percent of their licensed capacity, except for the private, nonprofit centers in Denver, where slightly over 90 percent of the licensed capacity is utilized.

So it is not at all surprising that some of the providers have waiting lists. I found that only about 6 to 10 percent of the unlicensed (I-H and FDCH) providers in either city had a waiting list containing one or more children. In fact, in Seattle none of the unlicensed FDCHs have an active waiting list of children seeking their services. Licensed FDCHs were slightly more likely to have a waiting list, with about 14 percent of these providers in Seattle and 19 percent in Denver having a list with one or more children on it during the period of the survey. Centers, however, were generally more likely to have a list of children waiting to enroll. About two-thirds of the nonprofit, private centers had such a list in Seattle and Denver, about three-fourths of public, nonprofit centers had one, and approximately half the private, for-profit centers in both cities also had waiting lists. In general, those who use child care need it immediately; so if a desired facility is not available, they go to a less-desirable facility or mode of service. This may help to explain the large percent of centers with waiting lists, especially the public centers. Since the survey was taken in May, and I find a substantial decline in child care use during the summer, the day care centers' waiting lists may reflect a desire for fall enrollment. This could be either for families planning ahead for first-time child care use for a particular child or for a desire to change from the child care facility or mode currently being used.

Another important consideration with regard to capacity is the availability of child care slots for children of different ages. One of the frequently heard complaints concerning child care services is the lack of facilities for toddlers, i.e., children under two years of age. Table 3-4 indicates that a substantial proportion of the children cared for by licensed and unlicensed FDCH operators in both Seattle and Denver, as well as for the public, nonprofit centers in Seattle, are toddlers. However, I do not have any indication of the possible unmet demand, according to the existence of a waiting list by age of child. In general, I find that centers were less likely to have children under two enrolled than were the other sectors. In fact, 85 percent of all the Seattle centers and almost 90 percent of those in Denver had no children under age two when interviewed, while in both cities almost none of the private, for-profit centers provided care for toddlers.

Aside from the age of the children cared for, it is of interest to note the average number of children cared for by the various provider groups. As shown in Table 3-4, with the exception of centers, providers in the different sectors in both cities care for approximately the same number of children, on the average; that is, the I-H providers in Seattle are comparable to the I-H providers in Denver with regard to the average number of children cared for, etc. For centers, the average number of children cared for in Denver is significantly higher than for Seattle. The variance is also greater for centers in Denver, where the largest center cared for 230 children. Table 3-4 also indicates that the public centers in Denver can be quite large, whereas the largest public center in Seattle had less than one-third the maximum enrollment found in Denver.

Another relevant factor regarding capacity is the number of hours of care provided. In the informal sectors, providers in Seattle spend far fewer hours taking care of children; I-H providers in Seattle showed an average of 21 hours of care per week versus 38 in Denver, and the unlicensed FDCHs in Seatttle provided an average of 30 hours of care per week versus 39 in Denver. In the formal sectors, the average hours of care per week in both cities was about 45.

I also found that there appeared to be substantial friction in the clearing of the market. For example, within the center sector I found that almost 60 percent of all centers in both cities had waiting lists, with almost three-fourths of the public, nonprofit centers stating that they had a waiting list. At the same time, I found that the average level of capacity utilization for Seattle centers was 85 percent, with the public centers utilizing only 78 percent of their capacity. In Denver the utilization rate was 95 percent for both the total, as well as for public centers.

That unused child care services and waiting lists exist simultaneously may indicate some frictions in the child care market. There are a variety of causes for friction in the operation of this market: child care service is a good that is not easily standardized, so demanders must search for a supplier who fits their needs;

Table 3-4

Age of Children Using Child Care (In Percent of Total) and Number of Children Cared For

	Seattle							Denver						
	Unlicensed		Licensed					Unlicensed		Licensed				
					Centers							Centers		
						Nonprofit							Nonprofit	
	In-Home	Family Day Care Homes	Family Day Care Homes	Total	Private	Public	For-Profit Private	In-Home	Family Day Care Homes	Family Day Care Homes	Total	Private	Public	For-Profit Private
Age (Percent of Total)														
Less than 2 yrs.	9.8	29.1	16.2	4.1	3.2	16.6	0.5	7.5	18.2	21.1	2.7	3.9	4.8	0
2–5 yrs. of age[a]	47.6	48.8	52.9	69.5	71.6	54.0	71.8	47.2	50.6	57.7	68.4	65.9	70.8	67.5
6 yrs. & over[b]	42.6	22.1	30.9	26.5	25.2	29.4	27.7	45.3	31.2	21.2	29.0	30.4	24.4	32.6
Mean age[c]	5.3	3.6	4.6	4.0	3.9	3.8	4.1	5.7	4.7	4.0	4.1	4.1	3.9	4.3
Average Number of Children Currently Enrolled or Cared For	1.9	3.2	5.2	41.9	46.1	29.6	41.1	1.8	3.7	4.6	60.1	54.3	59.9	64.6
Maximum Number Currently Enrolled	3	7	14	135	135	66	120	2	12	10	230	87	215	230

[a] 2–4 yrs. for centers.

[b] 5 yrs. and over for centers.

[c] Estimates for centers.

differences in the type of care, as well as in the hours of available care, contribute to the time needed to find desired child care; and special needs may also make a match between child and provider more difficult. I did find that care was more difficult to obtain for very young children, and for children with any but the most routine illness. As mentioned, it is a commonly heard complaint that not enough child care capacity is available for toddlers, children under the age of two. However, it was seen that a substantial proportion of the children cared for by licensed and unlicensed FDCHs in both cities, as well as public centers in Seattle, are toddlers. If child care users are trying to get toddlers into the other segment of the day care market, the complaint may have some validity, since only a small percentage of the children cared for in these other segments are less than two years of age. Although a large percentage of the informal sector providers will take care of children with a minor illness (e.g., a cold), the percentage drops sharply for licensed FDCH providers; and the percentage of centers that offer such care is negligible. Yet another possible reason for friction in the child care market is that information about available suppliers was not widely used. Although both cities have free referral services, I found that only 10 to 25 percent of all children were enrolled through the use of these services. Most of the other users learned of the available service through friends, neighbors, or relatives. These, then, are some of the possible causes for the simultaneous existence of underutilization of capacity and excess demand as seen in the existence of waiting lists.

Another important issue is the relationship between changes in supply and changes in price of child care services. Information on the reaction of supply to changing prices was more difficult to obtain than that about the current state of the market. The available information related to possible constraints on supply rather than the actual change in aggregate supply that might result from an increase in price. As has already been mentioned, the supply of labor for potential child care service seems unlikely to be an absolute constraint on the supply of child care. Other inputs, such as buildings or equipment, are also not likely to constrain the expansion of child care.

Income

This section highlights all the relevant data collected that was concerned with revenues, whether they came from fees or subsidies. The discussion will be grouped into two main subsections: subsidies and revenue and fees. A brief discussion of the relative importance of child care vendor earnings in total family income will also be included.

Subsidies

In Denver a private, nonprofit group, the Mile High Child Care Association (MHCCA), provides about one-fourth of all licensed child care. They operate under a contract with the City/County of Denver that pays (as of mid-1974) MHCCA about $7.50 per child per day for children enrolled in their centers and about $4 per child per day for children enrolled in their family day care homes.[28]

The children are from low-income families, coming mainly from WIN Program participants, AFDC families, or eligible Model Cities families. Users of MHCCA facilities make very little direct payment, if any, for child care services. A fee is charged if family income exceeds stipulated amounts, given family size. However, MHCCA never benefits from any fee charged to the user, since user fees are subtracted from the contract rate guaranteed by the county. The MHCCA also provides a general child care referral service for licensed care that is available to anyone in Denver.

Although MHCCA provides about one-fourth of all licensed child care in Denver, they provide a larger percentage of the licensed care for preschool children. Prior to late 1973, MHCCA facilities were concerned only with care for preschool children. Since that date, however, they have started to get into programs that will provide child care for all children less than 13 years of age.

Subsidy payment from the Department of Welfare in Denver goes directly to the vendor for centers. If the child is cared for by a FDCH operator, licensed or unlicensed, the subsidy payment is made to the vendor only upon the written request of the child care user. Subsidy payment for I-H providers, including relatives, is allowed and is made to the user. An I-H provider who is related to the user must be over sixteen and have foregone a paid position because of the child care duties in order for the child being cared for to be eligible for a subsidy.

The Seattle Welfare Department also allows subsidies to be paid for child care to I-H providers who are related to the child. One difference is that in Seattle the provider must be at least eighteen years of age. Reimbursement for I-H care goes only to users of the service; however, since August 1973, subsidy payments for centers and FDCHs (only licensed, since unlicensed FDCHs are illegal)[29] are made directly to the vendor. Moreover, since early 1974, two-headed families are also eligible for child care subsidy under stipulated conditions, mainly where both heads are working and/or in training or one head is disabled. In Seattle, vendors are also constrained to a maximum charge for subsidized children that is less than or equal to the subsidy rate. That rate for centers and FDCHs, as of mid-1974, was $5.31 per day for the first child in a family, $4.79 per day for the second child, and $4.26 for the third child, with an overall limit per family of $265 per month. For I-H care the subsidy rates cannot exceed $0.75 per hour for the care of one to three children, and $1 per hour if four or more children are cared for.

Table 3-5 shows the percent of child care users who are subsidized. There is very little intercity comparability in the percentages found, except for the fact that in both cities the public centers had far and away the largest percentage of users who were subsidized. In Seattle I found that the percent subsidized

Table 3–5
Subsidization of Child Care Users
(In Percent)

	Seattle							Denver						
	Unlicensed		Licensed					Unlicensed		Licensed				
			Family Day Care Homes	Centers						Family Day Care Homes	Centers			
						Nonprofit		For-Profit Private						Nonprofit		For-Profit Private
	In-Home	Family Day Care Homes		Total	Private	Public		In-Home	Family Day Care Homes		Total	Private	Public	
Fully Subsidized	8.2	9.2	27.0	28.9	24.3	71.3	21.6	35.4	20.7	15.7	17.8	5.1	45.4	0.2
Partially Subsidized	3.3	1.5	1.3	8.1	13.0	3.0	0.7	0	4.9	3.8	8.8	11.2	14.9	1.6
No Subsidy	88.5	89.2	71.7	63.0	62.7	25.7	77.7	64.6	74.4	80.5	73.4	83.7	39.7	98.2

was similar for the informal sector providers and the formal sector providers. These relationships were especially valid for the fully subsidized users. However, within the center sector, as pointed out previously, the percent of subsidized users was far greater for the public centers. In Denver the licensed and unlicensed FDCHs, along with all centers, had a roughly comparable rate of user subsidization, whereas the I-H providers showed the highest percentage of users being subsidized, not including the public centers.

In discussions with public and private agents concerned with child care in Seattle and Denver, I found that it was far easier for unlicensed vendors to be approved as recipients of child care subsidies in Denver than in Seattle, i.e., that children cared for by unlicensed vendors are more likely to be eligible for a subsidy in Denver. Moreover, the Denver agencies appear to be more liberal with regard to the payment of a subsidy for a child cared for by an I-H provider who is also related to the child being cared for. These reasons largely explain the much higher percent of fully subsidized children using unlicensed care in Denver.

Another implication from Table 3-5 is that the center sector in Denver caters to a higher-income clientele than does that sector in Seattle. In the former city, only about one-fourth of the users are subsidized; whereas in Seattle, over one-third are subsidized. This is even more glaring for the private, for-profit centers in Denver, where almost none of the users are subsidized, while over one-fifth of similar users in Seattle are subsidized.

I also have information on the amount of subsidy received per child by child care centers. Public centers, as expected, have the largest subsidy per enrolled child; ($939 in Seattle and $1199 in Denver); however, the private, nonprofit centers also have a sizable subsidy provided per enrolled child (approximately $540 in both cities). In fact, in Seattle both the private, nonprofit centers and the public centers receive about three-fifths of their total revenue per child from subsidies and other donations. In Denver, however, while private, nonprofit centers obtain about three-fifths of their revenue from subsidies and donations, public centers get 70 percent of their revenue from those sources. I also found that in both cities the subsidy is usually given on a monthly or annual basis.

For centers, a relationship was also found to exist between subsidies and revenues. From a crosstabulation of revenue per child against percent of enrolled children who were subsidized, I found that there is a statistically significant difference in the revenue per child according to the percent subsidized (as seen in Table 3-6). For example, in Seattle, over four-fifths of the centers with less than half their children being subsidized had gross revenue per child that was over $900. This implies that the center's gross revenue increases as they increased the proportion of users who were subsidized. This result holds for both cities and is somewhat pronounced in Denver. This finding indicates that differential pricing according to subsidy status may exist.[30] The data also suggest the possibility that revenue from subsidized children is a steadier and

Table 3-6
Crosstabulation between Revenue per Child and Percent of
Children Subsidized Centers

Gross Annual Revenue per Child (1973)	Percent of All Children Enrolled Who Are Fully or Partially Subsidized	
	Less than 50.0%	50% or more
Seattle[a]		
Less than $900.00	81.6	18.4
$900.00 or more	33.3	66.7
Denver[b]		
Less than $900.00	91.7	8.3
$900.00 or more	35.0	65.0

[a] $N = 62$; chi = square level of sig. .0004.

[b] $N = 44$; chi = square level of sig. .0003.

more reliable source of income. Moreover, the payment for subsisized children relative to nonsubsidized users is more likely to be made even if the child is absent for a short period. This leads to higher average revenue from subsidized children over the period of a year, for which period the preceding relationship was defined.

Earnings and Fees

Gross earnings per month per currently enrolled child were calculated for all sectors, as were the corresponding fees per hour. The results of these calculations are presented in Tables 3-7 and 3-8. In the unlicensed (informal) sector, in both Seattle and Denver, the earnings per child are very low, averaging about $20 to $30. Earnings per child rise somewhat for the licensed FDCH operators, at $42 per month in both cities. For centers, there is a more substantial increase in the average gross monthly earnings per child.[31] Both cities are roughly comparable in their earnings per child, with the public, nonprofit centers showing the highest earnings figure, approximately $140 per month per child in both Seattle and Denver. Table 3-7 also shows that there was a large variance in the gross earnings per child in all sectors for both cities, although almost all child care providers, except for centers, had gross monthly earnings per child of less than $100. In

Table 3-7
Gross Monthly Earnings

	Seattle							Denver						
	Unlicensed		Licensed					Unlicensed		Licensed				
					Centers							Centers		
					Nonprofit							Nonprofit		
	In-Home	Family Day Care Homes	Family Day Care Homes	Total	Private	Public	For-Profit Private	In-Home	Family Day Care Homes	Family Day Care Homes	Total	Private	Public	For-Profit Private
Gross Monthly Earnings per Currently Enrolled Child[a] (Dollars)	18	19	42	82	77	138	64	28	22	42	101	76	143	71
Maximum Gross Monthly Earnings for Currently Enrolled Child (Dollars)	102	104	131	190	186	190	107	66	99	143	275	238	275	114
Percent with Gross Monthly Earnings per Currently Enrolled Child < $100	96.0	96.3	93.9	74.2	75.8	22.2	95.0	100.0	100.0	95.2	61.4	84.6	23.5	85.7
Percent with Gross Monthly Earnings per Currently Enrolled Child > $200	0	0	0	0	0	0	0	0	0	0	11.5	7.7	23.6	0

[a]For I-H and both FDCH sectors this is gross earnings during April 1974 divided by the average number of children cared for during that reporting period; for centers it is total revenue, including subsidies, donations, etc. for 1973 per currently enrolled child during May 1974, with the revenue adjusted for May 1974 prices and the sum divided by 12.

Table 3-8
Fees per Child-Hour of Care

	Seattle							Denver						
	Unlicensed		Licensed					Unlicensed		Licensed				
				Centers							Centers			
					Nonprofit							Nonprofit		
	In-Home	Family Day Care Homes	Family Day Care Homes	Total	Private	Public	For-Profit Private	In-Home	Family Day Care Homes	Family Day Care Homes	Total	Private	Public	For-Profit Private
Average Hourly Fees (Dollars)	0.46	0.54	0.54	0.505	0.470	0.629	0.500	0.45	0.43	0.47	0.493	0.330	0.485	0.601
Maximum Average Hourly Fees (Dollars)	3.80	1.00	0.95	1.760	1.700	1.760	1.675	1.75	2.40	1.50	1.600	0.469	0.579	1.600
Percent with Average Hourly Fees between 50 and 75 Cents	26.2	51.9	68.2	25.9	28.0	25.0	23.8	10.4	17.3	28.9	18.2	0	40.0	23.6
Percent with Average Hourly Fees less than 75 Cents	91.8	81.5	90.2	94.4	96.0	87.5	95.2	87.5	91.3	94.6	87.9	100.0	100.0	76.5

Note: For I-H and FDCH operators this was calculated as the sum of the amounts paid per week for child care divided by the number of child care hours provided during that week; for centers the hourly fees were based on weekly fees paid for a standard 40-hour week, with that sum divided by 40.

the center sector, about three-fourths of the public centers had averaged more than $100 per month per child of gross earnings, with about one-fourth of the Denver public centers receiving more than $200 per month per child.

It is of some interest to compare these earning figures with standards of care, according to cost, estimated by others. The Children's Bureau of HEW established the following costs per child per month for mid-1974 for three levels of care in child care centers:[32]

Minimum	$136 per month per child
Acceptable	204 per month per child
Desirable[33]	254 per month per child

My survey data for centers in Table 3-7 show that, on the average, only the public centers in either city came up to the costs needed to meet the minimum standards of care.[34] Even when looking at the maximum earnings figure, I find that some public centers in Denver earn slightly more than is needed to maintain a desirable level of care, while some private, nonprofit centers in Denver are not too far below that figure. In Seattle, both nonprofit components are slightly below the acceptable level insofar as the earnings needed to sustain the required costs is concerned. Moreover, in both cities the private, for-profit centers have earnings that would prevent them from spending enough to achieve the minimum level of care, as developed by the Children's Bureau.[35]

Table 3-8 indicates that in Seattle the average fees in all sectors range from about 45 to 63 cents per hour, while in Denver the average goes from 33 to 60 cents per hour. In most cases, in both cities over nine-tenths of all children pay less than 75 cents per hour for care; in all cases, over three-fourths of the children are charged fees less than that amount. However, in Seattle there is a very large variance between the average and the maximum fees charged for all providers, except the nonprofit components of the center sector. In Denver the variance is very large for all but the FDCH provider, where the range between average and maximum is not as marked.

Finally, to see whether reasonable predictions for earnings could be made from the data collected, and to see whether there was any racial/ethnic differences in those predictions, gross quarterly earnings for the first quarter of 1974 were regressed against 17 independent variables for unlicensed FDCH operators in Denver and against 16 independent variables for licensed FDCH operators in Seattle and Denver (see Tables 3-9 and 3-10).

Using the estimated regressions along with the mean values of the independent variables, gross monthly earnings for the FDCH operators can be predicted.[36] The predicted values are all shown in Table 3-11. Dividing these values by the average number of children taken care of during the survey period, we find that the predicted gross monthly earnings per currently enrolled child is somewhat

Table 3-9
Parameter Estimates for Gross Quarterly Earnings in Denver[a] (Unlicensed FDCH) *(Dollars)*

Variables	Parameter Estimates: OLS (Standard Error)	
Weeks that provider has been FDCH operator (X_1)	0.0388	(0.0485)
Percent of total child care hours devoted to educational–developmental care (X_2)	22.54	(81.99)
Provider has previously worked in a day care center (X_3)	−111.45	(69.74)
Provider is age 30 to 49 (X_4)	5.70	(32.99)
Monthly expenditures on indoor equipment, supplies, and food (X_5)	0.049	(0.005)[b]
Child's fees are fully subsidized (X_6)	139.56	(36.38)[b]
Provider has a waiting list (X_7)	16.94	(58.45)
Provider is 19 years old or less (X_8)	−49.45	(58.55)
Child is not related to provider (X_9)	39.88	(30.81)
Provider is 50 years old or more (X_{10})	148.16	(44.96)[b]
Provider is Chicano (X_{11})	544.26	(227.60)[c]
Child is Chicano (X_{12})	−44.03	(72.75)
Provider is black (X_{13})	387.85	(229.52)
Child is black (X_{14})	98.38	(83.79)
Provider is white (X_{15})	592.06	(224.11)[b]
Child is white (X_{16})	−73.51	(72.35)
Weeks child has been cared for by same provider (X_{17})	−0.289	(0.194)
Constant	−440.92	(218.92)[c]

R^2 = 0.536
S.E. = 205.77
N = 104

[a]There were too few observations to estimate a similar regression for Seattle.

[b]Coefficient significant at 1 percent level.

[c]Coefficient significant at 5 percent level.

Table 3-10

Parameter Estimates for Gross Quarterly Earnings in Seattle and Denver (Licensed FDCH) *(Dollars)*

Variables	Parameter Estimates: OLS (Standard Error)			
	Seattle		Denver	
Weeks that provider has been FDCH operator (X_1)	0.068	(.056)	0.141	$(.056)^a$
Percent of total child care hours devoted to educational-developmental care (X_2)	973.35	$(107.15)^a$	14.59	(106.30)
Provider has previously worked in a day care center (X_3)	64.87	(58.75)	14.00	(56.25)
Provider is age 30 to 49 (X_4)	41.06	(43.43)	124.05	$(39.87)^a$
Monthly expenses on indoor equipment, supplies, and food (X_5)	0.015	$(.001)^a$	0.042	$(.003)^a$
Child's fees are fully subsidized (X_6)	149.17	$(36.59)^a$	−44.16	(50.88)
Provider has a waiting list (X_7)	250.45	$(39.36)^a$	2.42	(39.60)
Child is not related to provider (X_8)	154.48	(89.09)	237.44	$(100.40)^b$
Provider is 50 years old or more (X_9)	286.69	$(51.74)^a$	177.53	$(51.09)^b$
Provider is Chicano (X_{10})	−132.30	(317.99)	−25.26	(196.79)
Weeks child has been cared for by same provider (X_{11})	0.598	$(.246)^a$	0.834	$(.294)^a$
Child is Chicano (X_{12})	−93.29	(128.98)	−56.25	(109.72)
Provider is black (X_{13})	−120.32	(98.47)	−178.64	(194.43)
Child is black (X_{14})	179.64	$(69.88)^a$	70.20	(113.98)
Provider is white (X_{15})	−44.01	(89.12)	110.93	(190.20)
Child is white (X_{16})	72.07	(55.79)	−151.02	(95.22)
Constant	−2.18	(142.60)	50.42	(236.14)
R^2	0.400		0.390	
S.E.	429.10		367.26	
N	214		167	

[a]Coefficient significant at 1 percent level.

[b]Coefficient significant at 5 percent level.

Table 3-11
Predicted Gross Monthly Earnings
(Dollars)

| | Unlicensed FDCH | Licensed FDCH | |
	Denver	Seattle	Denver
All	$41.53	$215.44	$140.78
Per Child	11.19	41.65	30.89
Chicano[a]	43.70	131.10	128.47
Per Child[b]	11.77	25.34	28.19
Black[a]	39.03	226.07	119.49
Per Child[b]	10.51	43.70	26.22
White[a]	49.81	215.65	142.27
Per Child[b]	13.42	41.69	31.22

[a]In obtaining the predictions for the three ethnic/racial groups, I let the value of the variable for both the relevant provider and child equal one, while the other racial/ethnic variables were set equal to zero. For example, for the Chicano estimate I let the variable for "provider is Chicano" and "child is Chicano" equal one, while the black and white counterparts were set equal to zero.

[b]In each case the overall average number of children cared for in the separate sector and city was used as the division.

lower in each instance from values shown in Table 3-7. However, the predicted values are within one standard error of the actual measured earnings. I also found that the predicted earnings for blacks in Seattle is somewhat higher than the value for whites; but black predicted earnings in Denver is lower than similar values for whites or Chicanos. This was true for both licensed and unlicensed FDCH operators in Denver. This result is difficult to explain, but is consistent with the effect of race in the estimated cost equations, as reported in Chapter 7.

A final item worth examining is the importance of child care earnings to the individual provider and to the family of that provider.[37] As shown previously, the earnings of I-H and FDCH providers are rather low. Of the amounts earned, half to three-fourths of the providers in every sector said that it was their only source of *personal* income. However, no more than 12 percent of the providers in any sector in either city said that their child care earnings constituted 90 percent or more of their total *family* income. In fact, on the average, between 72 and 88 percent of the providers in both cities said that their child care earnings contributed one-third or less of their family earnings. The implication here is that in most instances child care earnings were a secondary source of family income. It appears that most of those day care providers are women who are classified as secondary workers but are part of the regular labor force. Others have preteenaged children; and in the absence of some earnings potential within an environment where they can provide care for their own children, they probably would also be in the labor market on, at best, a part-time basis, either in hours per week or weeks per year.

Not only was the earnings of I-H providers low, but many were required to do other tasks for the earnings received. I found that almost half the I-H providers in Seattle and about two-thirds in Denver were required to do at least one of the following household tasks:

Laundry or ironing for families

Light housework

Cook meals for family members other than children cared for

Heavy cleaning

Every provider that was required to perform these tasks said that the fees charged included payment for these additional tasks. Consequently, child care services are only one component of the I-H provider earnings.[38]

Costs—A Descriptive Review

Because the cost data collected for FDCHs is not comparable to the center cost data, I will not be able to make intersectoral comparisons in this section.[39] However, costs can be compared between Seattle and Denver for FDCHs and for centers separately.

Tables 3-12 and 3-13 show the costs for unlicensed and licensed FDCHs, excluding any imputed cost of the providers labor and any prorated share of the housing cost. Table 3-12 indicates that the costs in Seattle and Denver are quite similar for unlicensed FDCHs. In both cities, costs per month are low, with the bulk of the costs accounted for by expenditures on food. The net revenue obtained by subtracting those costs from average revenue was very low in both cities, especially for Seattle, where only $23 was left after the costs listed had been subtracted from the monthly revenue.

For the licensed FDCHs in Table 3-13 both costs and net revenues are much higher than for the unlicensed FDCHs. In the former sector there are some

Table 3-12
Costs and Revenue for Unlicensed FDCH Providers[a]
(for Recent Month)

	Seattle	Denver
Amount Spent on Indoor Equipment[b] (Mean)	$ 3.69	$ 1.96
Amount Spent on Program Supplies[c] (Mean)	5.72	5.46
Other Supplies, excluding Food[c] (Mean)	5.12	7.31
Amount Spent on Advertising (Mean)	0.59	0.04
Amount Spent on Food for Children[d] (Mean)	21.74	19.17
Total Cost	$36.86	$33.94
Revenue for Recent Month[e] (Mean)	60.35	82.52
Revenue Less Cost	$23.49	$48.58

[a]It has been assumed that there is no *additional* cost for maintenance of the home because of its being used as a facility for the provision of child care services.

[b]1973 average divided by 12 and adjusted for inflation from June 1973 to May 1974.

[c]Recent weeks cost multiplied by 4.3.

[d]Includes food used by own children while in the home with children being taken care of for pay.

[e]Revenue for first quarter of 1974 divided by 3 and adjusted for inflation from February 1974 to May 1974.

significant differences in the absolute amount spent on various items in Seattle versus Denver. But the main difference between the two cities in the relative weight of expenditures in the different categories of Table 3-13 is the amount spent on program supplies and the sum spent on advertising. In Seattle almost a fifth of all costs are for supplies and a tenth for advertising, while in Denver not quite a tenth of the costs are for supplies and almost a fourth for advertising. Otherwise the relative expenditure is about the same in the two cities. Moreover, the net revenue for the month is approximately equal in Seattle and Denver.[40]

Centers, unlike the other child care sectors, often have a large initial capital cost for buildings and equipment. Because of the lack of adequate data, I have not been able to estimate the capital costs of buildings. I have, however, been able to estimate the variable cost of day care center operations.[41] Table 3-14 shows these as an average per child, and as a ratio to total revenue.[42]

Table 3-13
Costs and Revenues for Licensed FDCH Providers[a] (for One Month during 1st Quarter, 1974)

	Seattle	*Denver*
Amount Spent on Indoor Equipment[b] (Mean)	$ 7.50	$ 4.83
Amount Spent on Program Supplies[c] (Mean)	21.50	6.97
Other Supplies, excluding Food[c] (Mean)	21.50	12.94
Amount Spent on Advertising	10.00	20.00
Amount Spent on Food for Children[d] (Mean)	51.00	38.00
Total Cost	$111.50	$ 82.74
Revenue for Recent Month[e] (Mean)	219.78	194.17
Revenue Less Cost for Month	$108.28	$111.43

[a]It has been assumed that there is no *additional* cost for maintenance of the home because of its being used as a facility for the provision of child care services.

[b]1973 average divided by 12 and adjusted for inflation from June 1973 to May 1974.

[c]Recent weeks cost multiplied by 4.3.

[d]Includes food used by own children while in the home with children being taken care of for pay.

[e]Revenue of first quarter of 1974 divided by 3 and adjusted for inflation from February 1974 to May 1974.

Monthly variable cost per child averaged $95 in Seattle and $107 in Denver. In Seattle the range was from $61 for the private, profit-making centers to $158 for the public centers, with the private, nonprofit centers falling about midway between these extremes. However, in Denver the range was about the same, but the private, nonprofit centers had average monthly variable costs about equal to those of the private, for-profit centers. If variable cost is estimated as a ratio to full-time equivalent enrollment rather than total currently enrolled, the average value increases by 7 to 12 percent, but the relationship between proprietary types does not change.[43]

The ratio of variable cost to total revenue for public centers in both cities, as well as for the private, for-profit ones in Denver, is surprising. For those centers the ratio is greater than 1.0, which means that variable costs take up over 100% of all revenues. Since total revenue was supposed to include all income received, it appears that in Denver the profit-making centers were, on the average,

Table 3-14

Relationship between Variable Cost, Children Enrolled, and Total Revenue

	Seattle				Denver			
	Total	Nonprofit Private	Public	For-Profit Private	Total	Nonprofit Private	Public	For-Profit Private
Monthly Variable Cost/ Currently Enrolled Children								
(Mean)	$94.84	$102.92	$157.57	$61.47	$107.11	$75.66	$160.46	$67.79
Variable Cost/ Total Revenue								
(Mean)	.94	.97	1.15	.83	1.00	.88	1.06	1.01
Mean Rate of Hourly Pay for Center Work	$ 2.71	$ 2.70	$ 3.18	$ 2.33	$ 2.62	$ 2.45	$ 2.95	$ 2.12

taking a loss and the public centers in both cities were incurring a fairly sizable debt.

In almost all cases, variable costs absorb most of the revenue brought into centers. This is largely due to the large percentage of total revenue that is made up of salaries and wages. Overall, 70 percent of the total revenue in Seattle and 66 percent in Denver is directed toward wages and salaries.[44] However, these percentages varied considerably according to proprietary type. In both cities the private, for-profit centers spent a relatively small percentage of their revenue on wages and salaries (less than half in both Seattle and Denver); while the public centers in Seattle had almost all their revenue spent on wages and salaries alone, and in Denver four-fifths went for that expense. Nonprofit, private centers had a somewhat lower percentage of revenue going to wages and salaries than public centers, but the percent so spent was still far above (about three-fourths in either city) those of the profit-making groups.

I found that the annual cost per currently enrolled child in public centers was from 2.5 to 4 times higher than for other center types in Seattle and from 2 to 3.25 times greater than for the other proprietary types in Denver.[45] From the data collected I have determined that the cost discrepancy was due to three main factors: (1) a lower average ratio of children to staff in public centers, (2) a somewhat higher average number of hours worked per week by public center employees, and (3) a much higher average hourly pay received by public center employees.

So it becomes apparent that for a given number of children, public centers used more paid help and that help was paid a larger amount for more hours worked. Moreover, it is well to remember that these factors may also be indicative of a higher quality of care.

The effect on the center's wage bill can be estimated if the minimum wage in effect on May 1, 1974 were to be paid by all centers. Table 3-15 summarizes the result of that calculation. On the average, centers would find that imposition of the minimum wage would raise their wage bill by from 2 to 3 percent, except for the private, for-profit centers in Denver.[46] In that case, the wage bill would increase by almost 12 percent.

I was also able to estimate the current market value of equipment and vehicles in the Seattle and Denver day care centers (see Table 3-16). In Denver I found that the for-profit centers have a substantially higher outlay for equipment and vehicles than either of the nonprofit types. However, this is largely due to the much higher value of vehicles for the profit-oriented centers. Taking only the ratio of the current market value of equipment to the number of currently enrolled children in Denver, I found that the profit-making centers have an expenditure on equipment per child about equal to the public centers. This is still quite different from what is seen in Seattle, where public centers have a far larger value of equipment and vehicles per child, as well as of only equipment per child, as do either the profit-making or the private, nonprofit centers. I also found that the current value per child of these items was greater in Seattle than in Denver, although the for-profit centers in both cities had values of equipment per child that were approximately equal.

Another cost issue is the provision of transportation services to users. Very few of the unlicensed FDCH vendors in either city provided such service, about 7 percent in Seattle and 3 percent in Denver. Of those who did in Seattle, most charged extra for that service; while of the few who provided transportation in Denver, almost all said that they did not alter their fee for this additional service.

Of the licensed FDCHs in Seattle, about a tenth provided transportation to and/or from the home of the children under their care. In about three-fourths of these cases, the fees paid did not include a charge for this service. Where it occurred, an additional assessment was made for transportation. In Denver almost none of the licensed FDCHs offered a transportation service.

In Seattle about a quarter of all centers provide transportation to and from their facility, with about half these having their regular fees include a charge for this service. The percentage providing transportation in Seattle ranged from 33 percent of the for-profit and public centers to about 17 percent of the private, nonprofit centers, with none of the public centers including the cost of transportation in the fees charged. In Denver less than 10 percent of all centers provided transportation, including none of the private, nonprofit ones, with about 6 percent of the public and 18 percent of the for-profit centers doing so.

Table 3-15
Effect on Center Wage Bill of Enforcement of the Minimum Wage[a]

	Seattle				Denver			
		Nonprofit		For-Profit		Nonprofit		For-Profit
	All Centers	Private	Public	Private	All Centers	Private	Public	Private
Number of Deficit Employees[b]	30	20	4	7	50	9	11	30
Additional Annual Wage Needed for Deficit Workers[c]	$ 14,975	$ 10,491	$ 1,877	$ 2,607	$ 26,509	$ 2,378	$ 3,712	$ 20,628
Total Number of Past Employees	283	175	52	56	302	82	150	70
Average Hourly Wage of All Paid Employees	$ 2,715	$ 2,702	$ 3,183	$ 2,326	$ 2,621	$ 2,451	$ 2,946	$ 2,125
Total Annual Wage Bill for All Paid Employees[d]	$897,427	$552,289	$193,323	$152,139	$924,521	$234,747	$516,139	$173,740
Percent that Added Wage Is of Total[e]	1.7%	1.9%	1.0%	1.7%	2.9%	1.0%	0.7%	11.9%

[a]The minimum wage for newly covered workers, effective May 1, 1974, was used, which was $1.90 per hour.

[b]A deficit worker is a regularly paid employee who earned less than $1.90 per hour during the survey week, May 1974. The number of deficit workers actually found in the survey of regular paid employees was adjusted, by the inverse of the proportion responding to the staff questionnaires, to estimate the total number of deficit employees among all regular paid workers. The inverse of the proportion responding was 1.7857.

[c]The additional annual wages needed for deficit workers was computed by adding the amounts that would be needed in order to bring *all* deficit workers up to the minimum wage level and then multiplying that total by the estimated average number of hours worked per year (1168). The estimated annual hours was derived by assuming that paid employees worked an average of 40 weeks per year. That figure was then multiplied by 29.2, which is the average hours that regular paid employees worked during the survey week.

[d]This is the product of line 3 multiplied by line 4 of the table, and the sum multiplied by the estimated annual hours of work (1168).

[e]Line 2 divided by line 5 and the result multiplied by 100.

Table 3-16
Current Market Value of Equipment and Vehicles

	Seattle				Denver			
		Nonprofit		For-Profit			Nonprofit		For-Profit
	Total	Private	Public	Private	Total	Private	Public	Private
Current Market Value of Equipment and Vehicles (Mean)	$5320	4742	6849	5577	4789	2460	4221	7157
Current Market Value of Equipment and Vehicles/ Currently Enrolled Child (Mean)	126.97	102.86	231.38	135.69	79.68	45.30	70.47	110.79
Current Market Value of Equipment/ Currently Enrolled Child (Mean)	97.33	87.55	210.07	74.94	61.61	30.94	70.42	72.34

Public Policy Implications

Few systematic studies of child care providers have been done, while interest in the area, as well as government intervention, have increased. For these reasons it seems worthwhile to summarize the implications of my findings for child care policy. It must be noted and kept in mind that the findings discussed below and the conclusions drawn apply only to Seattle and Denver and should not be uncritically generalized beyond those two cities.

1. Are There Barriers to Entry in the Day Care Market?

I found some barriers to entry into the day care market, but they were not substantial ones. Centers, and perhaps family day care homes, require capital investment, but the amount required is probably less than that required of most small businesses. There are also licensing and zoning requirements for formal sector providers, but the requirements are not particularly onerous. Complying with the licensing requirements necessitates a moderate increase in capital investment. Also, certification of compliance with the licensing and zoning requirements can delay the opening of a center or family day care home, but almost all the providers in the surveys had completed the process in less than two months.

The survey also found little evidence that entry into the market was more difficult for minorities. For the market as a whole, the racial composition of providers matched that of the children. Within some sectors of the market, I found more variation, but not enough to use as clear evidence of any pattern of discrimination.

2. Is Regulation Successful?

Regulation of the child care centers in both cities seemed moderately successful. Some family day care homes in both cities were unlicensed and therefore unregulated. There were fewer unlicensed homes in Seattle than in Denver, because a greater effort was made by the licensing authorities in Seattle. But in either city it seemed fairly easy for someone to take a few children into their home for care with little chance that they would be noticed by the authorities.

The regulations in force at the time of my interview were straightforward and relatively easy to enforce, and some of them were enforced by other agencies, such as the fire departments. Greater effort would be required to enforce more comprehensive regulations, and some problems might be expected if that were undertaken.

3. Would Additional Regulations Raise Costs Substantially?

Using the data collected in Seattle and Denver, estimates were made of the costs of compliance to the federal day care standards, including the Title XX amendments that were partially implemented on October 1, 1975 (see Chapter 8).[47] I found that there were a significant proportion of licensed child care operators who were not in compliance with existing and proposed federal standards. Especially heavy costs would have to be incurred by the private, for-profit centers that were not in compliance. On the average, however, the increases in the number of family day care homes or staffs of child care centers are significant but not overwhelming.

4. Are Direct Subsidies an Efficient Means of Supporting Day Care?

The evidence from the survey is especially equivocal on this point because the information on direct subsidies relates to 1973, while the cost data is from 1974.

However, if it can be assumed that subsidy levels remained relatively fixed for the two years, then the survey indicates that direct subsidies are not an efficient means of reducing costs to users of child care. In the sectors receiving direct subsidies, little reduction was seen in the charges to users. While this evidence argues against the use of direct subsidies to lower user charges, it is not necessarily evidence against the use of such subsidies. It may be that the direct subsidies were spent to upgrade the quality of the service provided and did not benefit the provider at all. However, the same result could be obtained by indirect subsidies to users, combined with greater regulation. Such a policy would give more control to parents and so would seem to be preferable.[48]

Aside from the four points discussed above, there are several issues concerned with the subsidy (revenue) side of public policy that arose from my analysis of the survey data. One of the critical issues with regard to the subsidization of child care services is whether the subsidy should promote the services or modes of service that are deemed to be desirable by the subsidizing agency, or some other nonuser group, or whether the subsidy should promote utilization of the mode of service that is revealed to be preferred by its use. For example, if care by members of the extended family is preferred, subsidy policy can promote such care by allowing payment to relatives, especially for in-home care. In Denver, where public agencies were more likely to allow such subsidy payments to be made than was true in Seattle, I found a far larger percentage using relatives as I-H providers. If subsidy payments were not allowed for relatives, the modal choice would probably be affected (see Chapter 4).

Another issue is the extent to which subsidy policy should promote the provision of special needs, such as sick child care or care during odd hours. The costs of these special services are generally higher than for the usual child care service offered, and the subsidy policy in effect will determine the availability of these special services.

Finally, it appears that child care providers are partially subsidizing users through the low average earnings that providers receive relative to their education and previous work experience, especially for in-home and family day care home providers. Enforcement of the minimum wage, especially for noncenter providers, would have serious implications for the fees and therefore for subsidy requirements.

Notes

1. My description of this sector is based on 25 I-H providers surveyed in Seattle and 20 in Denver.

2. My description of the unlicensed and licensed FDCH sectors is based on interviews with 214 licensed FDCHs in Seattle and 167 in Denver, as well as on 27 unlicensed FDCHs in Seattle and 104 in Denver.

3. Of the centers found within the limits of these cities, I obtained interview data from 67 out of 76 centers within Seattle and 47 out of 50 in Denver. Of those in Seattle, 21 were for-profit private, 35 were nonprofit private, and 11 were nonprofit public; the corresponding numbers in Denver were 17, 13, and 17. See Appendix 8C for more detail regarding the actual survey.

4. Some of the center data came from staff members. A separate staff supplement was given to each staff member with instructions to fill in the required answers and return the completed form to the center director. Although several follow-up procedures were initiated, the response rate for staff member supplements was disappointing, with about one-fourth of the centers in both cities returning no staff questionnaires. Of 372 volunteer workers only 33 (8.9 percent) returned completed forms. Fortunately, the response rate was much better for regularly paid staff. Of 1128 regular staff in both cities, 612 (54.3 percent) returned forms. I ran a series of 14 chi-square tests on a crosstabulation of the frequencies of several variables against the proportion of all regular staff members who returned their questionnaire. In Seattle none of the differences in the distributions were significant at the 5 percent level or better; while in Denver I found one significant difference for the total number of children currently enrolled. What I found in that instance was that centers with a smaller number of children enrolled were more likely to have over 25 percent of their total staff members return completed forms. In general, on the basis of those tests, it does not appear that there is any bias introduced in using data on the staff members who returned their questionnaire as representative of all regular staff members.

5. See Abt Associates, Inc., "Costs and Quality Issues for Operators," in *A Study in Child Care 1970-1971*, Vol. III; Seth Low and Pearl G. Spindler, "Child Care Arrangements of Working Mothers in the United States," Children's Bureau Publication 461, Department of Health, Education and Welfare, 1968; Richard R. Rowe et al., *Child Care in Massachusetts: The Public Responsibility*, Massachusetts Early Education Project, February 1972; Florence A. Ruderman, *Child Care and Working Mothers: A Study of Arrangements Made for Daytime Care of Children*, Child Welfare League of America 1968; Stanford Research Institute, "A Survey of Day Care in Seattle and Denver," May 1974; Unco, Inc., "A Profile of Federally Supported Day Care in Region X," Vol. 3 (Final Report), Department of Health, Education and Welfare, March 31, 1973; and Westinghouse Learning Corp. and Westat Res., Inc., *Day Care Survey—1970: Summary Report and Basic Analysis*, April 1971.

6. Low and Spindler, "Child Care Arrangements."

7. Ruderman, *Child Care and Working Mothers.*

8. Westinghouse and Westat, *Day Care Survey.*

9. Although the structure may, at other times, be used for non-child care activities.

10. This may simply be a reflection of relative spatial living patterns among Chicanos versus those found for whites or blacks.

11. As a measure of quality, this dichotomy is only a reasonable approximation for at least two reasons. First I was not able to obtain an independent assessment of the reliability of the self-designated type of care given; and second, there is some evidence that educational-developmental care can be harmful to the child. (See, for example, William J. Meyer, "Staffing Characteristics and Child Outcomes," paper prepared for the Department of Health, Education and Welfare, OS/ASPE/SSHD, January 1977).

12. Although I have presented my finding on some variables thought to influence the quality of care, I hesitate to draw firm conclusions from the results. The definition and measurement of the quality of day care have not been formulated objectively enough by educators to allow economists to make judgments about the adequacy of existing child care.

13. Other tasks grouped under the "other" category included cooking, household maintenance, etc., that could not be classed under the other categories used.

14. Including dental checkups, physical examinations, immunizations, TB tests. These data were available only for centers.

15. Much of the material on barriers to entry is concerned with licensing and zoning and is based on interviews conducted by Mae Stephen of SRI International.

16. This is not true for Seattle, where children must be in attendance for at least four hours before licensing is required.

17. Licensing is required for FDCHs in both cities, although the Seattle licensing agency appears to be more energetic or diligent in getting the unlicensed homes licensed.

18. If more than six children are cared for, an adult assistant must be used. Therefore, the maximum child/staff ratio remains 6:1. There has also been an attempt to classify FDCHs licensed for 7 to 12 children as minicenters, which would change their licensing requirements.

19. In general, it is not difficult to obtain a zoning variance that allows up to six children in an FDCH.

20. The new child/staff requirements proposed under the Title XX amendment to the Social Security Act will make the standards for FDCHs receiving federal funds a bit more stringent or costly (see Chapter 8).

21. Which, of course, is their own home.

22. These are long handles that need only body pressure to open the door. Theaters generally have them.

23. I examined the capital cost for FDCHs as well.

24. Almost 56 percent of the 108 changes made in 44 centers in Seattle were to meet fire or safety standards, in Denver almost 48 percent of the 108 changes in 35 centers were for these reasons.

25. Such as square feet of space used.

26. For I-H and FDCH vendors, the percent of capacity utilized was constructed as follows: (1) I obtained the maximum number of children taken care of for pay during any day of the week; (2) I multiplied that figure by the maximum number of hours that the provider took care of children for pay during each day of the week, which is my measure of capacity; (3) the sum of item 2 was then divided into the actual hours of paid care that the provider stated that she had worked during the week, which is the percentage of capacity utilized. For centers it represents the ratio of full-time equivalent enrolled children to licensed capacity, multiplied by 100; and in parentheses it represents the ratio of currently enrolled children to licensed capacity, multiplied by 100.

27. For centers, capacity utilization is measured as the ratio of current enrollment as of the survey date to the number of children for which the center is licensed to provide care. Since current enrollment includes part- as well as full-time children, the ratio sometimes exceeds 1.0.

28. These rates are considerably higher than the Welfare Department's child subsidy rates in Denver, which in 1974 were $3.00 per day for the first child in a family that used child care to $1.90 per day for each child beyond two from the same family that uses child care.

29. They are also illegal in Denver, although, as pointed out above, enforcement of the law in Denver was not as stringent in 1974 as it was in Seattle.

30. One reviewer suggested that such a positive relationship could be a reflection of higher wage bills at public centers, which have a much larger proportion of their users subsidized. This seems to be as reasonable a hypothesis as the one I suggested.

31. For centers, I really refer to gross revenue, since subsidies and donations are included; whereas for the other sectors, there is very little involved other than earnings.

32. The Children's Bureau figures were given as cost per child per year for 1968. I divided their figures by 12 to get a monthly average; then I adjusted their costs to reflect price-level changes to mid-1974.

33. A study of high-quality centers conducted by Abt Associates came up with a cost per month per child, adjusted for 1974 prices, of $259.

34. I assume that gross earnings are the total amount that will be spent; and therefore, it is equivalent to the actual costs incurred. This probably implies a downward bias as a result of volunteer help and donated supplies.

35. Assuming they were to at least cover full cost. Moreover, the importance of volunteer help and donated supplies is far less important for the private, for-profit component of the center sector. Also see Chapter 7 for another estimate of the cost of adequate custodial care.

36. The predicted value of gross quarterly earnings was simply divided by three to obtain monthly value for comparison with the data in Table 3-7.

37. The data available for this examination do not include Center staff.

38. However, see the estimate of the custodial component of child care presented in Chapter 7.

39. See Chapter 7 for a detailed discussion of estimated cost equations.

40. The net revenue shown has not been adjusted to take account of payments made by the licensed FDCH provider for paid help. In general, these payments are very limited. Only 8 to 9 percent of the providers in Seattle have either or both a paid bookkeeper or other paid assistant, while only about 4 percent of the providers in Denver paid for such help. Moreover, these services tend to be purchased on a very limited basis, and it appears unlikely that these payments would lower the average net returns by more than a few dollars per month. The issue is of even less importance for the unlicensed FDCH sector.

41. Includes salaries and wages, insurance, rent, all utilities, janitorial service, purchase of nondurable supplies, advertisement, food, and amount spent on leasing equipment.

42. In all cost and revenue estimates, price level adjustments have been made when a ratio is used and the numerator and denominator were not for the same period.

43. This is calculated by adding one-half of all part-time enrolled children to the total of all full-time enrolled.

44. Including fringe benefits raises this by about 5 percent.

45. It was found to be $1,960 in Seattle and $1,644 in Denver.

46. The percent change in Table 3–15 is more meaningful than the absolute amounts, since I did not receive the necessary data from about half the regular paid staff in centers.

47. Imposition of a more stringent child/staff standard for children under three, which is part of the Title XX amendment, has been postponed temporarily.

48. See Chapter 6 below for a discussion of the use of vouchers as a means of subsidizing child care.

Additional References

Bain, Joseph S. *Industrial Organization.* New York: Wiley, 1959.

Bourne, Patricia G. "What Day Care Ought To Be." *The New Republic,* January 12, 1972.

Breiter, Carl. "An Academic Proposal for Disadvantaged Children: Conclusions from Evaluation Studies." Paper presented at Johns Hopkins University, February 1971.

Campbell, D., and A. Erlbacker. "How Regression Artifacts in Quasi-Experimental Evaluation Can Mistakenly Make Compensating Education Look Harmful." In *Disadvantaged Child,* Vol. III, Helimuth, ed., Brunner-Mazel, N.Y., 1970.

Chambers, Jay. "An Analysis of School Size Under a Voucher System." Occasional Papers in the Economics and Politics of Education, No. 72-11, School of Education, Stanford University, November 1972.

Children's Bureau. "Standards and Costs for Day Care." Day Care and Child Development Council of America, Inc. and Department of Health, Education and Welfare, 1968.

Day Care and Child Development Council of America, Inc. "Alternative Federal Day Care Strategies for the 1970s." Child Care Bulletin No. 9, March 1972.

Jencks, Christopher, et al. *Inequality: A Reassessment of the Effect of Family and Schooling in America.* New York: Basic Books, 1972.

Fein, G. G., and A. Clarke-Stewart. *Day Care in Context.* New York: Wiley, 1973.

Moore, Thomas G. "The Purpose of Licensing." *Journal of Law and Economics* 4 (October 1961): 93–117.

Office of Child Development. "Day Care Licensing Study, Summary Report on Phase I: State and Local Day Care Licensing Requirements." Publication No. (OCO) 73-1066. Department of Health, Education and Welfare, 1973.

Rowe, M. P., and R. D. Husby. "Economics of Child Care: Costs, Need and Issues." In *Child Care Who Cares?* Pamela Roby, ed. New York: Basic Books, 1973.

Schultze, C. L., et al. *Setting National Priorities: The 1973 Budget.* Washington: Brookings Institution, 1972.

Stigler, George J. "The Theory of Economic Regulation." *The Bell Journal of Economics and Management Science* 2, No. 1 (1971):3–21.

Strober, Myra H. "Some Thoughts on the Economics of Child Care Centers." Paper read at 140th meeting of the American Association for the Advancement of Science, San Francisco, February 28, 1974.

Walters, A. A. "Production and Cost Functions: An Econometric Survey." *Econometrica* 31, Nos. 1–2 (April-July 1963):1–66.

Young, D. R., and R. R. Nelson, eds. *Public Policy for Day Care of Young Children: Organization, Finance, and Planning.* Lexington, Mass.: Lexington Books, D. C. Heath, 1973.

4

Substitution Among Child Care Modes and the Effects of a Child Care Subsidy Program

Philip K. Robins and
Robert G. Spiegelman

1. Introduction

During recent years, child care has become an important issue of public policy. In discussions of welfare reform, great emphasis is placed on developing comprehensive child care programs that can be integrated into a more general system of providing tax relief for the poor.[1] The Federal Revenue Act of 1971 contains a provision enabling low-income families to deduct a limited amount of work-related child care expenses on their federal tax returns. This law was liberalized in 1972, when both the income limitation and the maximum allowable child care deduction were increased.[2] In 1976 the law was changed again to allow families at all income levels to obtain a tax credit for 20 percent of qualified child care expenses. Qualified expenses are limited to $2000 for one dependent child and $4000 for two or more dependent children. Thus, at the present time, a substantial segment of the U.S. population is eligible for child care subsidies through the federal government.

The implementation of a national program of child care subsidies raises several questions of an economic nature that are relevant to public policy. First, in order to determine the costs of the program, policymakers must know what effect the program has on labor force participation. One would expect labor force participation rates to rise because a program that reduces the price of child care is similar to a program that increases the net wage rate.[3] Ditmore and Prosser estimate that the provision of free and adequate day care services to women with children leads to a 10 percentage point increase in their labor force participation rate.[4] Other studies that focus on the labor force participation behavior of women indicate that work effort is sensitive to changes in the net wage rate.[5]

Second, it is important to know the extent to which child care subsidies alter the distribution of child care arrangements among the population of

A somewhat shortened version of this chapter appeared in *Economic Inquiry, Journal of the Western Economic Association,* January 1978 under the title "An Econometric Model of the Demand for Child Care."

working women. Substitution among child care modes occurs because of a change in relative prices. In particular, the prices of market modes decrease relative to the (shadow) prices of nonmarket modes because the subsidies are generally restricted to market care (those modes for which a fee is charged). In a national survey conducted during 1972, Duncan and Hill report that in families where both heads work, about 35 percent use nonmarket modes of child care.[6] The costs of a national program depend, in part, on how many of these families would switch modes if the price of market care to them were lowered.

In this chapter we consider the nature of substitution among child care modes in a sample of two parent families with working mothers. Particular emphasis is placed on the effects of child care subsidy programs. No attempt is made to estimate the labor supply effects of child care programs.[7] We estimate an econometric model of the demand for child care using data from a survey given to families in the Seattle and Denver Income Maintenance Experiments.[8] Of the two-parent families in these experiments, approximately half are eligible to receive child care subsidies at a rate different from that associated with the federal income tax. Experimentally induced variation in the subsidy rate enables us to measure the marginal effects of a child care subsidy program.

In the next section we describe the sample used to estimate our model. In section 3 we define precisely what is meant by *child care mode* for purposes of this study. This definition plays a central role in the analysis. In section 4 we discuss the major factors influencing the choice of child care mode. In sections 5 and 6 the empirical model is presented along with the results. The final section discusses policy implications.

2. The Sample

The Seattle and Denver Income Maintenance Experiments consist of approximately 4800 families, 2000 of which reside in Seattle and 2800 in Denver. The experiments began in 1970 and are scheduled to end in late 1978. Approximately one-half the families in the experiments are eligible to receive negative income tax payments. These families are also eligible to receive child care subsidies at a rate greater than that available under the federal income tax.[9]

The needs of the experiments dictated that the sample be stratified on the basis of household income, ethnicity, and family status in addition to the geographic stratification. Assignment to a control or experimental group, however, was completely random within strata. As a result of the stratification, only low-income and lower middle-income families were included in the experiments, and black families, Mexican-American families, and families headed by women were oversampled.

The sample used for this study consists of a subset of 545 two-parent families in which the mother was working and at least one child was under thirteen years of age at the time a child care survey was administered (late 1972–early 1973). The mothers were asked questions regarding their type of child care arrangements and various economic and demographic characteristics of the family.

Table 4-1 presents means of various characteristics of the sample of 545 families. The average family income is $993 per month, which translates into about $12,000 annually. The sample is heavily weighted by black and Mexican-American families relative to their proportions in the national population, a reflection of the racial stratification used in the experiments. About three-fifths of the families reside in Denver and two-fifths reside in Seattle.[10] The average family has just over two children, and about one-fifth of the families had non-head adults living in the household. Approximately two-fifths of the sample are experimental families.

3. Major Modes of Child Care Services

The child care survey distinguishes among several types of child care arrangements. For analytic purposes these have been grouped into three mutually

Table 4-1
Sample Characteristics[a]

Characteristic	Sample Mean
Family Income per Month	$993
Hours of Work of the Mother per Week	34.2
Percent Black	41%
Percent White	45%
Percent Mexican-American	14%
Percent Residing in Seattle	43%
Percent Residing in Denver	57%
Number of Children under 13	1.8
Number of Children between 13 and 17	.5
Percent of Families with Nonhead Adults Living in the Household	20%
Percent Experimental families	42%

[a]$N = 545$.

exclusive and exhaustive categories, or modes. Two of the modes are market oriented, while the third is nonmarket.

The first mode is termed *formal market care* because it includes group arrangements that are purchased in the open market by the user and require a state license for the operator. The arrangements comprising this mode are day care centers and licensed family day care homes. In general, the level of services provided in day care centers is greater than the level provided in family day care homes, primarily because licensing requirements are more stringent and more strictly enforced. Nevertheless, the fact that the operations of both are subject to some form of regulation and that many subsidy programs are oriented toward these types of arrangements places them in a category different from other types of market care.[11]

The second mode is termed *informal market care* and consists of the remainder of child care arrangements purchased in the open market. Included in this mode are services provided by either a relative or nonrelative and taking place either inside or outside the family's home. The conditions determining placement into this mode are that the care is unlicensed and eligible for subsidization under the Seattle and Denver Income Maintenance Experiments.[12]

The third mode of care is distinguished from the other two in that no explicit monetary fee is charged for the service. Thus the care is not subject to the conditions of an economic market and is. hence termed *nonmarket care*. Moreover, none of the arrangements within this mode are eligible for subsidization under existing programs, except in rare instances. The mode almost exclusively consists of care provided by members of the household (other adults, older children, or the father at times when he is not working) and self-care by the child.[13]

Table 4-2 presents a percentage breakdown of the three modes of child care used by two parent families in the Seattle and Denver Income Maintenance Experiments. As the table indicates, only a small percentage of families reported using formal market sources. More than half the families reported using nonmarket sources.

4. Determinants of Child Care Mode

The traditional theory of consumer choice indicates that the principal determinants of the demand for a commodity are the price of the commodity, the prices of close substitutes, household income, and consumer preferences. In developing an empirical formulation of the modal choice problem, we rely on this framework to derive a testable model.

Price

In the case of market child care, variation in price exists primarily because of the availability of subsidies to certain families.[14] Our approach is to define the price

Table 4-2
Child Care Modes in the Seattle and Denver Income Maintenance Experiments[a]

	Number	Percentage
Formal Market Care	53	9.7
Day Care Center	35	6.4
Licensed Family Day Care Home	18	3.3
Informal Market Care	186	34.1
In-Home Care	145	26.6
Out of Home Care	41	7.5
Nonmarket Care	306	56.1
Total	545	100.0

[a]The sample consists of two parent families in which the mother worked and at least one child was less than thirteen years old at the time of the survey.

of market care on the basis of the subsidy rate available to a particular family. In the sample, families are eligible to receive subsidies from two sources. These include the federal income tax and the Seattle and Denver Income Maintenance Experiments. Under both of these programs, child care costs are treated as a work expense and are reimbursed fractionally according to the tax rate of the program. The reimbursement occurs through a reduction in the relevant tax base. This can be seen by the following:

$$T = t_1 T_B = t_1 Y - t_1 C \qquad (4.1)$$

$$G = S - t_2 T_B = S - t_2 Y + t_2 C \qquad (4.2)$$

where T = federal income tax liability
t_1 = federal income tax rate
T_B = $Y - C$ = the tax base (income Y less child care expenses C)
G = the income maintenance grant
S = the income maintenance guarantee
t_2 = the income maintenance tax rate

Equation (4.1) indicates that for families who itemize, the federal tax liability is reduced by an amount equal to $t_1 C$. Equation (4.2) indicates that for families receiving income maintenance benefits, the grant is increased by an amount equal to $t_2 C$. Thus, in both cases, the family receives a partial child care subsidy. If C is the same for similar-sized families, the differential subsidy between the two programs is $(t_2 - t_1)C$. In our sample the average value of t_1 is about 16 percent and the average value of t_2 is about 40 percent.[15] Thus families subsidized through the Seattle and Denver Income Maintenance Experiments have their child care expenses reimbursed at a rate that averages about two-and-one-half times greater than under the federal income tax system.

Because only market care is eligible to be subsidized, we expect an increase in the subsidy rate to increase the utilization of market care relative to non-market care. To draw this implication, however, requires that the shadow price of nonmarket care be held constant. The shadow price of nonmarket care varies systematically with the availability of other household members and the employment situation of the mother and father. In our empirical analysis, the number of teenage children in the household, the presence of nonhead adults, and the length of time spent away from home by the mother (her hours of work) are used as proxy variables for the shadow price of nonmarket care.

Income

It is likely that the child care decision is made by the mother. Because the mother has greater control over her own hours of work, she may weight her earnings differently than other family income when making the child care decision. Thus, in analyzing modal choice, it is useful to distinguish between earnings of the mother and other household income.

Assuming the price per unit of child care service is held constant, there is reason to hypothesize that earnings of the mother and other household income are positively related to the user of market care, because market care is generally of higher quality than nonmarket care. To the extent that child care is a joint product consisting of health, educational, and developmental services in addition to pure custodial care, one would expect income to be positively associated with the use of modes that provide more of these additional services (and presumably cost more). Group day care facilities, most notably day care centers, generally provide such additional services. Thus, relative to the other modes, the utilization of formal care should be positively related to income.[16]

Additional Determinants

In addition to price and income, there are several other determinants of child care mode that may reflect individual preferences or institutional restrictions. These include ethnicity, place of residence, and the age structure of children in the family. Variables representing these factors are also included in the empirical specification.

5. Empirical Specification

Because of the discrete nature of the child care decision, the multinomial logit probability model is used to analyze the data.[17] The model assumes that an individual chooses from a set of mutually exclusive and exhaustive alternatives. The empirical formulation of the model is as follows:

$$P_{ij} = \exp{(x_i\beta_j)} \left[\sum_{k=1}^{3} \exp{(x_i\beta_k)} \right]^{-1} \qquad i = 1, \ldots N; j = 1, 2, 3 \qquad (4.3)$$

where P_{ij} = the probability that the ith family selects the jth mode of child care

β_j = a column vector of parameters for the jth mode

x_i = a row vector of explanatory variables for the ith individual.

Since the addition of a constant to all parameters in equation (4.3) leaves the probabilities unchanged, a normalization must be imposed to identify the model. We choose to normalize all the parameters of the third mode (nonmarket care) to zero so that

$$P_{ij} = \exp{(x_i\gamma_j)} \left[1 + \sum_{k=1}^{2} \exp{(x_i\gamma_k)} \right]^{-1} \qquad i = 1, \ldots N; j = 1, 2 \qquad (4.4)$$

$$P_{i3} = \left[1 + \sum_{k=1}^{2} \exp{(x_i\gamma_k)} \right]^{-1} \qquad i = 1, \ldots N$$

where $\gamma_j = \beta_j - \beta_3$.[18] Thus the parameters in (4.4) may be interpreted as the effects of the x variables on the probabilities relative to the third mode.

The model is estimated by the method of maximum likelihood. The first-order conditions are nonlinear in the parameters and must be approximated by numerical methods. The algorithm used is the modified quadratic hill-climbing technique for maximizing functions.[19] The inverse of the information matrix provides a consistent estimate of the asymptotic variance-covariance matrix of the estimated coefficients.

The variables used in the empirical analysis, along with their definitions, are as follows:

Symbol	Description
PRICE	1 = eligible to receive a subsidy through the Seattle or Denver Income Maintenance Experiments. 0 = eligible to receive a subsidy through the federal income tax.[20]
EARNMOTH	Earnings of the mother in the month prior to the survey. ($1000's).
EARNFATH	Earnings of the father in the month prior to the survey ($1000's).
NONWAGE	Other family income in the month prior to the survey, including earnings of non-heads, all public and private transfers to the family, and capital income $1000's).
HRS05, HRS612, HRS012, HRS13+	Hours of work per week of the mother interacted with dummy variables describing the following age distribution of nonhead family members: none over 5, none under 6 nor over 12, none over 13 but at least one over 6 and one under 6, at least one over 13 and one under 13.
NUM04, NUM5, NUM612, NUM1317	Number of children aged 0-4, 5, 6-12, and 13-17 respectively.
OLDPRE	1 = at least one child under 6 and one over 6; 0 = otherwise.
OPERS	1 = nonheads over 17 living with family; 0 = otherwise.
BLACK, WHITE, CHICANO	1 = black, white, or Chicano family, respectively; 0 = otherwise.
SEATTLE, DENVER	1 = resides in Seattle or Denver respectively; 0 = otherwise.

6. Results

As indicated earlier, the experimental sample is not a random sample of the U.S. population, although it is random with respect to child care mode. However, even though the experimental sample is random with respect to child care mode, it is possible that the subsample of 545 families used to estimate the model is nonrandom in a way that biases the empirical results. For example, price effects are measured empirically by the average difference in subsidy rates between experimental and control families. Because the high tax rates of the experiments induce a reduction in work effort, experimental wives working at the time of the child care survey may be more strongly committed to working than control wives.[21] This commitment may be reflected in a greater demand for market care. Thus experimental-control differences in demand may exist because of a sample selectivity bias rather than differences in the subsidy rates.

Fortunately, it is possible to test for the existence of a sample selectivity bias by measuring experimental-control differences in the demand for market care prior to the experiment, using the sample of 545 families. If there are no experimental-control differences in the demand for market care prior to the experiment, then there is no selectivity bias. Such a test has been performed, and the results indicate no significant differences.[22] Thus experimental-control differences in the demand for market care can safely be attributed to differences in the subsidy rates.

Table 4-3 presents the maximum likelihood estimates of the model. In addition to the parameter estimates, two measures of the model's goodness of fit are also reported. One is a likelihood ratio statistic (χ^2) and the other (ρ^2) is analogous to the coefficient of determination in linear regression models.[23]

The coefficients in Table 4-3 can be interpreted in at least two ways. First, if the signs of the coefficients of a particular variable are the same for both formal and informal market care, the impact of that variable on use of the alternative mode (nonmarket care) is unambiguously of the opposite sign. Thus the coefficients reveal that subsidization of market forms of child care leads to a reduction in the utilization of nonmarket care. This result is statistically significant in both cities. Second, the coefficients of each mode relative to one another provide an indication of the odds of using one mode over another. The log of the odds of using mode j over mode k is given by

$$\log\left(\frac{P_{ij}}{P_{ik}}\right) = x_i \left(\gamma_j - \gamma_k\right) \qquad j \neq k \qquad (4.5)$$

The derivative of this expression with respect to x_i is equal to $\gamma_j - \gamma_k$. Thus the coefficients reveal that an increase in earnings of the mother (her wage rate)[24] leads to an increase in the odds of using formal market care over informal market care $(6.311 > 4.031)$.

The signs of the coefficients in Table 4-3 generally conform to our prior expectations. One surprising result is that neither of the coefficients of other family income is statistically significant. This suggests that the source of income is an important determinant of modal choice.

Table 4-3
Maximum Likelihood Estimates of the Child Care Model

Variable	Mode 1: Formal Market Care		Mode 2: Informal Market Care	
	Coefficient	Standard Error	Coefficient	Standard Error
PRICE · SEATTLE	1.120^b	.466	$.787^b$	.374
PRICE · DENVER	1.383^a	.740	.470	.521
EARNMOTH	6.311^b	2.510	4.031^b	1.614
EARNFATH + NONWAGE	.459	.569	.416	.414
HRS05	−.045	.033	−.005	.020
HRS612	$−.077^a$	.042	−.077	.021
HRS012	$−.089^b$	.037	$−.052^a$	.022
HRS13+	$−.119^b$	.041	−.035	.026
NUM04	.015	.311	−.215	.266
NUM5	.583	.455	.038	.331
NUM612	$−1.201^b$	.376	$−.831^b$	.182
OLDPRE	2.537^b	.760	2.717^b	.520
NUM1317	.395	.461	$−1.217^b$	.537
OPERS	−.102	.819	$−1.473^a$	.748
BLACK	1.523^b	.408	−.065	.257
CHICANO	.744	.767	−.033	.369
SEATTLE	.423	.480	$−.935^b$	.308
CONSTANT	$−2.990^a$	.889	−.365	.560
x^2		274.22^b	(d.f. = 34)	
ρ^2		.274		
Number of Observations		545		

[a]Indicates significant at 10 percent level.

[b]Indicates significant at 5 percent level.

Prediction

While the coefficients in Table 4–3 enable us to determine the direction of effect of a variable, they do not provide information about the size of the impact. In order to determine the size of the impact, we evaluate a series of probability estimates based on the results in Table 4–3. These probability estimates are presented in Table 4–4 for a select set of variables. Each is evaluated at the sample means of the other explanatory variables.[25] In addition to the probability estimates, the table also reports estimated asymptotic standard errors of the predictions.[26]

The probabilities in Table 4–4 reveal some interesting information regarding modal choice. First, families appear to be very sensitive to price. Let us assume that the market price of child care is $5 per day,[27] that the subsidy rate under the federal income tax is 16 percent,[28] and that the subsidy rate under the Seattle and Denver Income Maintenance Experiments is 40 percent. As a result of these subsidies, the price of child care to the user is $4.20 under the federal income tax and $3 under the Seattle and Denver Income Maintenance Experiments. Shifting from the federal tax program to income maintenance increases the utilization of market care by 14 percentage points in Denver and 18 percentage points in Seattle. These correspond to price elasticities of about –1.36 and –2.86 respectively. While the effects are about equally divided between formal and informal care, the relative impact is much greater for formal care. The estimated elasticities for formal care are –6.99 in Denver and –4.08 in Seattle. For informal care the estimated elasticities are –.85 in Denver and –2.40 in Seattle.[29]

Second, the demand for market care varies with the wage rate. An increase in the hourly wage by approximately $2 (from $1.30 to $3.40 per hour) increases the utilization rate of market care by 28 percentage points. This corresponds to an elasticity of about .91. While most of this impact is in the informal market, the relative impact is again greater for formal care. The estimated elasticity for formal care is about 2.5, while for informal care it is about .73.

Third, modal choice varies with family structure. In families with only younger children (under 5) the utilization rate of market care is about 70 percent. In families with only older children (between 6 and 12) the utilization rate is about 50 percent. If a teenager or other adult is also present, the utilization rate drops to 20 percent.

Finally, the utilization rates differ by ethnic group. In particular, blacks exhibit a higher utilization rate of formal market care than do whites or Chicanos. This may be somewhat of an artificial effect, however, attributable to institutional factors. In many urban centers a large proportion of formal facilities, particularly day care centers, are located in areas heavily populated by black families. Since we have not controlled for supply conditions in our analysis, we may be picking up location effects in our ethnic variables.

Table 4-4
Predicted Probabilities of Child Care Use for Selected Characteristics[a]

	Market		Nonmarket	Family Structure	Market		Nonmarket
	Formal	Informal			Formal	Informal	
Subsidy–Seattle				No Teenagers or Other Nonhead Adults Present			
Under Federal Income Tax	.06 (.02)	.16 (.04)	.78 (.04)				
Under Income Maintenance	.13 (.04)	.27 (.06)	.60 (.07)	1 Preschooler	.13 (.03)	.58 (.05)	.29 (.04)
Subsidy–Denver				1 School Age	.02 (.02)	.49 (.07)	.49 (.07)
Under Federal Income Tax	.03 (.01)	.33 (.04)	.64 (.04)	1 Preschooler and 1 School Age	.10 (.04)	.65 (.06)	.25 (.05)
Under Income Maintenance	.09 (.05)	.41 (.12)	.50 (.12)	Teenager Present			
Female Earnings (Wage Rate)				1 Preschooler	.04 (.03)	.17 (.06)	.79 (.07)
$200/month ($1.30/hour)	.02 (.01)	.17 (.04)	.81 (.05)	1 School Age	.01 (.01)	.11 (.04)	.88 (.04)
$300/month ($2.00/hour)	.04 (.01)	.23 (.03)	.73 (.03)	1 Preschooler and 1 School Age	.08 (.05)	.53 (.10)	.39 (.10)
$400/month ($2.70/hour)	.06 (.02)	.30 (.04)	.64 (.04)	Other Nonhead Adult Present			
$500/month ($3.40/hour) ,	.10 (.03)	.37 (.06)	.53 (.07)	1 Preschooler	.03 (.02)	.14 (.08)	.83 (.08)
Ethnicity				1 School Age	.01 (.01)	.08 (.05)	.91 (.05)
Black	.11 (.03)	.25 (.04)	.64 (.04)	1 Preschooler and 1 School Age	.06 (.05)	.49 (.17)	.45 (.16)
White	.03 (.01)	.29 (.04)	.68 (.04)				
Mexican-American	.05 (.03)	.27 (.06)	.68 (.07)				

7. Summary and Conclusions

Child care denotes any arrangement used by a working parent for care of a child, including self-care. This chapter has been concerned with factors that influence the demand for market modes of child care by two-parent families with working mothers.

Our results indicate that the demand for market care is significantly affected by demographic characteristics of the household. In families with teenagers or nonhead adults, market care is infrequently used unless there are children of both school and preschool age.

The demand for market care also varies with the female head's wage rate. The estimated wage elasticity for market care is about .9. The evidence also suggests that the demand for market care is price elastic and therefore susceptible to considerable change through a program of increased subsidization. Formal market care is particularly sensitive to changes in price.

Notes

1. Two studies that deal with the relationship between child care and welfare reform are Vivian Lewis, "Day Care: Needs, Costs, Benefits, Alternatives," in *Studies in Public Welfare,* Paper No. 7, U.S. Government Printing Office, July 1973, pp. 102-165, and Michael Krashinsky, "Day Care and Welfare," in *Studies in Public Welfare.* A recent book by Dennis R. Young and Richard R. Nelson, *Public Policy for Day Care of Young Children: Organization, Finance, and Planning* (Lexington, Mass.: Lexington Books, D. C. Heath, 1973), discusses public policy in the field of child care.

2. For a family with one child, the income limitation was $6000 in 1971 and the maximum allowable child care deduction was $600. The deduction was reduced dollar for dollar on income over $6000. In 1972 the income limitation was raised to $18,000 (with the deduction being reduced 50 cents per dollar on income over $18,000) and the maximum allowable child care deduction was raised to $2400 ($200 per month). The deduction was used on 1,569,000 returns in 1972, amounted to $1.1 billion, and had a tax value of about $275 million according to George F. Break and Joseph A. Pechman, *Federal Tax Reform—The Impossible Dream?* Washington: Brookings Institution, 1975.

3. A reduction in the price of child care may also lead to an increase in the fertility rate. See the studies in Theodore W. Schultz, ed., "New Approaches to Fertility," proceedings of a conference, June 8-9, 1972, published in *Journal of Political Economy* (March-April 1973).

4. "A Study of Day Care's Effect on the Labor Force Participation of Low-Income Mothers," Office of Planning, Research, and Evaluation, Office of Economic Opportunity, June 1973; child care subsidies may affect the husband's wage (and labor force participation) as well, but this possibility is not considered in their paper.

5. See, for example, Glen G. Cain, *Married Women in the Labor Force* (Chicago: Univ. of Chicago Press, 1966); William G. Bowen and T. Aldrich Finegan, *The Economics of Labor Force Participation* (Princeton, N.J.: Princeton Univ. Press, 1969); Glen G. Cain and Harold W. Watts, eds., *Income Maintenance and Labor Supply* (Chicago: Rand McNally, 1973). All find labor force participation rates of women to be quite elastic with respect to the wage rate.

6. Greg Duncan and C. Russell Hill, "Modal Choice in Child Care Arrangements," in *Five Thousand American Families—Patterns of Economic Progress,* Vol. III, Institute of Social Research, Univ. of Michigan, 1975, pp. 235-258.

7. See James J. Heckman, "The Effects of Child Care Programs on Women's Work Effort," *Journal of Political Economy,* Part II (March-April 1974):S136-S163.

8. For a description of the Seattle and Denver Income Maintenance Experiments, see Mordecai Kurz and Robert G. Spiegelman, "The Seattle Experiment: The Combined Effect of Income Maintenance and Manpower Investments," *American Economic Review* (May 1971):22-29; "The Design of the Seattle and Denver Income Maintenance Experiments," Research Memorandum No. 18, Center for the Study of Welfare Policy, Stanford Research Institute, May 1972.

9. Families receiving income maintenance benefits do not pay federal income taxes so that they are not subsidized by both programs.

10. The Seattle sample is smaller because Mexican-American families were only enrolled in Denver. The number of black and white families are about the same in Seattle and Denver.

11. One could argue that day care centers and licensed family day care homes should be analyzed separately because they provide different levels of services. Efforts to analyze them separately, however, proved unsuccessful because only a small number of families in our sample used these types of arrangements.

12. Child care arrangements by a nonrelative outside the family's home is equivalent to an unlicensed family day care home. In both Washington and Colorado (and in most other states) this constitutes an illegal operation because the states require licensing (presumably to ensure a minimum level of quality) whenever care is provided by a nonrelative outside the family's home. Our data do not permit us to distinguish between care by relatives and nonrelatives when care is provided outside the home. Thus we do not know the extent to which such illegal operations actually exist.

13. Our data do not permit precise delineation of the various arrangements within this mode.

14. Here we are assuming a competitive child care market and are referring to price per unit of constant quality child care services.

15. The Seattle and Denver Income Maintenance Experiments use four different tax systems. Two of these are constant tax systems at 50 percent and

70 percent, and two are declining-rate systems—one with an initial tax at 70 percent, the other with an initial tax at 80 percent, and both decline at a marginal rate of 5 percent per $1000 of taxable income. Since our sample consists of families with working mothers, the effective tax rates under the declining systems are somewhat lower than the initial tax rates and are lower than the overall tax rates facing other families in the experiments. The income maintenance experiments reimburse positive income taxes so that families are not subsidized by both programs. Positive income taxes are computed using data from the survey and the tax laws for 1972.

16. There is an implicit assumption here that quality and cost are positively related and that a positive income effect arises because the income elasticity of quality adjusted child care services is positive.

17. The multinomial logit probability model was developed by Henry Theil, "A Multinomial Extension of the Linear Logit Model," *International Economic Review* (October 1969):251-260; Daniel McFadden, "Conditional Logit Analysis of Qualitative Choice Behavior," in *Frontiers of Econometrics*, Paul Zarembka, ed. (New York: Academic Press, 1974); and Marc Nerlove and S. J. Press, *Univariate and Multivariate Log-Linear and Logistic Models* (Santa Monica, Calif.: Rand R1306/NIH-EDA, 1973). Representative empirical applications include J. G. Cragg and R. S. Uhler, "The Demand for Automobiles," *Canadian Journal of Economics* (August 1970):341-358; Nicholas A. Barr and Robert E. Hall, "The Probability of Dependence on Public Assistance," Department of Economics Working Paper No. 131, Massachusetts Institute of Technology, May 1974; and P. Schmidt and Robert P. Strauss, "The Prediction of Occupational Level Using Multiple Logit Models," *International Economic Review,* (June 1975):471-486.

18. The normalization used is arbitrary and is of no empirical consequence.

19. This technique is described in Stephen M. Goldfeld and Richard E. Quandt, *Nonlinear Methods in Econometrics* (Amsterdam: North-Holland, 1972).

20. A dummy variable is used to measure price rather than the subsidy rate because data on the latter are not available for the time period studied. Thus the model provides an estimate of the average difference between the subsidy rates available under the federal income tax and the Seattle and Denver Income Maintenance Experiments.

21. See Michael C. Keeley, Philip K. Robins, Robert G. Spiegelman, and Richard W. West, "The Labor Supply Effects Costs of Alternative Negative Income Tax Programs," *Journal of Human Resources,* forthcoming, for a discussion of the work effort response to the Seattle and Denver experiments.

22. The t statistics in a difference between means test is -.28 and the t statistic on the coefficient of a dummy variable in a more elaborate regression model is .70.

23. These statistics are described in McFadden, "Conditional Logit Analysis." The null hypothesis in the likelihood-ratio test is that the coefficients

of all explanatory variables (other than the constant terms) are equal to zero. The likelihood-ratio statistic is distributed as chi-square.

24. Since hours of work of the mother is also in the equation, the earnings effect is really a wage effect.

25. Because of the nonlinear functional form of the logit model, the size of the effect depends on the point at which the probability estimates are evaluated. We use the sample means because they represent the "typical" family in our sample.

26. The asymptotic variance of the predictions is given by:

$$V(\hat{P}_j) = \left(\frac{\partial \hat{P}_j}{\partial \hat{\gamma}}\right)' \, V(\gamma) \, \left(\frac{\partial \hat{P}_j}{\partial \hat{\gamma}}\right)$$

where $\hat{P}_j$ = predicted probability for mode $j; j = 1, 2, 3$

$\hat{\gamma}$ = the vector of estimated structured parameters = $\begin{bmatrix} \hat{\gamma}_1 \\ \hat{\gamma}_2 \end{bmatrix}$

$\dfrac{\partial \hat{P}_j}{\partial \hat{\gamma}}$ = the row vector of first partial derivatives of the probability function for mode j with respect to each of the estimated structural parameters, evaluated at the point of prediction

$V(\hat{\gamma})$ = the estimated variance-covariance matrix of the estimated structural parameters.

Like the probability estimates, the variance of prediction also depends on the point at which the probabilities are evaluated.

27. This is the average cost of child care experienced by families in our sample during the period studied.

28. This is an overestimate to the extent that families with child care expenses do not itemize their deductions or are ineligible for a federal income tax subsidy because the expenses are incurred for care by a relative (which is not deductible).

29. It should be pointed out that these price elasticities may be overestimated to the extent that our price variable is measuring effects of being in the experiment rather than changes in the price of child care. A similar upward bias exists if we have overestimated the size of the child care subsidy under the federal income tax. For example, under the extreme assumption of a zero federal income tax subsidy rate, the price elasticities for market care are -.97 in Denver and -2.04 in Seattle. However, if child care subsidies are available through programs other than the federal income tax, the price elasticities are underestimated. None of these biases are believed large enough to qualitatively affect our estimates.

5

Quality of Day Care: Can It Be Measured?
Jane Stallings and Mary Wilcox

The experience of the young child in day care is a matter of increasing significance and concern to students of early childhood, as well as to practitioners, parents, and legislators. Even though consensus may be found in the literature regarding the importance of the infant and preschool years to the child's development, very little is known about the environment or the daily experience of the child in day care.

As the demand for day care services grows, so does the need for answers to two important questions: What kinds of experiences should young children have in day care? What is quality care and how can it be measured?

The purpose of this chapter is to discuss these questions and to describe several instruments that have been developed to describe day care experiences and record indices of quality.

What is Quality Day Care?

Within the existing body of literature on day care, no common definition of *quality* can be found, and therefore the indices used to measure quality may vary. Attitudes toward child-rearing in general affect the values placed on various aspects of day care. Also, values change over time, and at any point they may vary between different social groups.

A survey of day care programs over the past three decades indicates several major shifts in opinion of what constitutes "good care." During and immediately following World War II, there was great concern that institutional care would result in social and emotional ills in the young. It was feared that children would feel abandoned in day care facilities and would become alienated from their parents. Efforts were made to provide the kind of warm, nurturing care it was believed the child received at home. Quality care was equated with nurturing care.

The 1960s saw a new interest in the cognitive development of children, and this interest inspired Head Start and other programs designed to assist the children of low-income and working families. The assumption was that to perform well in school, preschool children needed to experience school-like activities that would enhance language and cognitive abilities. During this time, quality care was considered closely related to programs that encouraged cognitive development.

According to a recent review of day care studies, attempts have been made in the 1970s to balance the emphasis on various aspects of child development.[1] Less stress is being placed on cognitive development in preschool programs, possibly because most educational intervention programs have not shown long-term educational gains. Instead, contemporary programs strive to foster integrated physical, emotional, social, and cognitive growth in children.

Reflecting both attitudinal and experimental differences, the indices of these major areas of growth may vary from study to study. However, the characteristics listed in Table 5-1 are those which appear most frequently in the literature and seem to be generally regarded as measurable indices of the quality of day care.[2]

Although there is some consensus that the variables shown in Table 5-1 are indicative of the quality of day care, the relative values assigned to them may vary. For example, some parents from inner-city neighborhoods might value most for their children a strong self-concept, while others value greater cognitive skills. Some parents from middle-class suburban areas might value task persistence most highly, while others favor problem-solving and curiosity.

Table 5-1
Child Growth Variables

Social-Emotional Development

    Dependency
    Autonomy
    Aggression
    Self-Control
    Social Involvement
    Self-Concept
    Prosocial Behavior
    Social and Emotional Harm
    Compliance/Obedience

Language and Cognitive Development

    Language Development
    Memory
    Skills and Concept Learning
    Reflectivity
    Task Persistence
    Generation of Ideas
    Problem Solving
    Curiosity

Physical and Motor Development

    Self-Help Skills
    Safety
    Health
    Motor Development

Practitioners might regard cognitive skills as most desirable, and policymakers may be most concerned with health and safety.

In addition to variations according to differing values, measurement of quality in day care is affected by opinions on definition. For example, some aggression is acceptable and normal for children of certain cultures and certain ages—how much aggression is acceptable and at what point it does not reflect a quality setting is debatable. Similarly, the acceptable degree of dependency or autonomy of children varies with culture and social class, and the assessment of quality in day care is related to this variation.

To some, a quality day care setting is one that is most like the child's own home; they believe this type of setting is most likely to enhance the child's social and emotional development. Others believe that the day care environment should be structured and predictable, regardless of the child's own family setting.

Despite these differences of opinion on the relative merits of various day care settings and the differing values placed on some of the indices of quality in day care, there is agreement among early childhood experts, practitioners, and parents that all aspects of child development must be reflected in an evaluation of day care and its quality. Our next question then becomes: Given some agreement on definitions and priorities, can quality be measured adequately?

Can Quality Be Measured?

It is not the intent, nor is it possible at this time, to resolve differences in definitions and priorities. The purpose of this section is to show that given agreement on the variables that reflect quality care (such as those on Table 5-1), and given agreement on their definitions, an accurate description of quality care can be recorded.

One of SRI's tasks for the National Day Care Cost-Effects Study was to identify existing observation instruments and critique them for their appropriateness to the day care setting. Table 5-2 includes child-growth variables from the list of variables in Table 5-1 and the specific instruments chosen to measure them. Descriptions of the observation instruments are given in the following section, and samples of those instruments are included in the appendixes.

In addition to assessing child growth, it is important to study the caregiver behaviors related to child growth. However, little data are available to describe the kind of day care practices that are likely to contribute to child growth. Most evaluations of the quality of day care have selected independent variables, such as teacher/child ratio, professional training, group size, and extended services. While it is easy to collect these data, the variables do not sufficiently describe the kind of care children receive because they are based on the assumption that better-trained people with fewer children will provide better care. This may or may not be true. There are many examples of untrained but experienced

Table 5-2

Child Outcome Variables and Observation Instruments Selected for Phase II of National Day Care Cost-Effects Study

Variables	Instrument
Social-Emotional Development	
Dependency	Prescott-SRI Child Observation System
Autonomy	Prescott-SRI Child Observation System
Aggression	Prescott-SRI Child Observation System
Self-Control	Prescott-SRI Child Observation System
Social Involvement	Prescott-SRI Child Observation System
Self-Concept	
Prosocial Behavior	
Cooperation	Prescott-SRI Child Observation System
Helping	Prescott-SRI Child Observation System
Compliance/Obedience	SRI Preschool Observation System
	Prescott-SRI Child Observation System
Social and Emotional Harm	Prescott-SRI Child Observation System
	SRI Preschool Observation System
Language and Cognitive Development	
Language Development	Preschool Inventory
Reasoning Skills and Concept	
Learning	Prescott-SRI Child Observation System
Reflectivity	Prescott-SRI Child Observation System
Task Persistence	Prescott-SRI Child Observation System
Generation of Ideas	Prescott-SRI Child Observation System
Problem Solving	Prescott-SRI Child Observation System
Curiosity	Prescott-SRI Child Observation System
Physical and Motor Development	
Self-Help Skills	SRI Preschool Observation System
Safety	Prescott-SRI Child Observation System

caregivers who provide a large number of children with a warm and supportive environment in which they thrive.

The missing link is how caregivers actually interact with children. In the past, studies have not examined the caregiver processes. To this end, SRI has developed four observation instruments that can systematically record not only the independent behavior of the caregiver and the children but also their interactions in the natural day care setting, whether a center or a home. The instruments are the following:

SRI Preschool Observation System (adult-focused)—for use in day care centers

Prescott/SRI Child Observation System (child-focused)—for use in day care centers with three- and four-year-old children

SRI Infant Observation System—for use in day care homes or centers

Carew/SRI Observation System (adult- and child-focused)—for use in day care homes.

SRI Observation Instruments

Because of the value of recording the interactions that occur between the care-giver and the children or among the children themselves, each of the observation instruments is discussed in the following section and samples of the instrument are included in the Appendixes.

SRI (Adult-Focused) Preschool Observation System

The SRI Preschool Observation System is adult-focused and provides a description of a day care center or classroom, a record of activities that occur, and a record of the interactions that occur between adults and children. The system was designed to assess a variety of instructional methods. In this system, a principal caregiver in the classroom is regarded as the focus person.

The observation system consists of four sections: Classroom Summary Information, Physical Environment Inventory, Classroom Snapshot, and Five-Minute Interaction. The Classroom Summary Information records the number of adults and children in the classroom and the duration of the class. The Physical Environment Inventory describes the center or classroom space and the materials available to the children.

The Classroom Snapshot yields data on the nature of the activities of each adult and child in the classroom and the size of the groupings. From this section, information is obtained on how the caregiver spends her time and with whom; how the aides spend their time and with whom; how frequently children engage in cognitive activities; how frequently children play together; how frequently children cry; how frequently they are comforted.[3]

The Five-Minute Interaction can be used to observe both group interactions and individuals alone in an activity. It consists of a series of frames in which each action of the person being observed is recorded in four categories: who is speaking, who is being addressed, what the message is, and how the message is being delivered. A total of 63 frames, one after the other, can record an entire interaction or, in the case of individuals alone, describe nonverbal action over a five-minute period. Based on these data, the researcher can examine the caregiver's teaching style, control system, and socializing techniques.

Each observation booklet is made up of one set of Classroom Summary Information and Physical Environment Inventory grids and four sets of Classroom Snapshot and Five-Minute Interaction frames. Identification Information and

Classroom Summary Information sections are coded once an hour, Physical Environment Inventory is coded once a day, and the Classroom Snapshot and Five-Minute Interactions are coded four times an hour for four-and-one-half hours per day. This provides a total of 18 snapshots and 18 Five-Minute Interactions in one day.

Using all the observation data, we can answer such questions as: How supportive is the caregiver to the child in distress? How frequently does the caregiver instruct the child in cognitive tasks? Does the caregiver control child behavior through reason or arbitrary rules? Does the caregiver respond to the children's questions or requests for help? Is the caregiver mostly positive or negative in her statements? Are the caregivers more supportive when the child ratio is smaller? Do better-educated caregivers provide more cognitive activities? Does the caregiver show pleasure in being with the children? Details of this observation system are provided in Appendix 5A.

Prescott/SRI Child Observation System (Child Focus)

The Prescott/SRI Child Observation System was developed at SRI to assess a wide range of child behaviors including dependency, aggression, social involvement, cooperation, obedience, task persistence, and self-help skills. Each child in the National Day Care Cost-Effects Study was observed for three separate 30-minute sessions in the natural classroom and also in two structured situations. In the structured situations, the child was observed for his ability to share and cooperate when the toy resources were limited and when they were plentiful. This provided data to assess social behaviors. Details of this system are provided in Appendix 5B.

SRI Infant Observation System

A third instrument, the SRI Infant Observation System, was developed to observe caregivers who have infants in their charge. This instrument can assess the quality of attention the adult gives the child during routine tasks, such as diapering, feeding, or changing clothes. Some specialists in child development believe that infants who are spoken to directly and treated with respect and sensitivity from the time they are born will develop greater understanding of what is expected of them and will be more cooperative and less fretful.[4] The SRI Infant Observation System can record whether the caregiver is:

Paying attention to the infant during caregiving activities

Announcing to the infant what will happen next

Explaining what is happening

Waiting for the infant's response after each announcement, explanation, or question

Allowing the infant to participate in the task as much as possible

Encouraging the infant to become proficient at whatever part of the task is possible for him

Enjoying the task and being involved in it

Waiting for the infant to focus on the task again if the infant becomes playful or teasing and enjoying the teasing and playfulness while it is occurring.

Behaviors of the infant can be recorded on the same instrument. If adults treat the infant as a person to be respected rather than as a doll or an object, certain outcomes are expected of the infant. The infant is expected to:

Pay attention to the adult and the task

Cooperate and participate in the task as much as possible

Achieve mastery of whatever part of the task is possible for him

Enjoy the task and be involved in it.

Details of this system are provided in Appendix 5C.

Carew/SRI Observation System (Adult and Child Focus)

This observation instrument was developed for use in the National Day Care Home Study.[5] In the Adult Behavior Codes section, the behavior of the caregiver is recorded at 20-second intervals. Through this instrument, facilitating, instructional, management, and comforting techniques of the caregiver can be recorded. In the Child Codes section, the behavior of the child is recorded, including the child's activity, the person to whom the activity is directed, the emotion of the behavior and the language used. The adult and child codes are used six times per hour to record what the caregiver and specific children in the home are doing. In addition to recording spontaneous interaction, observations are made in three structure situations, in which the caregiver reads a book to the children and shows them how to use two new toys. Use of the structured situations assures the researcher that some common events will occur in each home. Details of this system can be found in Appendix 5D.

Training Observers

To collect useful observation data on any of the instruments, it is important to select observers carefully and to establish an excellent training program. The day care study observers in each case were selected from the community in which day care centers were to be observed. The criteria for hiring included a college education and experience with young children. Observers received 7 to 12 days of training, and each was required to pass an extensive test of coding videotapes of day care activities. Each observer was also monitored by a staff trainer in the natural situation in day care centers.

Analysis of Observation Data

In addition to developing the observation technology, analytic techniques have been developed for examining process and outcome data. In some studies of day care, tests are administered to the children to examine social, emotional, cognitive, and physical growth. The observer-child outcomes and the test-child outcomes can be correlated with the observed behaviors of caregivers. In this way, it is possible for researchers to examine the relationship between quality of care and child growth. Quality can be assessed by using the data to answer questions such as:

Do caregivers who praised children for helping each other have children who are more willing to share toys?

Do caregivers who praise children for accomplishments in cognitive tasks have children who score higher on a school reading test?

Do children who have more gross-motor and fine-motor equipment to play with score higher on tests of motor ability?

Summary

Parents, children, teachers, educators, psychologists, researchers, and policymakers are all stakeholders in day care. All parties are interested in the quality of day care. Although there is no consensus on an exact definition of *quality,* most people agree that children should be provided care where they are safe, happy, and will grow socially, emotionally, cognitively, and physically.

Observation technology now makes it possible to study what caregivers actually do with children and to assess how the experiences of children in child care settings relate to their growth and development. It is expected that this technology and instrumentation will enable researchers to describe the variations that do exist in the quality of day care as indicated by the variables discussed in this chapter. For example, do caregivers who have more education provide more language development activities for children than caregivers who have less education? Do caregivers have conversations with children less frequently when the ratio of children to caregiver is higher? In homes with a high ratio of children, are less affection and more negative emotions shown by the caregivers; that is, does the caregiver express more angry, irritable, critical or demeaning behavior?

With such information, policymakers could base policy on factual data; they could recommend in-service training programs for caregivers, and parents could make wiser choices about the kind of care they want for their children. Centers that provide cognitive, structured programs may develop children who score higher on school readiness tests; similarly, more open exploratory center programs may develop children who are more creative in their behavior. Day care homes with a low child ratio may provide a more nurturing environment for younger children.

These are just a few examples of the kind of information that is expected to result from current observation technology. Hopefully, further research will improve this technology and consequently the quality of care that is provided.

Notes

1. See U. Bronfenbrenner, J. Belsky, and L. Steinberg, "Day Care in Context: An Ecological Perspective on Research and Public Policy," report prepared for the Office of the Assistant Secretary for Planning and Evaluation, Department of Health, Education and Welfare, December 1976.

2. The child-growth variables listed in Table 5-1 were compiled by SRI staff and consultants for the National Day Care Cost-Effects Study, which was sponsored by the Office of Child Development, Department of Health, Education and Welfare. The study focused on the behavior of day care children between the ages of three and five years and the behavior of their caregivers. See Jane Stallings and Mary Wilcox, "Report of Field Testing of Instruments for the National Day Care Cost-Effects Study," prepared for the Day Care Services Division, Office of Child Development, Department of Health, Education and Welfare by SRI International, Menlo Park, Calif., 1976.

3. In all day care studies performed by SRI, the caregivers have been female.

4. See E. Pikler, "Learning of Motor Skills on the Basis of Self-Induced Movements," *Exceptional Infant Studies in Abnormalities* (New York: Brunner Mazel, 1970); E. Pikler and A. Tardos, "Some Contributions to the Study of Infants' Gross Motor Activities," *XVI International Congress of Applied Psychology* (Amsterdam: Swets and Zeitlinger, 1969); Sally Provence and R. C. Lipton, *Infants in Institutions* (New York: International Universities Press, 1962); H. L. Rheingold and N. Gayly, "The Later Effects of an Experimental Modification of Mothering," *Child Development* 30 (1950):363-372; Margaret Ribble, *The Rights of Infants* (New York: Columbia Univ. Press, 1965); and K. S. Robson and H. A. Moss, "Patterns and Determinants of Maternal Attachment," *Journal of Pediatrics* 77 (1970):976-985.

5. This study, which is now in its second phase, is sponsored by the Office of Child Development, and is designed to assess the quality of care given in home facilities.

Appendix 5A
SRI Preschool Observation Instrument (Adult-Focus)

Classroom Summary Information

The Classroom Summary Information is found on the first page of the instrument. To fill in the circles accurately, the observer must obtain the following information from the caregiver, teacher, or aide.

Number of Children Enrolled and Number of Children Present

The number of children enrolled is the number of children who are officially registered in a particular center or classroom (column A). The number of children present is the number of children who are in attendance on the observation day (column B). Figure 5A-1 shows that 35 children were enrolled in the center and 29 children were present on a given day.

Number of Teachers/Caregivers, Aides, Volunteers, and Parents/Visitors

The coding for one caregiver and one aide who regularly work in the center and two volunteers and no parents present on the observation day is shown in Figure 5A-2.

Total Class Duration

Total class duration is the period of time during which the center is open to children. Because all children may not arrive or leave at the same time, the total class duration begins when the first child arrives and ends when the last child leaves. For example, a day during which children arrive at 8:30 A.M. and leave at 12:00 noon would be coded as shown in Figure 5A-3.

Physical Environment Inventory

The Physical Environment Inventory is divided into six categories. Only those items which apply to the center or classroom being observed are coded.

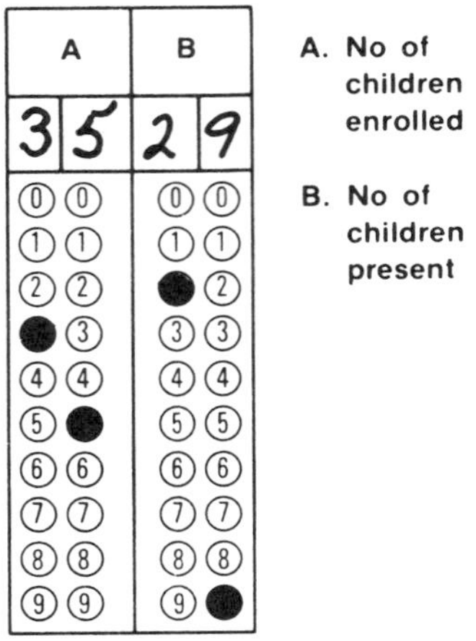

A	B

3 5 2 9

A. No of children enrolled

B. No of children present

Figure 5A-1.

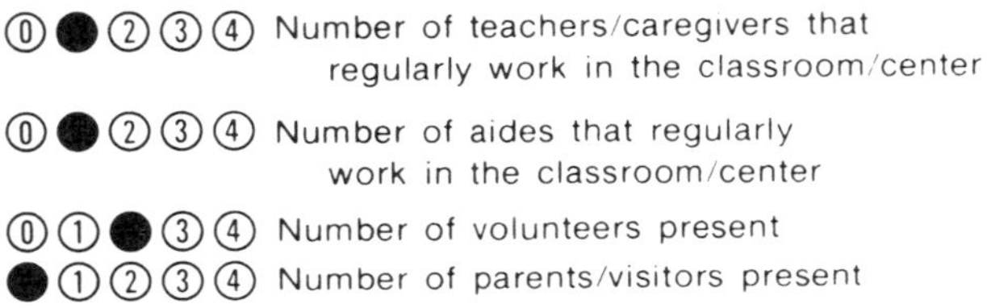

Number of teachers/caregivers that regularly work in the classroom/center

Number of aides that regularly work in the classroom/center

Number of volunteers present

Number of parents/visitors present

Figure 5A-2.

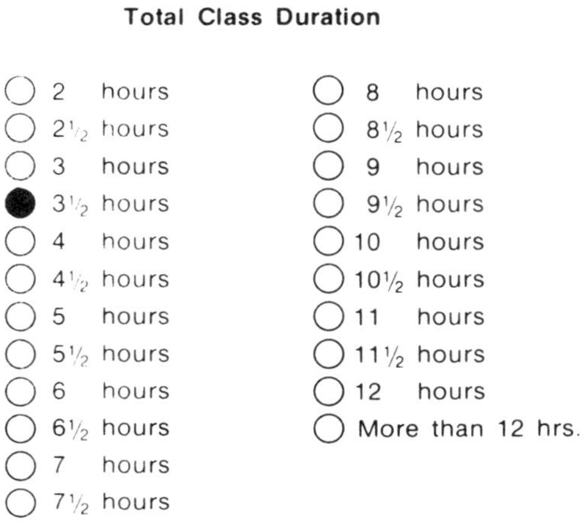

Total Class Duration

○ 2 hours
○ 2½ hours
○ 3 hours
● 3½ hours
○ 4 hours
○ 4½ hours
○ 5 hours
○ 5½ hours
○ 6 hours
○ 6½ hours
○ 7 hours
○ 7½ hours

○ 8 hours
○ 8½ hours
○ 9 hours
○ 9½ hours
○ 10 hours
○ 10½ hours
○ 11 hours
○ 11½ hours
○ 12 hours
○ More than 12 hrs.

Figure 5A-3.

Space Selection

This section describes the choice children have about the space or area they use. Only the item that applies is coded. If there is a lot of choice for children regarding the activities or space they are involved in, it would be coded as shown in Figure 5A-4.

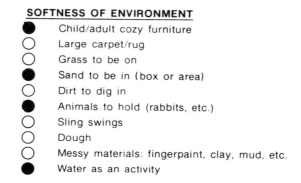

Figure 5A-4.

Softness of Environment

Softness of the environment refers to the malleability and comfort of the children's surroundings. An example of softness would be sling swings rather than wooden swings or craft materials that children can mold and shape rather than crayons and scissors. If the center has, for example, bean bag chairs, guinea pigs, water in the doll house sink, and a sandbox, this would be coded as shown in Figure 5A-5.

SOFTNESS OF ENVIRONMENT

- ● Child/adult cozy furniture
- ○ Large carpet/rug
- ○ Grass to be on
- ● Sand to be in (box or area)
- ○ Dirt to dig in
- ● Animals to hold (rabbits, etc.)
- ○ Sling swings
- ○ Dough
- ○ Messy materials: fingerpaint, clay, mud, etc.
- ● Water as an activity

Figure 5A-5.

Play Equipment (Present or Used)

Play equipment includes fixed-form materials that have limited uses. The example in Figure 5A-6 shows that in the center being observed, there is an area with dress-up clothes, books on shelves, children using floor blocks, a few children hammering nails, bikes parked outside, puzzles in boxes on a shelf, and children sitting on child-size furniture.

PLAY EQUIPMENT Present and/or Used

● Ⓤ Dramatic play props
● Ⓤ Structured games and puzzles
● Ⓤ Books, magazines, comic books, etc.
Ⓟ Ⓤ Water play
● Ⓤ Large vehicles to ride
Ⓟ Ⓤ Live animals to hold
Ⓟ Ⓤ Outdoor physical: slides, swings, climbers
Ⓟ Ⓤ Construction, table-type toys: lego blocks, tinker toys, etc.
Ⓟ Ⓤ Work tools
Ⓟ ● Floor blocks
Ⓟ Ⓤ Small wheel toys, cars, trucks, etc.
Ⓟ ● Skill equipment: carpentry/sewing, cooking equipment, etc.
Ⓟ Ⓤ Art materials: pencils, crayons, paper, scissors
Ⓟ Ⓤ Other
Ⓟ ● Child sized furniture, tables and chairs

Figure 5A-6.

Space or Play Equipment Problems

This category describes problems that may be present with the space or play equipment in the center. If there appear to be no problems, "None" is coded. If there are no trees, the swing has severely frayed ropes, and close quarters cause friction between two groups of children, the coding in Figure 5A-7 would be used.

SPACE OR PLAY EQUIPMENT PROBLEMS

○ None
● Lack of shade
● Broken or shabby equipment
○ Space is used as a pathway for other people
● Two groups in one space which are interfering with one another
○ Little privacy for children
○ Any combination of 2 or more special problems

Figure 5A-7.

Space Available

Space available is defined as any room where children are permitted to be, either by free choice or with adult permission. A play yard is an area divided or separated from other areas by a fence of any kind that requires a gate or door-way for entry. Secure safety fences/gates have latches or locks that discourage children from leaving the premises unattended. If there is one large play area with a swimming pool, sandbox, and swings, it is considered as only one play yard. However, if two yards adjoin one another and there is a playroom, and a safety latch on the fence, the coding in Figure 5A-8 would be used.

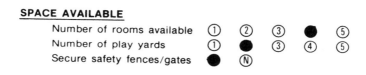

SPACE AVAILABLE

Number of rooms available ① ② ③ ● ⑤
Number of play yards   ① ● ③ ④ ⑤
Secure safety fences/gates ● Ⓝ

Figure 5A-8.

Storage Patterns

This category refers to how toys and materials for child use are stored. It does not refer to materials for adult use, such as food, dry paints, cleaning fluids, and the like. If some closets containing toys and materials for children are open and items are accessible, "Open" is coded. If closets are closed but not locked, "Closed" is coded. If toys and materials are kept in locked closets and are not available to children except when adults get the materials out, "Locked" is coded. If all three storage patterns are present in a center, the coding would be as in Figure 5A-9.

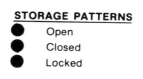

STORAGE PATTERNS
● Open
● Closed
● Locked

Figure 5A-9.

Classroom Snapshot

The Classroom Snapshot is coded just before the Five-Minute Interaction is coded. The snapshot attempts to record the distribution of adults and children within the activities that are occurring at the beginning of the observation. Essentially, the snapshot assesses (1) the activities occurring, (2) the materials used within these activities, (3) grouping patterns, (4) teacher and aide respon-sibilities, and (5) children in activities independent of adults (see Figure 5A-10).

Reliability Sheet ○

ACTIVITIES

				ONE CHILD	TWO CHILDREN	SMALL GROUPS	MEDIUM GROUPS	LARGE GROUPS
NON-WORK	T ○	A ○	P ○	T ①②③	①②③	①②③④	①②③④	①②
CLIMATE	T ○	A ○	P ○	A ①②③	①②③	①②③④	①②③④	①②
1. Child is	T ○	A ○	P ○	P ①②③	①②③	①②③④	①②③④	①②
Arriving or Departing				i ①②③	①②③	①②③④	①②③④	①②
2. Being Nurtured, Comforted				T ①②③	①②③	①②③④	①②③④	①②
				A ①②③	①②③	①②③④	①②③④	①②
				P ①②③	①②③	①②③④	①②③④	①②
				i ①②③	①②③	①②③④	①②③④	①②
3. Being Disciplined				T ①②③	①②③	①②③④	①②③④	①②
				A ①②③	①②③	①②③④	①②③④	①②
				P ①②③	①②③	①②③④	①②③④	①②
				i ①②③	①②③	①②③④	①②③④	①②
4. Child Uninvolved or Aimlessly Wandering				T ①②③	①②③	①②③④	①②③④	①②
				A ①②③	①②③	①②③④	①②③④	①②
				P ①②③	①②③	①②③④	①②③④	①②
				i ①②③	①②③	①②③④	①②③④	①②
5. Observing	T ○	A ○	P ○	T ①②③	①②③	①②③④	①②③④	①②
	T ○	A ○	P ○	A ①②③	①②③	①②③④	①②③④	①②
	T ○	A ○	P ○	P ①②③	①②③	①②③④	①②③④	①②
				i ①②③	①②③	①②③④	①②③④	①②
EXPRESSIVE				T ①②③	①②③	①②③④	①②③④	①②
6. Group Sharing, Planning or Singing				A ①②③	①②③	①②③④	①②③④	①②
				P ①②③	①②③	①②③④	①②③④	①②
				i ①②③	①②③	①②③④	①②③④	①②
7. Social Interaction			c ○	T ①②③	①②③	①②③④	①②③④	①②
	Observer		2 ○	A ①②③	①②③	①②③④	①②③④	①②
			s ○	P ①②③	①②③	①②③④	①②③④	①②
				i ①②③	①②③	①②③④	①②③④	①②
RECEPTIVE				T ①②③	①②③	①②③④	①②③④	①②
8. Stories, reading or telling, listen-				A ①②③	①②③	①②③④	①②③④	①②
ing to stories or music on records				P ①②③	①②③	①②③④	①②③④	①②
				i ①②③	①②③	①②③④	①②③④	①②
9. Teacher Directing, Children				T ①②③	①②③	①②③④	①②③④	①②
Responding: dancing to music,				A ①②③	①②③	①②③④	①②③④	①②
using instruments, listening games				P ①②③	①②③	①②③④	①②③④	①②
(e.g. Simon says) marching				i ①②③	①②③	①②③④	①②③④	①②
10. Instruction (alphabet, colors,				T ①②③	①②③	①②③④	①②③④	①②
shapes, numbers)				A ①②③	①②③	①②③④	①②③④	①②
				P ①②③	①②③	①②③④	①②③④	①②
				i ①②③	①②③	①②③④	①②③④	①②
11. Instructed Food Preparation				T ①②③	①②③	①②③④	①②③④	①②
(cooking, baking, carpentry,				A ①②③	①②③	①②③④	①②③④	①②
sewing, making a product)				P ①②③	①②③	①②③④	①②③④	①②
				i ①②③	①②③	①②③④	①②③④	①②
12. Teaching Practical Skills				T ①②③	①②③	①②③④	①②③④	①②
Acquisition (Body Care Instructions:				A ①②③	①②③	①②③④	①②③④	①②
tooth brushes, toileting, eating, tie				P ①②③	①②③	①②③④	①②③④	①②
shoes, dress, wash, wipe nose)				i ①②③	①②③	①②③④	①②③④	①②
VISUAL				T ①②③	①②③	①②③④	①②③④	①②
13. TV as entertainment				A ①②③	①②③	①②③④	①②③④	①②
				P ①②③	①②③	①②③④	①②③④	①②
				i ①②③	①②③	①②③④	①②③④	①②

Figure 5A–10. SRI Classroom Snapshot.

		ONE CHILD	TWO CHILDREN	SMALL GROUPS	MEDIUM GROUPS	LARGE GROUPS
14. Looking at Picture Books, Slides, or Movies	T	①②③	①②③	①②③④	①②③④	①②
	A	①②③	①②③	①②③④	①②③④	①②
	P	①②③	①②③	①②③④	①②③④	①②
	i	①②③	①②③	①②③④	①②③④	①②
USE OF MATERIALS 15. FIXED RULE OBJECT Table games, Puzzles	T	①②③	①②③	①②③④	①②③④	①②
	A	①②③	①②③	①②③④	①②③④	①②
	P	①②③	①②③	①②③④	①②③④	①②
	i	①②③	①②③	①②③④	①②③④	①②
LIMITED EXPLORATION (FIXED FORM) 16. Leggo, Tinker Toys, Peg Board, Felt Boards, Cutting Materials, Stringing Beads/Macaroni, etc.	T	①②③	①②③	①②③④	①②③④	①②
	A	①②③	①②③	①②③④	①②③④	①②
	P	①②③	①②③	①②③④	①②③④	①②
	i	①②③	①②③	①②③④	①②③④	①②
MALEABLES AND EXPLORATORY 17. Sand, Dirt, Animals, Bugs, Plants, Dough, Clay, Fingerpaint, Paints, Pasting, Water Play, Color Crayons Collage	T	①②③	①②③	①②③④	①②③④	①②
	A	①②③	①②③	①②③④	①②③④	①②
	P	①②③	①②③	①②③④	①②③④	①②
	i	①②③	①②③	①②③④	①②③④	①②
18. Unusual/Creative	T	①②③	①②③	①②③④	①②③④	①②
	A	①②③	①②③	①②③④	①②③④	①②
	P	①②③	①②③	①②③④	①②③④	①②
	i	①②③	①②③	①②③④	①②③④	①②
DRAMATIC PLAY 19. Dress-up, Trucks, Dolls, Doll house furniture	T	①②③	①②③	①②③④	①②③④	①②
	A	①②③	①②③	①②③④	①②③④	①②
	P	①②③	①②③	①②③④	①②③④	①②
	i	①②③	①②③	①②③④	①②③④	①②
MOTOR 20. ACTIVE PLAY—LARGE MUSCLE Bike Riding, Jungle Gym, Running, Jumping, Dancing, Active Games	T	①②③	①②③	①②③④	①②③④	①②
	A	①②③	①②③	①②③④	①②③④	①②
	P	①②③	①②③	①②③④	①②③④	①②
	i	①②③	①②③	①②③④	①②③④	①②
PROGRAM SCHEDULE RELATED 21. Transition: Clean up, Hand washing, tying shoes, putting on coat, toileting, getting ready to go out	T	①②③	①②③	①②③④	①②③④	①②
	A	①②③	①②③	①②③④	①②③④	①②
	P	①②③	①②③	①②③④	①②③④	①②
	i	①②③	①②③	①②③④	①②③④	①②
DOING WORK/HELPING 22. Setting table, Passing food/drinks, cleaning floors, washing windows, putting away toys	T	①②③	①②③	①②③④	①②③④	①②
	A	①②③	①②③	①②③④	①②③④	①②
	P	①②③	①②③	①②③④	①②③④	①②
	i	①②③	①②③	①②③④	①②③④	①②
23. Lunch or Snack	T	①②③	①②③	①②③④	①②③④	①②
	A	①②③	①②③	①②③④	①②③④	①②
	P	①②③	①②③	①②③④	①②③④	①②
	i	①②③	①②③	①②③④	①②③④	①②
24. Nap or Rest	T	①②③	①②③	①②③④	①②③④	①②
	A	①②③	①②③	①②③④	①②③④	①②
	P	①②③	①②③	①②③④	①②③④	①②
	i	①②③	①②③	①②③④	①②③④	①②

25. Adult Custodial, Prepare Materials	T ①②③	A ①②③④	P ①②③④	o ①②③④
26. Program Planning	T ①②③	A ①②③④	P ①②③④	o ①②③④
27. Program Peripheral	T ①②③	A ①②③④	P ①②③④	o ①②③④

For This Snapshot Only

Number of Caregivers in Center ⓪①②③④⑤⑥⑦⑧⑨
Number of Parents in Center ⓪①②③④⑤⑥⑦⑧⑨
Number of Children in Center ⓪①②③④⑤⑥⑦⑧⑨
⓪①②③④⑤⑥⑦⑧⑨

Number of Children Crying ⓪①②③④⑤⑥⑦⑧⑨
⓪①②③④⑤⑥⑦⑧⑨

Figure 5A–10. Continued

In the snapshot, the day care center activities are listed on the left with groups of circles in five columns on the right. The numbers that appear in these circles refer to the number of groupings in the categories identified by the column headings. Within each activity are four rows of circles with a letter designating each row: T (teacher), A (aide), P (parent or other person), and i (child independent of any adults). To use the snapshot, the observer scans the room in which the observation is taking place and marks the appropriate circles that describe how people in the room are grouped for each activity. The circles are read in relationship to both the column and row in which they appear. For example, in Activity 12, if the "2" circle in the "Two Children" column in the "A" row is coded, it is interpreted to mean that two aides are each instructing one group of two children in some kind of practical skill. This circle therefore refers to two groups of two children, since one aide cannot be with two groups at the same time. The snapshot records each person in the room at the time the observation is made.

Five-Minute Interaction

The Five-Minute Interaction records the behavior of the caregiver and all interactions she has with children or other adults. This record is made by using numeric and alphabetic codes that identify specific people or behaviors (see Figure 5A-11). This record identifies the speaker (Who), the person being spoken to (To Whom), the content of the Message (What), and several possible modifiers that explain the message (How). Figure 5A-12 shows three verbal statements (beginning with the teacher telling the child to shut the door). The set of frames following show that the child complied, that is, he shut the door. The next set of frames indicate the teacher praised the child. It is possible to record reliably 60 of these sentences in a five-minute period. During an hour, four of these five-minute interactions can be completed. If the observer records the behavior of adults and children for five hours, 20 such five-minute interactions will be obtained per day.

Whom/To Whom

T	Teacher
A	Aide
P	Parent
V	Volunteer/Visitor
C	Child
D	Different Child
Td	Toddler
I	Infant
S	Small Group (2-7)
M	Medium Group (8-12)
L	Large Group (13+)
O	Other

What

1	Command
2	Direct Question
2G	Open-Ended Question
3	Response
4	Instruction
5	Adult Self-Related Activity or Conversation
6	Center-Related Statements and Activity

What (continued)

7	Support/Comfort
8	Praise/Acknowledge
9	Correction
10	No Response
11	Rejects
12	Observing/Attending
T	Touch
NV	Nonverbal
X	Movement

How

T	Task
B	Behavior
U	Utilitarian
N	Negative
P	Positive
H	Happy
G	Guide
Pu	Punish
S	Sad
Dp	Dramatic Play
M	Materials
R	Rule

Figure 5A-11. Five-Minute Interaction Codes.

1. Teacher: "Shut the door."

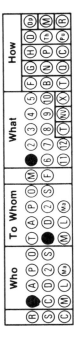

In our system, this command is coded TC1. The teacher (T, "Who" column) has given a child (C, "To Whom" column) a command (1, "What" column).

2. John: Walks to the door and shuts it.

Coding: CT3NVX. The child (C, "Who" column) responds (3, "What" column) with movement (X, "What" column) to the teacher's (T, "To Whom" column) command.

3. Teacher: "Good, John."

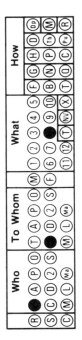

Coding: TC8. The teacher (T, "Who" column) praises (8, "What" column) the child's (C, "To Whom" column) compliance.

Figure 5A–12. Example of a Coded Interaction

Appendix 5B
Prescott-SRI Child
Observation System

The codes in the Prescott-SRI Child Observation System are divided into four main categories: Integrates, Thrusts/Initiates, Receives, and Defends/Responds.

The first category, Integrates, includes all those behaviors where the child integrates several behaviors such as involvement with task or understanding of the social situation. The code is used if the child watches or observes others or things, gives attention, participates, requests assistance, reacts with anger or gives up, contributes ideas, comforts another, or fights with another.

The second category, Thrusts/Initiates, includes behaviors that are initiated by the child, not in response to another's request or suggestion. It includes wandering about or waiting, moving with purpose or plan, selecting or suggesting an activity, asking for information or attention; giving opinions or directing others, and intruding.

The Receives category is used to record suggestions, comments, and questions that the child is receiving. It includes receiving requests or orders, suggestions, information, guidance, questions, comfort or praise, corrections, restraint, punishment or pain, intrusion, and rejection.

The Defends/Responds category is used to record the child's response to input. It includes giving no response, whining, crying, refusal to comply, asserting one's rights, and an active appropriate response. The Code Display Sheet in Figure 5B-1 shows the total list of behaviors in each category.

Integrates		Thrusts/Initiates		Receives		Defends/Responds	
I1	Monitors environment (looks, watches)	T1a	Does nothing, wanders	R1	Receives orders or minor behavioral corrections	1	No response
I2a	Maintains passive-attention activity	T1b	Moves with purpose	R2	Receives request/offer to play or share	2	Avoids, withdraws
I2b	Maintains open-ended, expressive activity	T2a	Selects activity alone				
I2c	Maintains closed, structured activity	T2b	Selects activity with others; suggests new activity; asks to join				
I3a	Asks for assistance, help with task	T3a	Asks for information	R3	Receives information/ help—task	3	Cries, whines (D3)
I3b	Quits activity after difficulty; gives up	T3b	Asks for permission to share materials, asks for turn				
I3c	Reacts with anger to difficulty						
I4ᵃ	Considers, contemplates, tinkers	T4	Gives opinions, preferences, information, comments	R4	Receives general comments, questions	4	Refuses to comply (D4) verbalized
I4b	Adds a different prop or new idea						
I4c	Sees pattern, gives structure; solves problem						
I5a	Offers sympathy, comfort	T5a	Asks for comfort, reassurance	R5a	Receives comfort, affection	5	Defends rights, asserts ownership (D5)
I5b	Shares, helps, offers affection	T5b	Asks for attention, recognition; expresses pride	R5b	Receives praise		

I6a	Participates in group activity—passive attention	T6a	States rules; tattles	R6a	Receives rules, corrections with explanation
I6b	Participates in group activity—open, expressive	T6b	Gives orders or directs others in task	R6b	Receives threats, discipline, restraint
I6c	Participates in group activity—closed, structured			R6b-N	Receives physical punishment
					6 Hostilely asserts rights; anger (D6)
I7-N	Participates in hostile exchange	T7a	Intrudes unintentionally	R7a	Receives unintentional intrusion or disruption
		T7b	Intrudes playfully	R7b	Receives playful intrusion
		T7b-N	Intrudes hostilely	R7b-N	Receives hostile intrusion
				R8a	Receives rejection, refusal
				R8b	Experience accident
					7 Active, appropriate response

AS   Attends to self
TT   Temper tantrum
NC   Not clear
OL   Other language
RP   Role play
Ng   Negative

Figure 5B-1. SRI/Prescott Child Observation System Code Display Sheet.

Appendix 5C
SRI Infant Observation
Codes

The SRI Infant Observation Instrument consists of a series of interaction frames. Each frame is put together somewhat like a sentence made up of the following categories: Who, To Whom, What, and How.

The "Who" and "To Whom" columns refer to the caregiver, parent, another adult, child or children, or the environment. "What" refers to the behavior expressed, such as a request, an explanation, praise, or a correction. "How" refers to the setting and/or the affective manner in which the behavior occurs. Figure 5C-1 provides a description of each code.

Who to Whom Column

C   — Caregiver, Parent
A   — Adult
I   — Infant
D   — Different Child
2   — Two Children
E   — Environment

What Column

1	— Request/Question	Code 1 is used for any request, command or question. A response is expected.
2	— Comply	Code 2 is used when an adult or child does what is expected.
3	— Noncomply/Protest	Code 3 is used when an adult or child does not do what is expected; child protests.
4	— Announce/Explain	Code 4 is used when an adult tells/explains to the child what the adult will do next to or with the child.
5	— No Response	Code 5 is used when there is no response from the child or from the adult.
6	— Action/Comment	Code 6 is used for action or comments which may or may not be related to the task.
7	— Acknowledge/ Reflect	Code 7 is used when an adult approves or recognizes what a child is doing. Also when an adult reflects back to the child what is going on with the child.
8	— Praise	Code 8 is used for excessive "fuss" over a child.
9	— Correct	Code 9 is used when the attempt is made by an adult to change or modify a child's actions.
10	— Wait	Code 10 is used when an adult is waiting for a response from the child, or the child from the adult. There is the expectation that a "dialogue" is possible.
11	— Distract	Code 11 is used when an adult tries to distract the child during a caregiving activity by the use of an unrelated toy or noises, gestures or words unrelated to the task.
12	— Attend/Listen	Code 12 is used when both the adult and child are attentive and focused on each other or on the task.

NV	— Nonverbal	When the action is not accompanied by words, NV is coded in the WHAT column, together with the appropriate number WHAT code.
RT	— Restraining Touch	Code RT when the adult holds the child firmly back from something he would rather be doing.
X	— Example/Model	Code X is used when the adult shows the child what action is required or how to do the action.

Hows

T^1	— Task 1	Attempt to involve child in task.
T^2	— Task 2	Child involvement in task process.
T^3	— Task 3	Mastery of task by child.

Figure 5C–1. Description of Codes: SRI Infant Observation Instrument.

M	– Mechanical/ Lipservice	Code "M" is used when the adult goes through the routine of diapering, feeding, bathing mechanically, without really involving herself in the task.
F	– Firm	Code "F" is used when the adult's tone is matter-of-fact. Tone is objective, no-nonsense, but is not demeaning. Code "F" does not exclude kindness or gentleness.
I	– Intrusive	Code "I" is used when the parent takes over the task; is reflective of own emotions rather than those of her child. Parent does not give space for the child.
T	– Temper Tantrum	Code "T" is used when the child has an uncontrolled burst of anger and crying.
N	– Negative	Any displeasure, irritability, fretful, or negative tone of voice.
P	– Positive Affect	Any pleasure, smiling, laughing, warm tone of voice, pleasure in task.
Pa	– Passive	Use "Pa" when the adult handles/picks up the child like an object or talks about the child in the third person. Child remains uninvolved.
H	– Playfulness/Humor/ Teasing	Code "H" when the child and/or adult is teasing and acting playful.
O	– Offering Choice	Use code "O" when an adult suggests options to the child and respects the answer or reaction.
Co	– Cooperating	Use code "Co" when a child actively helps with tasks or facilitates the task getting done.
C	– Crying	Use code "C" when a child is crying.

Who	To Whom	What	How
C A ◯ ◯	C A ◯ ◯	1 2 3 4 5	T1 M T Pa Co
1 D 2 ◯	1 D	6 7 8 9 10	T2 F N H
E	E	11 12 NV RT X	T3 I P O C

Figure 5C–1. Continued.

Appendix 5D
Carew/SRI Observation
System (Adult and
Child Focus)

The Carew/SRI Observation System consists primarily of an Adult Behavior
Code (adult focus) and a Child Code (child focus) instrument.

The Adult Behavior Code (ABC) Frame

The adult focus instrument is used to record the behaviors of the adult, usually
the principal caregiver. Each ABC coding frame has 10 dimensions 8 of which
describe the caregiver's behavior toward children during three-second observation intervals (see Figure 5D-1). The "Who" column identifies which caregiver is being observed. The "Whom" column identifies the person with whom

W h o	Auxil- iary	Whom	FACILITATE		CONTROL			E m o t.	L a n g.
			How	What	How	What	Explain		
(M1)	(CV)	(C1) (OC) (TE)	(PS) (LI) (MD)	(CN)	(DG)	YES	(+)	(EN)
(OP)		(C2) (GP) (PP)	(AF) (FS) (GM)	(SC)	(AS)	(NO)	(-)	(SP)
(OR)	(SV)	(BA) (AD) (HP)	(CM) (DP) (PN)		(AV)		(NU)	(BO)
	(PC)	(YC) (DR)	(FE) (ET)					(NO)
	(HS)		(WK) (NT)					
(C)	(RA)		(NA)					

Figure 5D–1. Adult Behavior Code (ABC) Frame.

she is interacting. "Facilitate-How" describes what the caregiver is doing during
the three-second interaction. "Facilitate-What" describes the activity context in
which the caregiver relates to a child (usually this is the activity that the child is
involved in during the interaction with the caregiver). The "Control" codes
describe the caregiver's method of controlling the children's behavior, if she has
tried to do so. "Emotion" describes the feeling conveyed by the caregiver's
behavior as positive, negative, or neutral. The "Language" column designates
whether the caregiver used English words, Spanish words, both, or no words
during the interaction. The "Auxiliary" column includes codes for caregiver

131

behaviors that do not facilitate or control children's activities; rather, they indicate limited or no interactions between caregiver and children.

The Child Code (CC) Frame

The child code frame is used to record the behavior of the child upon whom the observer is focusing her attention. The CC frame has seven dimensions, five of which describe the focus child's involvement or lack of involvement in an activity during the three-second observation intervals (see Figure 5D-2). The "Who" column indicates whether the focus child is within the observer's visual range. The "Whom" column identifies the person with whom the child is interacting. The "Activity" column describes the activity in which the child is engaged as he interacts with others, while the "Auxiliary" codes indicate limited or no interaction between the focus child and others. "Mode" describes the child's manner of participation in the activity, that is, whether he initiates or receives/responds to the actions recorded in the frame. The "Emotion" column describes the effect displayed by the focus child.

Who	Activity			Auxil-iary	Whom	Mode	Emot.	Lang.
FC	PS	LI	MD	CV	SF OC	AC	+	EN
OR	AF	FS	GM	TR	MI GP	RV	-	SP
	DS	DP	PN		BA AD		NU	BO
	AT	FE	ET	OB	YC			NO
	AS	WK	NT	BL				
C	CN		NA					

Figure 5D-2. Child Code (CC) Frame.

Vouchers for Child Care: The Santa Clara Child Care Pilot Study
Susan Stoddard

Underlying the various theoretical and empirical studies of child care service delivery is a question central in policy planning: What is the appropriate form of service delivery in the area of child care? The current child care delivery system is characterized as a "nightmare" of alternative funding sources, regulations, eligibility requirements, and operational models of service.[1]

Several policy analysts in the last few years have recommended voucher models of service delivery as the solution to the question of the provision and type of child care services. For instance, Nelson and Young ask,

> What should be the form of subsidy to day care? The clear implication of our discussion here is that subsidy should be implemented through a voucher-type system. There is no need that parents actually handle pieces of paper in the form of voucher certificates. What is important is that subsidy facilitates consumer choice by its attachment to children and not particular centers. Thus when a day care center admits a child, it knows that a subsidy check will be forthcoming, and when it loses a child it loses the corresponding subsidy.[2]

While policy analysts have recommended vouchers as desirable alternatives for service delivery from a theoretical point of view, the evidence in demonstration of such programs has been less than encouraging. In the day care voucher component of the Gary, Indiana, Income Maintenance Experiment, the child care voucher system went virtually unused.[3] And in other related social services, the voucher concept has been less than a total success. In Alum Rock, California, the much-heralded education vouchers experiment has fallen far short of original expectations.[4] A hasty conclusion from these experiences is that voucher systems do not work well in the delivery of social services. But it is also possible that it is the demonstrations, not the vouchers themselves, that have been difficult to implement and interpret.

This chapter discusses the implementation of a demonstration of vouchers in child care service delivery, the Child Care Pilot Study, implemented by the California State Department of Education and the County Superintendent of Schools' Office in Santa Clara County, California.

What Is a Voucher?

Simply stated, a *voucher* is a certificate or "chit" with buying power.[5] Food

133

stamps are vouchers. Applying the voucher idea to social services, the voucher would be an alternative to direct provision of services (often with only one possible supplier), on the one hand, and to unrestricted cash grants, on the other. Vouchers, by limiting in some sense where and when money can be spent, allow the government to influence spending and choice of services by consumers but give service consumers purchasing power. Vouchers, by allowing consumers to choose and purchase services, may create markets for services within social service systems. Voucher proponents have argued that vouchers would introduce the benefits of the marketplace into service bureaucracies that have typically been characterized as monopolistic, unresponsive, and unable to perform. By introducing consumer purchasing power through vouchers, more competitive markets may be achieved in service delivery systems. In particular, competition should have the effect of lowering price. For both the consumer and the producer, vouchers ideally might have a desirable effect. Indeed, numerous analysts have recommended vouchers for social services because of the anticipated market effects.

The social service area in which the voucher concept has been most developed is elementary education. In the late 1960s and early 1970s, the voucher idea developed as a result of policy recommendations in the field of education. Christopher Jencks and others at the University of Wisconsin explored, for OEO, the equity and efficiency implications of educational vouchers. Jencks' policy work built upon earlier conceptual work[6] dating back to Adam Smith (in *The Wealth of Nations*). Jencks' recommendations to OEO resulted in the issuing of a federal Request for Proposal (RFP) to test educational vouchers. Consequently, educational vouchers became the most visible of social service voucher recommendations.

While policy analysts have recommended vouchers as desirable alternatives for service delivery from a theoretical point of view, the evidence in demonstration of such programs has been less than encouraging. In Alum Rock, California, the much-heralded education voucher experiment resulting from the Jencks/OEO work has, as mentioned previously, not been very successful. Concerning Alum Rock, Eliot Levenson of Rand points out that,

the prime aim of the "transitional" voucher experiment in Alum Rock was to change the operation of a school system from a public monopoly to a market system, where parent choice determines the amount and variety of schooling. After three years of operation, [however] the basic changes envisioned prior to initiation of the experiment had not occurred as planned.[7]

In fact, we should expect that it is very difficult to create a competitive market within service delivery organizations. Most of our human and social service delivery systems have been organized as large bureaucracies, because of the failure of the market to provide and distribute needed services. Implementation of a voucher as a part of a complex and established service system, such as an elementary school district, is not straightforward, as the researchers in Alum Rock have discovered.

Voucher outcomes associated with competition and the market model depend upon several assumptions concerned with the supply and demand sides of the purchase. While "pure competition" does not exist, there are a number of common-sense conditions that should be satisfied if the market effects are to be expected.[8]

1. The consumer must have information on the service alternatives available. Information should include:
   a. information on alternatives available,
   b. price of the alternatives,
   c. quality of the service.
2. Consumer should have the means to evaluate outputs.
3. Consumer should have control of significant resources to make the system respond.
4. Cost of change of service facing consumer should not be prohibitive.
5. There should be realistic alternative choices among suppliers.
6. There should be freedom to offer significantly varying products.
7. Cost of entry into the system with innovative products should not be prohibitive.

If competition is the avenue for improvement of services, as many voucher proponents have argued, then these are rather obvious conditions. The organization of voucher plans in service delivery systems can compromise these conditions. For example, in Alum Rock several restrictions on the voucher model impeded the creation of markets and competition in the district. Many of the "market" conditions were traded away before the experiment began. Some features of the Alum Rock "transitional" model that severely compromised the "voucher" concept were that:

1. The demonstration would initially involve public schools only, with 6 of the 24 district schools participating.
2. Teacher job tenure and seniority rights were guaranteed.
3. Children already attending a school and their younger siblings were guaranteed "squatters rights."[9]

Features of the education voucher system that were not compatible with the goals and standard operating procedures of the Alum Rock school district were not fully implemented or were discarded; that is, the "pure" voucher as planned did not come to be because of the constraints on implementation inherent in the delivery model itself.[10] But policy analysts argue that public school districts are more structured and inflexible than other service systems.

There is continued interest in exploring the application of vouchers to other social services. Child care services are often mentioned as a service area where vouchers might be used effectively.

Why Are Vouchers Recommended Particularly for Child Care Services?

Two major social purposes predominate in child care delivery philosophy and influence the form of child care services and their organization. Public provision of child care services addresses two major objectives: *social service objectives* (heritage of the day nursery movement, reflected in the aim of Title XX, to help economically dependent families achieve self-sufficiency) and *educational objectives* (heritage of the preschool movement of the twentieth century, reflected in such legislation as California's Child Development Act of 1972). While there are two major aims of child care services, the form the program takes can vary widely.

For instance, in California, the Department of Education is the state agency primarily responsible for child care programs; programs for which the Department of Education is responsible include:[11]

Children's centers;

Campus centers;

Migrant child care centers;

California state preschool programs;

School-age parenting and infant development;

Innovative programs (AB99);

Community-based centers.

These programs vary in input components required. Variation can be defined in terms of eligibility requirements, funding sources, center auspices, number of children enrolled, educational components, parent participation, health services, nutritional requirements, social services, required evaluations, teacher qualifications, use of assistants or aides, ages of children served, hours of daily operation, and the adult/child ratio.[12] While there is such program variation, essentially, subsidized care has been provided in three major forms:

Group care: children's centers and other group care;

Family day care homes: homes licensed for the care of children, usually licensed for up to six children, including the mother's own, in a private home;

In-home care: care, or babysitting, in the child's own home.

Voucher proponents argue that there are a number of conditions in the current system that make a voucher approach (allowing parents to choose and purchase the preferred type of care) desirable.

1. *Costs.* The cost of publicly subsidized care has been high. Critics of the present delivery system have pointed out that the costs of publicly subsidized care often exceed the costs of privately provided services. For instance, in California, the 1974 legislative analyst's report cited the following significant cost differences among delivery systems types: "the average operating cost in publicly subsidized day care centers was $1.16 per child hour. Eliminating the extremes, we found a cost range from $.69 to $1.74 per child-hour. By contrast, the child-hour cost in nonsubsidized centers averaged approximately $.52, or only 45% of the cost in subsidized centers." Average cost in family day care homes was approximately $.49 per child hour.[13]

2. *The eligibility requirements of particular day care suppliers restrict the choice possible to parents.* One obvious result of the fragmented funding pattern in child care services is that different groups of subsidized clients are eligible for different care arrangements. For instance, people who are working may be eligible to use different care than people who are in training. Change in family or work situation may require change in a child's care arrangement. Some voucher supporters stress the importance of parental choice, and the importance of reducing the structural barriers imposed by eligibility requirements of multiple fund-sources.[14] Eligibility restrictions on choice could be reduced in the design of a voucher plan which allows "spending" for alternative types of eligible care.

3. *Little assurance that the public knows the best form of child care to deliver.* If the "technology" of child care were more developed, if we had an assurance that public providers knew the one best child care provider model for both children and families, the existing system would not be so troublesome. But we know from the literature that there is no assurance that a particular form of child care is "better" than another. While there are a number of studies of programs trying to demonstrate the cost-effective approach to the delivery of quality child care services, in fact there is little hope in the short run of conclusively arguing for a particular type of care. In the absence of longitudinal data, there is no sure way of determining the effect of the various program inputs on program outcome. Some analysts are awaiting the results of the OCD-funded National Day Care Study for definitive analysis of major child care delivery models.[15] The California Department of Education Pilot Study data is also viewed as a potential source of analysis.[16] But others would argue that analysis will not be possible at the level necessary to determine the appropriate child care service for individual families and specific children, and that this allocation should be made by the parents, not determined by the system. A voucher system would allow parents to evaluate and select the best alternative, and the parent would assume responsibility for the quality decision.

4. *An organizational argument.* Child care services are currently provided in diverse forms. Even the programs directly funded by public monies are in a variety of forms, as has been pointed out. There is no real system, and many

agencies are involved in providing different child care services. The services are already decentralized to a certain degree. Availability of child care services in a variety of forms satisfies one of the major voucher assumptions.

5. *Quality.* There is continuing research as to what is meant by *quality* in day care experience. But it is apparent that in many cases, the services provided both privately and publicly are deficient by any standard of quality. The survey carried out by the National Council of Jewish Women, and reported by Mary Dublin Keyserling in *Windows on Day Care,* found 11.4 percent of the nonprofit centers visited to be "poor" in quality.[17] For day care homes, 14 percent were found to be "poor" in quality. The current system is not guaranteeing quality, and the voucher theory argues that a more responsive supply may generate more "quality" child care, in addition to stimulating development of alternative child care services responsive to parent preference.

These characteristics of child care services seem compatible with the voucher approach to subsidy alternatives. In California, the Department of Education has conducted a demonstration of a form of voucher plan for child care subsidy. This demonstration, the Santa Clara County Pilot Study, provides policymakers and child care researchers with a range of information on the implementation of a child care voucher system.

The Santa Clara County Pilot Study

The Santa Clara County Pilot Study should be considered in the context of the history of child care services in California. Of all the states, California has an exceptional record of public responsibility for child care programs, and of questioning both responsibility and form.

Federal legislation during World War II amended the Lanham Act of 1942 and made it possible for school districts to establish group care, using federal funds. In California, enabling legislation was passed in 1943 and school districts were authorized to establish Child Care Centers. Thus the involvement of the State Department of Education with child care began in a time of emergency. Notably, in California, the state chose to retain the program after the war. This program continued and was renamed Children's Centers Program.

The Department of Social Welfare also assumed a role in child care services. In 1967, when amendments to the Social Security Act required that the state name a single agency to receive federal aid for a variety of services including child care, the single state agency designated in California was the Department of Social Welfare, which already administered welfare and social service monies.[18]

Since the early 1970s, several legislative changes have finally placed child care under the aegis of the Department of Education. In AB 1244 (1973), the California Legislature declared "the need for a two-year Pilot Study to develop and test a coordinated child care delivery system which shall provide the parent with a choice in selecting quality child care at costs responsive to the parent's willingness and ability to pay."[19]

The objectives of the pilot study, as contained in AB 1244, pertain to information needed to implement a new delivery system statewide to be administered by the Department of Education. Research needs identified in the legislation focus on information on existing child care services and users, and on various aspects of the delivery system to be tested. The objectives of the pilot study were specified as follows.

(a) To measure the effectiveness and efficiency of a delivery system which permits the eligible parent to select and purchase child care services based on a fee schedule requiring the parent to pay a proportionate share of the child care costs; to determine the existing types of care and range of services; to measure changes in the use of these services and development of alternative types of care as determined by parent choice; to stimulate a variety of alternative child care resources; to describe the demographic characteristics of the population seeking these services and their incidence by type of service selected; and to assess the costs of delivering these services.

(b) To determine the applicability of the fee schedule described in Section 16729; to define the income level at which the fee schedule no longer applies as measured by its limited utility in aiding low-income families to obtain or maintain employment; to define appropriate eligibility criteria and priorities for services; and to define appropriate standards for cost and quality of types of care and services.

(c) To develop and evaluate appropriate eligibility and certification procedures and parent fee payment procedures; to identify informational needs and accountability requirements of the child care delivery system; and to develop and evaluate appropriate monitoring and accountability mechanisms required by the system.

(d) To develop the management guidelines, policies, and techniques for administering the system statewide and to develop strategies for phasing out the existing system and introducing the new system on a statewide basis.[20]

Note that while a parent-choice system was specified, the exact design of the delivery system was not. The spirit of the legislation was consistent with voucher thinking, and the designers of the pilot study developed, in the first year after the legislation was passed, a model of a voucher-type delivery system. Details of the design and implementation phases of this model are documented elsewhere.[21] By July 1975, approximately a year after AB 1244, the pilot study delivery system was ready to serve clients in Santa Clara County. The pilot study service model developed in response to the legislative objective in a form of voucher model and might be characterized by the following simple description of change. The state provides:

A subsidy of 20 to 100 percent of child care costs, based on the fee schedule to be tested.

Choice of care. The payment system eliminates some of the restrictions on where a state child care dollar can be spent. The purchaser is free to use family day care homes and private day nurseries and centers, as well as publicly subsidized programs.

Information on types of care available, through counselors located at four information and referral centers in the county.

Referrals to licensed caregivers with vacancies ("live" referrals).

Consumers receiving such state services, in turn, agree to provide:

Detailed information on their households and their use of child care.

Cooperation with the experiment and with the reporting procedures.

This system of exchange requires backup systems of research management and data collection, of administration of the subsidy, of management of the information centers through which the exchange takes place, and of monitoring and evaluation of the process of the experiment. The particular service delivery model and backup systems of this experiment are the "how to do" response to the legislation, but they are not delineated there. AB 1244 is not specific about the type of model or the nature of the study. The model and backup systems have developed, some by deliberate project design decisions and some as organizational responses to the design or to the child care environment.

Management of the project was in the County Superintendent of Schools' Office in Santa Clara County. The client contact with the system was through four field offices with information and referral counselors. (Later in the study, these counselor functions were centralized in the county office.)

The Child Care Pilot Study system, as implemented, was made up of two important components: a *reimbursement system* (the voucher system), for providing subsidies to eligible parents, and an *information and referral system.* The information and referral function was seen by the pilot study designers as an important component of the voucher-type delivery system, providing consumers with information they would need to make "informed choices."

Description of the Pilot Study Voucher Design

A voucher is, by definition, restricted consumer purchasing power. Vouchers are not unrestricted cash but are issued for purchase of specific services or products. Therefore, any voucher design will include a number of design choices. Most of the important choice dimensions are discussed below, with a clear example of what the particular choices are in the pilot study model. It is important to note that this model is but one of a number of variations possible under the rubric of a child care voucher system, that each of these design choices may relate to the particular service environment of this model, that each of the choices may have a direct effect on demand and supply and on outcome, and that any analysis of the process and results in Santa Clara are specific to this particular model.

What the Voucher Can Purchase and Where It May Be Spent

Vouchers are in fact subsidy dollars limited to the purchase of some defined set of goods and/or services. Food stamps, for instance, may be used for a variety of food supplies, but not for liquor and cigarettes. The design of a voucher system will always include some definition of the commodities that can be purchased. In addition, there will be an identification of the appropriate places for the transaction, which may involve licensing, credentialling, or otherwise certifying locations where the vouchers may be "spent."

In the pilot study model, the parent may contract for child care services with any licensed provider of out-of-home care. Licensed child care is available in California from a variety of types of providers: family day care homes, private centers, and public centers. Reimbursable care can be full-day or part-day (including extended-day) care. In-home (residential) care and private schooling for kindergarten and beyond are specifically excluded. Unlicensed day care homes or day nurseries are likewise ineligible. It has been estimated that 75 percent of family day care homes in California are unlicensed. Such homes are not eligible for reimbursement under the regulations of the pilot study. (It should be mentioned that early in the study, some participants advocated inclusion of unlicensed care in the experiment, since licensing is an important issue in child care administration and unlicensed care is a significant percentage of total supply. But the public sponsorship of the demonstration and the close relationship with the licensing agencies—the Department of Education and the Department of Health—precluded the inclusion of unlicensed care.)

Are the Supply System Prices Regulated?

The design of a voucher system may specify limits or actual unit amounts to be paid for goods or services. The purchasing power of a voucher may be expressed in dollar terms or in unit amounts. In a child care system, for instance, a voucher might be designed for hours of child care (then reimbursing at some regulated rate) or dollars. In addition, the suppliers of services might be required to guarantee limits on amounts charged to voucher users. Or there may be no restriction on the amount that providers charge.

Pilot study providers are asked to record their usual fees and to attest that the fees charged to parents using the voucher subsidy are regular "market" fees. However, this is in no way a binding agreement in the pilot study model, and no system was set up for monitoring price disparities between subsidized and non-subsidized users.

Who Is an Eligible Client?

Voucher systems, as subsidy mechanisms, are accompanied by eligibility requirements for potential clients. Eligibility requirements may be based on income, family size, residence, citizenship, and so on. All the social programs supported by public funds are accompanied by such eligibility restrictions.

For this demonstration, residents of Santa Clara County with children under fifteen years of age were eligible to apply for a subsidy, regardless of income. The research purposes of the study imposed special eligibility requirements for the first year or so of service delivery; only a percentage of those applying for a subsidy were selected as recipients. After the research sample was selected, all such applicants were eligible for subsidy. The family was eligible whether or not the child or children were currently enrolled in licensed care. Payment would begin only after enrollment in licensed care.

What Is the Fee Schedule?

Along with the list of eligibility requirements, voucher design will include some schedule for determining level of reimbursement. Many of the social services are delivered on some form of "sliding scale." These scales or fee schedules are resource-allocation mechanisms for distribution of services.[22] The California Legislative Analyst's Office, in its December 1975 report entitled "Current Issues in Publicly Subsidized Care," states that there were 56,000 children receiving publicly subsidized care in 1975-1976 in California, with over 50,000 in child care centers. Usually such centers have waiting lists. These 56,000 children represent only a fraction of those children potentially eligible for subsidized child care services in California.[23] Over one million AFDC children are potentially eligible.[24] One of the changes in implementing a voucher system is the change from subsidy tied to supply to subsidy tied to consumers. The amount and distribution of such subsidy is determined by the fee schedule.

One of the primary purposes of the pilot study was stated as testing the applicability of a proposed new fee schedule. Before the model was implemented, however, there was some problem with which fee schedule to use. On June 1, 1975, the project reported that,

The Pilot Study fee schedule is currently a source of concern. Development of an extended fee schedule has been seriously hampered by changes in federal law. Revisions of income tax regulations significantly changed allowable child care deductions. More importantly, Title XX of the Social Security Act requires that a new statewide fee schedule be established for all Title IV-A programs. At this time, no Title XX fee schedule has been developed. As a consequence, it is likely that it will be necessary to revise the Pilot Study fee schedule at some later date. The implications for such a change are difficult to assess without knowledge of the configuration of the new statewide fee schedule.[25]

The fee schedule in the study varied over the two-year period of service delivery as to the actual upper limit on amount reimbursed. But basically, the fee schedule was a linear sliding scale based on family income and family size. Clients in the lowest income group were reimbursed for the full amount of their child care expenses, subject to a limit on the maximum allowable rate per hour of care ($1.14 per hour for regular care and $1.35 per hour for infant care).[26] Clients in the highest income group were reimbursed for 20 percent of their child care costs, subject to the upper limits on cost per hour. Rates of reimbursement for clients in middle-income ranges were based on a straight-line schedule and ranged from 20 to 99 percent.

Who is Paid? (Does the System Pay the Consumer or the Provider?)

A voucher is, in fact, a guarantee of payment for goods or services for consumption. Will the payment be made to the provider or to the consumer?

Reimbursement mode was investigated in the experiment. In the early months of the demonstration, 50 percent of the subsidy checks went directly to the consumers (that is, the users were themselves able to cash in certificates showing how much child care they had used the previous month). In the other 50 percent of the cases, the eligible care provider received the subsidy check directly (in other words, the state paid part of the bill directly). After September 1976, all new clients received their checks directly. By varying the way in which payment was made, the demonstration was able to test alternatives to the question "Who is paid?"

When Payments Are Made

In some voucher systems, a subsidy coupon may be issued in advance of purchase of services. The consumer is then able to purchase, using the coupons like cash. Food stamps are an example. In other cases, payment is made based on reimbursement for a portion of actual consumption, and must be made after the fact.

In the pilot study model, payments, whether to client or to provider, were sent after the end of the month, after clients submitted a monthly reimbursement form indicating the number of hours of child care consumed for the month, the amount spent for child care and any changes in income, labor force participation, or other personal information. On the monthly reimbursement form, the number of child care hours, and the total amount spent, must have been verified and signed off by the relevant child care provider and the parent applying for reimbursement.

Are the Vouchers to Serve as Some
Kind of Behavioral Incentive?

In some social service delivery systems, subsidy may be used as an inducement for particular, "desirable" client behavior. For instance, there are, in Work Incentive Programs, specific monies available for those willing to seek gainful employment.

In the pilot study there were no requirements that parents using the system be employed or seeking employment. The one behavioral incentive that was central to the pilot study was the willingness of clients to complete detailed survey questionnaires and detailed personal and financial information to be used in research of their child care use and preference.

Is There an Arrangement for the Quality of the Supplier?

In centralized, direct service delivery, the agency is often directly responsible for guaranteeing the quality of services delivered. With vouchers, consumers assume a good deal of the responsibility for choosing "quality" goods or services. However, a situation of "let the buyer beware" may not be appropriate for social services. In transferring to a voucher system, agencies may need to substitute alternative quality-assessing systems. By limiting eligible supply to licensed suppliers, the pilot study relied on state licensing procedures for regulation of quality.

Ability of Supplier to Screen Clients or Applicants

One possible use of a voucher system might be to guarantee an open supply of publicly subsidized services. For instance, there might be regulations that would prohibit screening on the part of any potentially eligible provider of services. In the pilot study model there was no regulation of supplier's normal screening of client applicants in this financing plan.

What Provisions Are Made for Consumer Information?

Thus far, the rules listed for a reimbursement system, and the pilot study model, do not include consideration of the consumer-information dimension of consumer choice. Choice implies the availability of information on the available supply. There are a variety of ways that designers of a reimbursement system could choose to handle the issue of consumer information. It could be assumed, for instance, that consumers will gather their own information, and that providers will have the incentive, in the "market" structure, to advertise and create a market-information situation. Or it could be the case that the public agency responsible for the subsidy will also assume some responsibility for assuring public-information sources on supply existence and quality.

The delivery system that developed in the pilot study included an information and referral system. In the early part of the study, counselors in four community information and service offices supplied information on care available, and gathered salient data and applications for the subsidy. In the later months of the study, this process was centralized, since almost all (97 percent) the contacts with the counselors were by phone rather than in the office. The information and referral counselors provided "live" referrals (i.e., of homes and centers with vacancies) to clients. This required updating a child care directory for the area. Also, counselors were to provide standardized information on the different major types of child care available, to minimize counselor influence on parent choice of care. The importance of the information procedures on the meaning of the parents' voucher choices was stressed throughout the study.[27]

These rules constitute major design decisions made in the development of the pilot study model. As is clear in the preceding discussion, the pilot study model is but one of many alternative designs that might have been tested in looking at "choice" models for the delivery of child care services. The value of looking at the pilot study model is not in seeing this as the one most appropriate voucher design for child care services, but as one design that has been tested in the field in a major subsidy program over a two-year service delivery period.

The Pilot Study Experience

The model has expanded significantly the use of an alternative supply of child care services within the system of publicly subsidized care in Santa Clara County in California. In the first 18 months of operation, the pilot study provided a total of $820,866 to 2905 families with 3774 children. The services of as many as 1116 separate child care providers in Santa Clara County were subsidized. Three types of providers were involved, all licensed or accredited. Unique identification numbers of participating providers were recorded for 846 family day care homes, 211 private centers, and 59 public centers.[28] The demonstration took three years, with the first year being devoted to planning and design. There were two years of actual program operation. As the first major child care voucher model, the pilot study broke new ground and, not surprisingly, experienced a number of implementation problems and design changes. And, while two years is a long time as far as the study and refinement of a delivery model are concerned, it is a very short period for any supply effects to occur. In fact, the paradox in voucher demonstrations is that in short-run programs there is little opportunity to test the important longer-run market rationale for use of vouchers. But preliminary findings from pilot study data reveal effects on demand and supply of child care services resulting from the implementation process of this particular model.

What were the Demand and Supply Conditions in the Implementation of This Particular Model?

In order to answer this question, let us review separately a number of specific questions on demand and supply.

Was There an Adequate Supply of Child Care Services Available for Parent Choice?

At the beginning of the pilot study, there was assurance from child care professionals in the county that there were adequate vacancies in child care services to allow parents a choice in the type of care selected.[29] In addition, the expansion of the allowable subsidized providers to include all licensed care increased the pilot study clients' options for care arrangements. Thus, at a macro level, there would seem to be a realistic alternative choice available in the model. On a micro level, however, there were a number of problems. First, there was a problem in finding certain special types of care. Infant care was difficult to find. Also, some geographical areas did not have an adequate supply. Special needs, such as after-school care or evening care, also were difficult to locate. Further, the on-the-books capacity figures often did not correspond to the actual operating capacities of centers and homes. A family day care mother, for instance, may prefer to care for two or three children, even though licensed to care for six. So there was great variation in the number of vacancies that might be estimated from license and use statistics and actual vacancies in the centers and homes.[30]

How Could Consumers Obtain Information on the Supply Available?

To make an informed choice, the consumer should have information on the service alternatives available. Information should include: alternatives available, price of the alternatives, and quality of service.

The pilot study model was specifically designed with an information and referral system; counselors and counselor aides provided information to clients on vacancies in child care in their geographical area. Counselors were instructed to provide consumers with "referrals" to at least three alternative child care providers and to inform clients of the differences between family day care homes and center care. In implementing the model, a number of problems in providing information became apparent:

(a) The counselors themselves were more satisfied in helping "place" children than in providing information. Therefore, the tendency in the field offices was more toward placement than dispensing information only. Repeated instruction from the project specialist in charge of research did not succeed in assuring complete and unbiased information.

(b) It was difficult and time consuming to keep an up-to-date information source on "vacancies." In fact, the decision to supply "live" referrals brought major expenses to the study: the cost of one "set" of referrals was roughly $50.[31]

(c) The system could not provide clients with "quality" information other than that the child care provider was licensed. The counselors could, and did, refrain from giving recommendations to centers or homes that had been subject to frequent complaints.

(d) The system was able to give information on approximate costs. But this information was better obtained from the provider.

(e) The decision to give "live" referrals was made so that providers were not "bothered" when they had no vacancies. While this did assure that clients did not have to "shop" through numerous unavailable providers before finding a vacancy, it did limit the clients' information on available care. Clients, when evaluating the system of information, did mention that they would like "quality" information, something difficult, if not impossible, to provide in such a system.

Consumers' ability to evaluate child care outputs is by no means easy to assure. There have been few studies of the effect of child care services on children in the short run, let alone long-run effects. Evaluation is more likely to be concerned with *process,* what goes on in a day care center, or *inputs,* such as the availability of equipment, space, and trained staff. The pilot study staff did encourage parents to visit the child care providers to observe operations. Some suggestions on this parent observation were provided in a "Consumers Guide to Choosing Child Care," published by the pilot study and distributed to clients.[32] Consumers were encouraged to "search," to visit a number of suppliers. The extent of client search is not known. But in one follow-up study carried out by the pilot study, it was recorded that almost half (49.8 percent) of the clients did not contact another provider before selecting the one being used.[33] (Many children already in licensed care at the beginning of the study remained with their original providers. Therefore, use of the voucher did not, in these cases, involve "search.")

Were Significantly Varied Child Care Alternatives Available?

The pilot study system did make the subsidy available to any provider licensed to care for children. *Within the requirements of licensing,* providers were free to differentiate their "product." The requirements of licensing do place some limitations on the programs, but programs were free to vary on the provision of meals, composition of staff, availability of equipment, and so on. A problem in differentiation of supply is in identifying alternative types. Other than the rubrics, "family day care homes," "public centers," and "private centers," the pilot study system itself did not provide identification of the dimensions of alternative choice. These distinctions were left to the parents, in investigating alternatives. Except for the limit on cost per hour eligible for subsidy, there was no system restriction on the providers' pricing of service. Cost per child hour does not in itself provide differentiation. Cost differences between alternative types of care proved surprisingly small: the average price charged by providers to parents (before reimbursement) was $.88 per child hour. Average costs were $.84 per hour for public centers, $.92 for private centers, and $.82 for family day care homes. All are significantly lower than the maximum reimbursement rates.[34]

*Did Consumers Have Control of Significant Resources
To Make the Supply System Respond?*

The pilot study provided approximately $2.1 million in subsidy over the two-year period of the study. Most of the subsidy money was distributed in the last half year of services. This was due to the length of time that it took to complete the stratified research sample of clients. Table 6-1 shows the number of families served each month, through January 1977. Note the rapid increase of families after September 1976. This is due to the change in eligibility policy in the pilot study. After September 1976, the sampling procedure was eliminated, and all eligible clients were accepted for service.[35]

Pilot study subsidies supported, in part, the child care costs of approximately 4000 children. Average length of time participating in the study was 5.5 months. A rough estimate of the total number of child care providers in the county during the study period is given in Table 6-2.

Therefore, approximately one-fifth of the total licensed care slots and one-tenth of all licensed and unlicensed care were subsidized in part by the study. The scale of publicly subsidized care in Santa Clara County during the study period was as follows: in fiscal year 1975-1976 (July 1, 1975-June 30, 1976) child care facilities in Santa Clara County contracted with the State Department

Table 6-1
Families Served Each Month
from August 1975 to January
1977

	Monthly Total
August 1975	38
	170
	311
	423
	487
	555
	671
	818
	941
	972
	968
	965
	935
September 1976	1189
	1687
	2011
	2010
January 1977	2007

Table 6-2
Total Number of Care Providers in Santa Clara County During Study (Estimate)

Estimated Total Licensed Capacity, Family Day Care Homes, June 76	6,985
Estimated Total Capacity, Centers and Nursery Schools	10,078
	17,063
Estimated Capacity in 100 Additional Centers and Nursery Schools Listed in a Local 4-C Directory without Capacity Figures (Assume 50 Slots/ Center in 100 Centers).	5,000
Total Licensed Care Estimate:	22,063
Estimate Unlicensed Family Day Care Homes (Assume 300 Percent of Licensed Family Day Care).[a]	20,955
Total Supply Estimate	43,018

[a]The estimate of 300 percent unlicensed is from: Office of the Legislative Analyst, State of California,\"Current Issues." In some studies this would be an underestimate of the ratio of unlicensed to licensed care.

of Education for \$5,457,230 in subsidy funds. (This includes payments for fees in the Standard Agreement with Welfare, Campus Programs, AB 99 Projects, and Migrant Workers Center. It does not include state preschools.) In fiscal year 1976-1977, \$6,047,871 was included in the funding applications.[36] These figures do not include pilot study funds; thus, in the two years of pilot study services, the pilot study payments accounted for roughly one-sixth of all child care subsidy funds in the county generated through Department of Education contracts.

Was This Increase Adequate To Bring About
Change in the System?

During the pilot study, there was little change in the number of child care centers in the county.[37] The supply inventory carried out by the Santa Clara County Community Coordinated Child Development Council reported 290 centers and nursery schools in February 1975 and 300 in January 1976 (1977 figures will be available soon).[38] The number of family day care homes rose dramatically, however. In January 1975 there were 1468 homes; in January 1977 there were 1964 homes, or an increase of 35 percent.[39] Many consumers requested that their family day care homes become licensed, so that they could be a part of the subsidy system. The effect may not have been an increase of actual supply but rather of the number of licensed suppliers.

Did Consumers Have Enough "Leverage" To Influence
Resource Allocation in the Supply System?

It is unlikely that, in fact, they did, in the brief period of the demonstration. Particularly in the first months of study, there were not many families participating, although there were often a number of pilot study clients enrolled with one supplier.[40]

In fact, evidence in the system is that the resource allocation was much more affected by suppliers. Suppliers have more ability to organize than do child care consumers. In the last months of the pilot study, when the discontinuation of subsidy was imminent, there was a great deal of attention given in the state legislature to continuing the subsidy for one more year. While continuation of the subsidy would directly benefit the individual consumers involved in the study, it was supported strongly by the providers and "child care professionals" who throughout the study had a significant role in planning and operations.

Could New Providers Enter the System Easily?

One of the important goals of a voucher system is that the supply system will be responsive to consumer demands. Are suppliers able to enter the system with different products and attempt to capture a part of the market? In fact, in the pilot study there is evidence that family day care homes perhaps were able to enter easily into the supply system and did. But there is little evidence that new day care centers entered, inspired by the subsidy system. The short-term nature of the study (at first scheduled for one year of subsidies and later extended for a second year) would not provide enough incentive for programs with major start-up costs. There was no seed money for new programs included in the funding. The start-up costs for centers, with staffing, space needs, equipment, and so on, may have in fact been prohibitive. Family day care homes, however, may need little or no modification, and the scale is so limited that the start-up costs may be minimal, especially for an unlicensed home already providing child care services.[41] So, the cost factor may have been especially helpful to family day care homes in the short run; in the long run, expectations would be changed, and then there might be an incentive for centers to enter the market with innovative products.

Conclusions: Vouchers for Child Care—What Makes Sense?

This detailed examination of the design of the Santa Clara Pilot Study voucher model illustrates how the design of a voucher system is influenced by the organization in which it develops and how the design then directly influences performance of the voucher system. The range of possible voucher designs is very large. System designers should consider many alternatives before choosing one particular voucher design for any system.

In Alum Rock, and again in the pilot study, there is evidence that service organizations exert tremendous constraints on the implementation of voucher models, and that there is pressure in the system to "neutralize" the very innovations that justify the adoption of vouchers in the first place—namely, the innovations that allow consumer choice and the right to purchase desired service alternatives. This tendency of organizations should be anticipated in planning for the implementation of voucher models for child care systems, as for other services.

In the pilot study model, almost every "market" condition is compromised in the implemented system, even though the designers of the system were interested in the effects of a voucher model. Some of the difficulty in attaining a "free market" voucher condition was inherent in the study itself: for instance, the short length of time for the demonstration placed severe limits on consumer expectations, and therefore, probably consumption of child care services or change of employment patterns, and certainly influenced provider investment decisions. In other instances, organizational decisions affected the design—for instance, the decision to include only licensed care as eligible, or to accept clients according to a stratified random sampling selection process, or to provide only "live referrals."

The pilot study had many legislative objectives, many of which were addressed by special research projects on supply and consumer use of child care. The overall objective to demonstrate an alternative system that provided "choice" to consumers was implemented in the pilot study model. There were some effects that can be attributed to the model: family day care home licensing increased dramatically and, even though there is no way to control for other effects in the environment, there is reason to suspect that the pilot study provided adequate incentive for many homes to apply for licensing. The price of child care per child care hour realized by pilot study consumers was significantly lower than the usual maximum reimbursible rate in the publicly subsidized system in California.

Perhaps the demonstration was most successful in its task of gathering data on child care suppliers and consumers, data that will provide a rich research resource for years to come on costs, quality, and consumer preferences in child care. As to testing a voucher delivery system, how successful is this project as a voucher model? What can we learn from this system?

The system has provided voucher proponents and child care delivery system planners with one model of delivery and a detailed record of its implementation difficulties and successes. Procedures for all phases of the pilot study delivery model are recorded and available to others interested in implementing a similar delivery system.

The pilot study provides an exaample of how the market assumptions inherent in voucher proposals for service delivery should be examined carefully in advance of program implementation if the argument for a voucher system is being made primarily on expectation of market effect on supply.

Considering the design of a child care voucher system, there are a number of points that may be particularly useful:

There should be adequate supply of child care on a micro level. Estimates of the availability of care should include consideration of geographic distribution and availability of special care.

There should be some system for consumers to obtain information on available care. All aspects of the system should be as bias free as possible and should not include severe restrictions on the information available to clients.

The manpower needs of a voucher system can vary greatly from a traditional delivery system. If a voucher system is to be implemented in an existing system, the role changes from a direct service function to an information and payment function should be considered carefully.

Voucher systems involve clients, providers, and delivery agencies in a complex system. Decisions on policy involving one component should be considered carefully as to the effects on the other components. For example, the decision to do "live referrals" in the pilot study protected providers from frequent, fruitless inquiries but restricted consumer information and affected the character of the information function greatly.

System accountability (both accountability of consumers and providers) is an important component of a voucher system. In the pilot study, sanctions were not specifically developed as a part of the delivery system design; the need for sanctions became apparent as the study progressed. Although it is not possible to anticipate every possible difficulty in a distribution system, the design of a sanctioning system is important. For instance, in the pilot study, while providers were asked to certify that clients would be charged fees equal to other clients, there was no system to check or enforce this condition.

A system of ongoing evaluation is important to the implemenation of a voucher system. For the pilot study, which included an information function, this included monitoring the information for bias and for completeness as well as monitoring the payments to clients, the completeness of data, the eligibility of clients and providers, and so on. Experience of other distribution programs, such as Medicare and food stamps, should be considered in the design of the appropriate monitoring and accounting systems.

If the market effect is to be realized, the system should be implemented at a scale adequate to ensure consumer impact on the overall supply system.

Entry into the system should be facilitated. Innovative forms of service may require start-up costs. It could be compatible with the goals of voucher models to make seed monies available to providers interested in providing alternatives to current delivery models.

It is apparent that a voucher itself does not assure quality child care or consumer clout. In the pilot study, one delivery model has been operationalized. The systems necessary to provide reimbursements for use of child care have been developed and the loopholes closed one by one during the two years of program implementation. All voucher conditions were not satisfied by this model, but many of the "rules" or choices in the pilot study model—eligibility, payment procedures, fee schedule, requirements on using licensed care—might be varied while retaining basic systems in the model and taking advantage of the lessons learned and the procedures developed in Santa Clara County. It is apparent that in child care today, the exploration of alternative delivery systems is an important agenda item. The experience of the pilot study should be of interest to policymakers and child care planners, both as a resource on child care information and use and as an example of the promise and the difficulties inherent in voucher service delivery recommendations.

Notes

1. Patricia Bourne et al., "Day Care Nightmare: Child Centered View of Child Care," Working Paper No. 145, Institute of Urban and Regional Development, Berkeley, California, February 1971.

2. Dennis R. Young and Richard R. Nelson, *Public Policy for Day Care of Young Children* (Lexington, Mass.: Lexington Books, D.C. Heath, 1973), p. 65.

3. Lois B. Shaw, "The Utilization of Subsidized Child Care in the Gary Income Maintenance Experiment: A Preliminary Report," November 1974.

4. Eliot Levinson, "The Alum Rock Voucher Demonstration: Three Years of Implementation," Paper P-5631, Rand Corporation, Santa Monica, April 1976.

5. In fact, it is not necessary to have a physical coupon or chit, so long as the government commitment to share or absorb the cost is established.

6. *Education Vouchers: A Report on Financing Elementary Education by Grants to Parents,* Center for the Study of Public Policy, Cambridge, Massachusetts, December 1970.

7. Levinson, "Alum Rock Voucher Demonstration."

8. This list is adapted from conditions set out by Anthony Downs. See "Competition and Community Schools," in A. Downs, *Urban Problems and Prospects* (Chicago: Markham, 1970), pp. 264-293.

9. Rand, "A Public School Voucher Demonstration: The First Year at Alum Rock. Summary and Conclusions" R-1495/1-NIE, June 1974, pp. 2-3. (In April 1972, OEO awarded Rand a contract, subsequently renewed by the National Institute of Education (NIE) for the study and analysis of the Alum Rock demonstration.)

10. Levinson, "Alum Rock Voucher Demonstration."

11. "California's Major Child Development Programs," California State Department of Education, Office of Child Development, October 1975.

12. Ibid.

13. Office of the Legislative Analyst, State of California, "Current Issues in Publicly Subsidized Child Care," Sacramento, December 1975, pp. 16, 22.

14. John E. Coons and Stephen Sugarman, *Choice* (Chicago, Ill.: University of Chicago Press, In Press).

15. The instruments being used for that study are described in Chapter 5.

16. Office of the Legislative Analyst, "Current Issues."

17. Mary Keyserling, *Windows on Day Care* (New York: National Council of Jewish Women, 1972).

18. Office of the Legislative Analyst, State of California, "Publicly Subsidized Child Care–California," Sacramento, August 23, 1974.

19. In the Child Development Act of 1972 (AB 99), the Legislature designated the State Department of Education as the "single state agency" to administer child care programs. AB 99 directed the State Department of Education to take over statewide administrative responsibility for publicly subsidized

child care. There was, however, no implementation schedule. AB 1244 (1973) provided further direction.

20. Ibid.

21. The study staff and consultants have prepared detailed reports of procedures and a detailed chronology of program implementation as a part of the final report. Contributors have included: Connie Hellyer, Ernie Hudson, Kathy Moroney, Susan Stoddard Pflueger, David Ramirez, and Robin Wolfson.

22. For a detailed analysis of alternative child care fee schedules, see Terrance F. Kelly, "Fee Schedules and Social Services," Working Paper 963-9, Washington, Urban Institute, undated.

23. James R. Smith, "Policy Implications and Methodology of Data Collection," Child Care Pilot Study, October 31, 1975.

24. Ibid.

25. California State Department of Education, "Interim (Progress) Report," Child Care Pilot Study, June 1, 1975, p. 3.

26. The maximum reimbursible rate in effect during the last months of the pilot study service delivery.

27. Smith, "Policy Implications."

28. The monthly reimbursement forms (MRFs) indicate 1035 separate provider identification numbers. There is reason to believe that this figure is higher than the actual number of unique providers, since (1) providers leaving the system and returning later would be assigned a new number and thus appear twice on the list, and (2) sometimes provider numbers were changed or reassigned.

29. Telephone interview with Carol Conner, Department of Social Services, San Jose, California, March 13, 1975.

30. Child Care Pilot Study, Final Evaluation Report. Part 1. First Draft, "Child Care Pilot Study Delivery System," May 1977, pp. 299–301.

31. Ibid., "Cost Analysis," p. 314.

32. Child Care Pilot Study, "Consumers Guide to Choosing Child Care," 1976.

33. Child Care Pilot Study, "Delivery System," p. 250.

34. Ibid., p. 289.

35. Ibid., p. 283.

36. Office of Child Development, California State Department of Education, Sacramento. See Child Care Pilot Study, "Delivery System," p. 261.

37. During the time that the Pilot Study was in operation, County population figures show a *decline* in the number of children of child care age in the population.

38. These figures are from directories published annually be the Community Coordinated Child Development Council of Santa Clara County, Inc. (4-C Council), 425 W. Hedding Street, Suite 213, San Jose, CA 95110 (408-288-7106).

39. Family day care statistics are from the Santa Clara County monthly reports to State Department of Health, Program Analysis and Statistics Section.

40. Child Care Pilot Study, "Delivery System," p. 291.

41. See Chapter 3 for more data on relative costs of FDCHs.

Estimating Cost Equations for Child Care
Arden Hall

This chapter reports the results of an attempt to estimate cost equations from the data on child care providers collected in a survey undertaken in Seattle and Denver. Cost equations are relationships between the amounts of various inputs used in the production of a good or service and the cost of the output. My purpose in estimating these relationships is to understand what the important determinants of child care cost are, to derive a relationship that will predict the cost of a unit of child care produced with a specified set of inputs, and to learn about the tradeoff between cost and quality in child care.

The estimation of a cost equation for child care is complicated by the nature of the output. One of the simplifying assumptions usually made in the study of cost equations is that outputs are homogeneous between firms. While this is never strictly true, the assumption is a reasonable abstraction from reality in many situations. Unfortunately, child care is not one of these. Comparisons of the amount of service produced by different child care providers fail to capture important differences in their products. The additional dimension in which child care services must be measured is that of quality. Correctly accounting for quality differences is complicated by the fact that there is no general agreement on what constitutes quality in child care. Other studies of child care costs have avoided the difficulty by simply equating quality and cost.[1] For a given quantity of care, they have assumed that differences in cost reflect equivalent differences in quality.

This study takes a different approach. A charge for each child for a standard 40-hour week of service was calculated. It was assumed that on a weekly basis, the relationship between the charge and the quantity of care is proportional, e.g., that the charge for two weeks of care is double that for a single week. To account for quality differences, variables were included in the cost equation that should affect the quality of care. This approach does not result in an explicit relationship between child care quality and cost because no single measure of quality is constructed. However, the goal of the study is to produce a cost equation that will exhibit the important cost relationships for child care, and that goal is accomplished. This approach also makes it possible to estimate the cost of custodial care, i.e., child care that approximates the care that would be provided by the mother herself. The concept of quality in child care and the rationale for my choice of indicators of quality are discussed briefly below.

157

Quality in Child Care

Quality of child care service is something that researchers in the field have had great difficulty in defining and measuring. However, there is a typology, with which most researchers would agree, from which we can draw implications for the construction of a model for child care costs. This typology divides child care quality into two groups of attributes. One group has to do with the interaction of child and provider and the environment or atmosphere of the place where the child receives care. High-quality care is equated with a "warm nurturing atmosphere" and a provider who is attentive and takes an affirmative and encouraging attitude toward the child. This group of attributes measures quality more in terms of the determinants of the child's feelings about the experience than in terms of the effect of the experience upon his growth or development. Of course, the child's attitudes toward a place where he must spend much of his time inevitably affects his development. The distinction is made to contrast this group of attributes with another that also affects child development and involves the deliberate manipulation of the child's experience to bring about some specific change in that development.

The only easily quantifiable indicator of quality of the first type is the staff/child or child/provider ratio. Most studies that have addressed the issue of child care quality have concluded that the staff/child ratio is crucial to the quality of care.[2] The relationship between the staff/child ratio and child care cost is clear. Because labor is the most important input to the production of child care services, higher staff/child ratios must significantly increase costs.

The behavior of providers toward children is as important as the staff/child ratio but much more difficult to evaluate. Fortunately, differences in provider behavior should not have strong effects upon costs. Judgments of the provider must be so subjective and opinions of desirable provider behavior so various that the market could not accurately differentiate prices on the basis of this aspect of child care quality. Thus variation in the staff/child ratio should summarize the effect of the first group of quality attributes upon child care cost.

The second group of attributes of child care quality involves the activities in the home or center that are designed to directly affect child development. Together these attributes represent the quality of the child care program. Deliberate attempts at affecting the child's development range from simply a careful choice of the toys with which he may play through the establishment of a detailed and specific curriculum. This group of attributes is somewhat easier to quantify, at least approximately. The Westinghouse study, for example, classifies providers as giving either custodial, educational, or developmental care.[3] Although measures of this group of attributes can be more explicit, there is less agreement about the level of quality associated with different types of developmental care. Different types of care are expressions of different theories of child development. In terms of its own theory, each particular type of care is best, but no generally accepted judgment of program quality exists.

However, the cost implications of differences in this group of quality attributes is relatively straightforward. Care that includes special equipment, more highly trained providers, or many peripheral services must be more expensive. Depending upon the theory consulted, custodial care that does not include extensive activities designed for child development may or may not be of minimum quality; but regardless of theory, it is a less-expensive form of child care. Since our sample provides information on the education, training, and experience of providers, as well as the type of activities provided for the children, it has been possible to identify the attributes in this group that affect cost.

The cost equations estimated here include the child/provider ratio and various variables reflecting differences in programs. It cannot be claimed that the resulting cost equations will give great insight into the constituents of child care quality, but they should adequately reflect the effect of quality differences on costs.

The Labor Input

The most important indicator of quality in explaining the variation in the weekly charge for child care is the amount of provider time available to each child. In value terms, labor is by far the most important input to the production of child care services. It is nearly the only provider input to in-home care. Additional inputs are used by other types of providers; but even in child care centers, which should use the greatest proportion of additional inputs, wages and benefits averaged 73 percent of gross income in the sample. Thus the relationship of labor input to the charge per child is central to the cost equation for child care.

Since the model seeks to explain the variation in the charge per child for a fixed period of care, the relevant amount of labor input can be represented by the ratio of children to providers. This ratio decreases as the attention given to each child increases and vice versa. The exact relationship of this quantity to the charge per child is not immediately obvious. At one extreme, the charge per child may be determined independent of the ratio of children per provider. All variation in the charge may be explained by the quality of the labor input and the amounts of other inputs.

At the other extreme, an argument can be made that it is the total charge for a provider's service rather than the charge per child that is determined by the quality of the service and the quantity of other inputs. If the number of children to be cared for is not large, the addition of another child should not greatly increase the effort required of the provider. This implies that over some range of the number of children per provider, the total charge should be approximately constant for a given provider's service. Such a relationship seems most probable for in-home providers. Since the total charge is the product of the charge per child and the ratio of children to providers, this relationship implies that the charge per child should be inversely proportional to the child/provider ratio.

These two possible relationships between the charge per child (C), the child/provider ratio (R), and the variables representing quality of the service and amounts of other inputs (Q_i) can be represented by the equations:

$$C = a + \sum_i^{\frac{1}{2}} b_i Q_i \tag{7.1}$$

$$CR = d + \sum_i^{\frac{1}{2}} e_i Q_i \tag{7.2}$$

Equation (7.2) can also be expressed as:

$$C = \frac{d}{R} + \sum_i^{\frac{1}{2}} e_i \frac{Q_i}{R} \tag{7.3}$$

The true function is likely to be somewhere between the two extremes, and some experimentation has led to an intermediate model of the form:

$$C = f + \frac{g}{R} + \Sigma h_i \frac{Q_i}{R} \tag{7.4}$$

The model in (7.4) requires the child/provider ratio as a variable, but the nature of the child care service makes it difficult to define a single child/provider ratio. The number of children cared for over any time period of reasonable length may vary for a number of reasons. Parents' differing needs, children's illness, or school attendance may cause substantial variations in the number of children present in a day care facility at any particular time.

An additional complication in relating the child/provider ratio to cost is that the number of children actually enrolled may not be the number preferred by the provider. Differences between the actual and the desired child/provider ratio may be reflected in the charge. Two providers equipped to handle the same number of children may charge differently if their average attendance is different. The provider with lower average attendance would wish to charge a higher hourly rate to maintain his hourly wage. Parents may be willing to pay this higher rate because they are purchasing essentially a lower child/provider ratio. This argument implies that differences between actual and desired attendance rates could affect costs. It was hypothesized that if differences in attendance caused any variation in cost, increases in the average proportion of the children in attendance to the number regularly enrolled would decrease cost. To capture this effect, the ratio of average attendance to maximum attendance was included as an independent variable in the cost equation.

Quality of the Program

Several indicators of the quality of child care vis-à-vis the child development activities pursued by the provider can be identified. The education and experience of the providers and the type of activities provided are examples of such indicators. Taken together they only represent a general understanding of the nature of this aspect of quality in child care service. The exact relationship between the indicators and the quality of child care is unknown because no operational definition of *quality* exists. A cost equation incorporating indicators of the quality of the service will not directly relate cost and the quality of care. It follows that a cost equation including quality indicators cannot be used to estimate the cost of a given level of quality of care unless that level can be defined in terms of the indicator variables.

There is only one level of quality that can be defined in terms of indicator variables in a way that could be accepted by experts in the field. Care that is almost purely custodial in nature should be identified because it would correspond to a minimum level of each of the variables that are identified as indicators of quality. Thus a cost equation incorporating the indicators of quality in child care service will permit the estimation of the cost of custodial care. This cost is an appropriate variable for the determination of child care policy, so informed policy decisions can be made without a complete understanding of quality variations in the provision of child care services.[4]

Limitations of Quality Indicators

While the cost of custodial care can be estimated from a function incorporating indicators, little insight will thereby be gained into the nature of child care quality. Developmental care in general has a higher cost, but some types of developmental care may be costless or even lead to decreases in cost. Thus the cost equation will identify not the cost of purely custodial quality care, but the quality of care with the lowest cost. Since the estimates are to be used to provide a lower bound estimate of costs for policymakers, this is not a serious drawback. Improvements on pure custodial care that were costless or resulted in cost savings presumably should always be used.

Even for those elements of quality that increase costs, the cost equation is likely to provide little insight. The variables available to account for quality are only indicators; while they are known to be correlated with quality, their exact relationship to quality and their interrelationships with each other are unknown. It is likely, however, that variables used as indicators of quality are highly intercorrelated. Variables indicating the quality of labor, age, experience, education, and race, for example, will be interrelated in other ways than in their mutual relationship to the cost of child care. Such interrelationships will cause the coefficients of variables used as indicators of quality to be inaccurately estimated. But it is the relationship among these variables and not their joint effect upon child care cost that is inaccurately estimated. Again, inability to accurately define quality will not detract from the estimates of the cost of custodial care. However, the intercorrelations of the quality indicators will severely limit the information about the quality of child care obtainable from cost-equation estimates.

Other Inputs to the Production of Child Care Services

While labor is the most important input to child care services, it need not be the only input. For in-home providers, those who care for children in the children's own home, the parents normally provide whatever other inputs are used. The cost of these inputs should therefore not affect the charge for child care. Another group of providers, the family day care home operators, bring children into their own homes and presumably supply nearly all inputs to the production of the child care services. However, most of the inputs besides labor used in the production of child care are the services of various pieces of capital equipment, which the family of the provider also consumes. The accepted view of these inputs is that they represent the excess of capital services not consumed by the provider's family and, as such, do not add to the cost of child care. For this reason, and because it would be very difficult to identify the part of these capital services used in child care, I have ignored these inputs in the estimation of the cost of child care for family day care homes. However, an attempt was made to identify differences between the capital goods held by family day care homes and similar homes that do not provide child care. The results of this analysis are presented in Appendix 7A at the end of this chapter.

The contribution of other inputs to cost in child care centers cannot be ignored, since these inputs are used exclusively for the production of child care services. Detailed information about the value and type of capital used in child care centers was collected in the interview. For analysis it was necessary to aggregate the variables into a manageable set. The aggregation was done in value terms, and the result was a single variable that measures the value of all capital equipment used in child care except buildings and grounds. Including a measure of the contribution of buildings and grounds proved difficult because the appropriate data was not often provided by the child care center. Two measures were investigated but not used: square feet of floor space and building cost, either rent or mortgage payment.

Other Services Provided with Child Care

Other services are often provided concurrently with child care, and their price is included in the child care charge. Variables were added to equations for each mode of care to account for these services. In-home providers sometimes provided various housekeeping services while they cared for children, and variables were added to account for the cost of these extra services. Both in-home and family day care home providers occasionally kept children with them overnight.

Presumably the hourly charge for an overnight stay was much lower, since it required little labor from the provider. Since the charge variable is standardized for 40 hours of any type of care, some adjustment for overnight stays was necessary. The adjustment was made by adding a variable in the cost equation that counted the number of overnight stays made by the child in the week of observation.

Subsidies

Subsidies for child care can either be direct, i.e., given to the provider to pay for operating expenses, or indirect, i.e., given to parents to help them pay for the child care used. Indirect subsidies should not have an effect upon charges made by providers because they do not affect costs. However, direct subsidies should affect costs and charges and their effect should be controlled for in estimating cost equations.

Combining Provider Types

While it differs in detail between different types of providers, the child care service is basically very similar for all providers. This implies that cost equations for different provider types should be similar. The similarity should also extend across cities. In the estimation of cost equations, this similarity can be used to advantage. So long as the few differences between provider types and cities are accounted for within the equation, the data can be combined in estimating cost equations. Combining the data for different provider types will produce more precise estimates than could be obtained if cost equations for each provider type and city were estimated separately. However, the way in which the combination should be done and the variation across providers that should be allowed in a combined regression are not obvious, a priori. Fortunately there is a flexible statistical test, the Chow test, that facilitates the comparison between separate and combined models and between different forms of the combined model. A strong belief in the similarity of the cost equations for different types led me to impose a 1 percent significance level for rejecting tests of combined regressions in favor of separate regressions.

Cost Equations for In-Home and Family
Day Care Home Providers

The estimated cost equations presented below are based upon a survey of child care providers in Seattle and Denver conducted in 1974 (see Appendix 8C).

These data for both provider types and cities were combined to estimate cost equations. Some variables were allowed to vary across provider types and cities. The variables chosen and the rationale for their choice are discussed below. The test of the hypothesis that these regressions could be combined had a significance level of 2.5 percent, within the 1 percent level established for rejecting the hypothesis.

The model given in equation (7.4) was estimated except that the dependent and independent variables were all multiplied by the child/provider ratio (R) to remove heteroskedasticity.[5] The complete regression is displayed in Table 7–1. Table 7–2 breaks the regression into six cost equations, one for each provider type and city combination.

Four variables were allowed to vary between cities and provider types. The constant and the ratio of the average number of children in attendance to the maximum number were allowed to vary for each city and provider type combination. The race variables were allowed to vary between cities only, but the Chicano dummy for Seattle was suppressed because of the small number of Chicano providers in that city. The child/provider ratio was allowed to vary across provider types only. These variables were chosen to vary because they seemed the most important in explaining child care costs and the most likely to affect costs differently for different provider types or in different cities. The relationship between the ratio of children per provider and the cost of child care is the basis for the model and is likely to vary across provider type and city. Both that ratio and the ratio of average to maximum attendance were allowed to vary. Subsequently, it was discovered that there was very little variation across cities in the coefficient of the child/provider ratio, so it was only varied across provider types. In the model, the constant represents a fixed charge for the provider's time that is shared by each of the children. As such, it is an important part of the model and is likely to vary across provider types and cities. If the race of the provider affected his charges, the effect should only differ between cities. Any race effect should be similar for all provider types in a city, so race dummies were allowed to vary across cities only.

The results for parameters that did not vary across provider type or city are most conveniently discussed before the equations are separated. Some of these were included to account for charges other than regular child care. A variable was included for all types and cities counting the number of times the child stayed with the provider overnight. The sum of all hours spent with the provider was used to calculate a standard 40-hour charge; and if some of those hours represented overnight stays, then the charge would be a weighted average of the charge for regular care and the charge for overnight care, with the weight depending upon the number of overnight stays. It was hypothesized that overnight care was cheaper per hour than regular care, and this implies that the coefficient for *OVRNT*, the variable representing the number of overnight stays, should be negative. The regression confirms this hypothesis. The coefficient for *OVRNT* is significantly negative and is of appropriate size. Remembering that the dependent variable is the product of the charge per child and the child/provider

Table 7-1

Combined In-Home and Family Day Care Home Regressions, Dependent Variable: C·R

Variable	Definition	Coefficient in Dollars (Standard Error)
C	The charge for a forty hour week of care	—
R	The child/provider ratio	—
Constant		105.01* (32.43)
SEAIH	Dummy for Seattle in-home providers	−40.98 (40.84)
SEAHU	Dummy for Seattle unlicensed family day care homes	−46.72 (35.97)
SEAHL	Dummy for Seattle licensed family day care homes	−56.30 (31.46)
DENHU	Dummy for Denver unlicensed family day care homes	−72.00* (34.19)
DENHL	Dummy for Denver licensed family day care homes	−73.55* (31.69)
RIH	Child/provider ratio for in-home providers	5.19 (5.04)
RHU	Child/provider ratio for unlicensed family day care homes	13.24* (1.56)
RHL	Child/provider ratio for licensed family day care homes	20.98* (.68)
SPTCIH	Ratio of average to maximum attendance for Seattle in-home providers, expressed as a percent	−.57 (.34)
SPCTCHU	Ratio of average to maximum attendance for Seattle unlicensed family day care homes, expressed as a percent	−.48* (.21)
SPCTCHL	Ratio of average to maximum attendance for Seattle licensed family day care homes, expressed as a percent	−.69* (.07)
DPCTCIH	Ratio of average to maximum attendance for Denver in-home providers, expressed as a percent	−1.02* (.31)
DPCTCHU	Ratio of average to maximum attendance for Denver unlicensed family day care homes, expressed as a percent	−.29* (.14)
DPCTCHL	Ratio of average to maximum attendance for Denver licensed family day care homes, expressed as a percent	−.59* (.09)

Table 7-1 — *Continued*

Variable	Definition	Coefficient in Dollars (Standard Error)
EDUC	The provider's years of education	1.32* (.66)
	The provider's years of experience	.03 (.28)
PREWORK	A dummy indicating whether the provider has ever held another full-time job	−8.23* (3.84)
INHOME	A dummy for family day care homes only, indicating whether the provider has ever been an in-home provider	−4.81 (3.22)
HOME	A dummy for in-home providers only, indicating whether the provider has ever worked in a family day care home	1.38 (12.75)
CENTER	A dummy indicating whether the provider has ever worked in a day care center	−13.25* (4.92)
PCTDEVL	The percent of care consisting of activities classified as developmental	.06 (.09)
SBL	A dummy indicating a black provider in Seattle	22.21* (4.69)
DBL	A dummy indicating a black provider in Denver	−9.51 (5.22)
DCH	A dummy indicating a Chicano provider in Denver	2.12 (6.36)
COOK	A dummy for in-home providers only, indicating that they cooked meals besides caring for children	−3.13 (14.81)
LAUND	A dummy for in-home providers only, indicating that they did laundry besides caring for children	19.41 (13.63)
OVRNT	The number of times the child stayed overnight with the provider	−7.46* (3.25)

Number of observations: 1750

$R^2 = .56$

Standard error: 56.25

Asterisks indicate coefficients that are significantly different from zero at the 5 percent level.

Table 7-2

Combined Regression Separated by City and Provider Type

Seattle In-Home Providers

$CR = 64.03 + 5.19R - .57PCTCHLD + 1.32EDUC + .03EXPER - 8.23PREWORK$
$\quad + 1.38HOME - 13.25CENTER + .06PCTDEVL + 22.21SBL - 3.13COOK$
$\quad + 19.41LAUND - 7.46OVRNT$

Seattle Unlicensed Family Day Care Homes

$CR = 58.29 + 13.24R - .48PCTCHLD + 1.32EDUC + .03EXPER - 8.23PREWORK$
$\quad - 4.81INHOME - 13.25CENTER + .06PCTDEVL + 22.21SBL - 7.46OVRNT$

Seattle Licensed Family Day Care Homes

$CR = 48.71 + 20.98R - .69PCTCHLD + 1.32EDUC + .03EXPER - 8.23PREWORK$
$\quad - 4.81INHOME - 13.25CENTER + .06PCTDEVL + 22.21SBL - 7.46OVRNT$

Denver In-Home Providers

$CR = 105.01 + 5.19R - 1.02PCTCHLD + 1.32EDUC + .03EXPER - 8.23PREWORK$
$\quad + 1.38HOME - 13.25CENTER + .06PCTDEVL - 9.51DBL + 2.12DCH$
$\quad - 3.13COOK + 19.41LAUND - 7.46OVRNT$

Denver Unlicensed Family Day Care Homes

$CR = 33.01 + 13.24R - .29PCTCHLD + 1.32EDUC + .03EXPER - 8.23PREWORK$
$\quad - 4.81INHOME - 13.25CENTER + .06PCTDEVL - 9.51DBL + 2.12DCH$
$\quad - 7.46OVRNT$

Denver Licensed Family Day Care Homes

$CR = 31.46 + 20.98R - .59PCTCHLD + 1.32EDUC + .03EXPER - 8.23PREWORK$
$\quad - 4.81INHOME - 13.25CENTER + .06PCTDEVL - 9.51DBL + 2.12DCH$
$\quad - 7.46OVRNT$

ratio, we see that a provider with three children will charge approximately $2.50 less for 40 hours of care for each overnight stay included in that 40-hour period.

Dummy variables indicated whether in-home providers cooked or did laundry while they provided child care. Neither variable was significantly different from zero. While there must have been some additional charges for these services, there were too few providers performing these additional tasks for the charge to be measured accurately. No variable representing direct subsidies was included in the estimated equation because only one provider in the sample of 1750 reported any direct subsidy.

Seven variables were included in the regression in order to capture the effect of quality differences upon the cost of child care. In general these variables exhibit the behavior that was hypothesized earlier. They are colinear and, as a result, have large standard errors and erratic values. Four out of the seven are not significantly different from zero at the 5 percent level. The variables are constructed so that larger values are expected to have a positive effect upon costs, and yet three of the variables have negative coefficients, two of which are significantly different from zero. For one of these, the dummy indicating whether the provider has ever held a full-time job, the negative coefficient may not be so surprising. If the provider has never had a full-time job, this may indicate that she has a high reservation wage relative to others with her skill and training. She would only work if she received a higher wage than is normally paid to people with the same qualifications. That such people exist, and that lack of previous work experience would indicate them, seems reasonable, but that anyone would make use of their services is somewhat surprising. Other equally qualified people offer their services at a lower price, so competition should assure that only those demanding lower wages would be employed. The reason that such people are employed may be that they possess qualities that make them especially attractive to their employers but that are not generally available in the market for child care providers. For example, the provider may live nearby or be related to the children and thus offer greater convenience or security to the parents. Such circumstances offer a plausible explanation for the negative coefficient on the previous employment dummy.

The negative coefficient on the dummy variable indicating whether the provider had ever worked in a child care center was also significantly less than zero. No explanation for this result is apparent. However, the decrease in the charge per child for an average number of children per provider caused by the variable is not large.

Three continuous variables were included to measure quality differences. Years of schooling had a significant effect upon the cost of care, increasing the charge about 43 cents per week for each year of education, when a provider cares for three children. Surprisingly, neither the provider's experience nor the proportion of the children's time occupied in developmental activities had a significant effect upon the cost of care. A variable measuring the provider's age was used in preliminary regressions; but it was found to be insignificant and highly colinear with other variables, so it was dropped.

Racial variables were only varied across cities; and because of the small number of Chicanos in Seattle, the variable representing Seattle Chicanos was dropped. Neither of the racial dummies for Denver were significantly different from zero, indicating no strong support for the hypothesis of racial discrimination. However, in Seattle, black providers received significantly more money for their services than did whites. The positive coefficient might have resulted from a spurious correlation between the dummy for black providers in Seattle and a variable that affects cost but that has been excluded from the regression. For example, race might be correlated with the location of the provider in the city, and the areas in which black providers tend to work might have higher than average charges. This possibility and several other plausible correlations have been investigated without result. The coefficient for black providers in Seattle remains unexplained.

Custodial Care

Custodial care must be defined in terms of specific values of the independent variables in the regression reported above. The values I have chosen to represent the custodial level of care for these variables are shown in Table 7-3. Summed, they add $7.60 to the equivalent wage in Seattle and $4.96 in Denver. None of the extra services was included in custodial care, and only two quality variables were given nonzero values. Using an appropriate data base from another study, I found that the average education of lower-income working women was approximately 12 years in Seattle and 10 in Denver (see Chapter 4). Since custodial care should approximate the care provided by the mother, at least in terms of quantifiable measures, this led me to choose 12 and 10 years of education as the amount appropriate for custodial care. The *PREWORK* dummy was set to 1 because it seemed likely that lack of previous work experience may indicate a provider who is reluctant to work and insists upon a higher than normal wage. Although I used a value of zero for the experience variable, the coefficient is so small that the choice of any reasonable value for the variable would cause very little change in the cost of custodial care.

Table 7-3
Values of Parameters for Custodial Care

Variable	Seattle	Denver
OVRNT	0	0
COOK	0	0
LAUND	0	0
EDUC	12	10
EXPER	0	0
INHOME	0	0
HOME	0	0
CENTER	0	0
PREWORK	1	1
PCTDEVL	0	0

Individual Equations

Substituting the values in Table 7-3 into the cost equations yields the equations in Table 7-4. It should be noted that the coefficients of the child/provider ratio are constrained to be equal across cities for each provider type and the race variables are constrained to be equal across provider type for each city. Despite the constraint on the child/provider ratio, the two unconstrained variables, the constant, and *PCTCHLD,* the variable measuring the ratio of average attendance to the maximum, have the same relationship between provider types for each city. Thus, for each city, in-home providers have the largest constant and licensed family day care homes the lowest. A similar relationship holds for *PCTCHLD.* The consistency of these results for both cities supports the validity of the constraint on the coefficients of the child/provider ratio across cities.

The coefficients of the child/provider ratio and *PCTCHLD* are significant against zero in most cases (see Table 7-1). Only for in-home providers is either not significantly different from zero at the 5 percent level. Thus, for all family day care homes, the hypothesis that the provider's wage does not depend upon the number of children in her care can be rejected.

The calculation of the cost of custodial care for each city and provider type requires the choice of values for *PCTCHLD* and the child/provider ratio. For each city and type, providers were found whose average attendance was equal to their maximum. Thus a value of 100 percent for *PCTCHLD* was chosen as appropriate for custodial care. The number of children per provider was found to be as high as 12 in some family day care homes. This ratio seems to be too high to ensure adequate custodial care for children. Both cities have regulations imposing a maximum of 6 children per adult in family day care homes. This seems to have been an effective limit for almost all family day care homes. Less than 7 percent reported averaging more than 6 children per provider. Because it

Table 7-4
Reduced City - Provider Type Regressions

City and Provider Type	Equation
Seattle In-Home	$CR = 71.62 + 5.19R - .57PCTCHLD + 22.21BL$
Seattle Unlicensed FDCH	$CR = 65.88 + 13.24R - .48PCTCHLD + 22.21BL$
Seattle Licensed FDCH	$CR = 56.30 + 20.98R - .69PCTCHLD + 22.21BL$
Denver In-Home	$CR = 109.96 + 5.19R - 1.02PCTCHLD - 9.51BL + 2.12CH$
Denver Unlicensed FDCH	$CR = 37.96 + 13.24R - .29PCTCHLD - 9.51BL + 2.12CH$
Denver Licensed FDCH	$CR = 36.41 + 20.98R - .59PCTCHLD - 9.51BL + 2.12CH$

was an effective limit for most firms, and because it seems a reasonable maximum to ensure adequate custodial care, a child/provider ratio of 6 was used in calculating the charge for custodial care for family day care homes. Neither Seattle nor Denver regulate in-home providers, so there is no established maximum child/provider ratio for this type of day care. However, the 6 to 1 ratio for family day care homes seems a reasonable maximum for these providers also. Only one provider in either of the two cities had a higher child/provider ratio. Substituting these values for *PCTCHLD* and the child/provider ratio yields the estimates of the cost of custodial care in Seattle and Denver in 1974 shown in Table 7-5.

The estimated charges for custodial care are consistent across provider types for each city. For neither city is the difference between licensed and unlicensed family day care homes large. There is a sizable difference between the two types of family day care homes and in-home providers, but this may be a product of the way the results are presented rather than a true difference between the provider types. In-home providers typically care for the children of only one family, while family day care homes may have children from several different families. Thus a three-child family must accept a child/provider ratio of 3 if the parents hire an in-home provider but can get a child/provider ratio of 6 in a family day care home. The relevant weekly costs for in-home care for a three-child family are $29.06 in Seattle and $41.84 in Denver per child, while the costs for care in a family day care home are those in Table 7-5. Thus the conclusion to be drawn from Table 7-5 is that in-home care is less expensive than other care on a comparable basis but not that it is a cheaper alternative for most users.

Differences in cost may also be a result of differences in services provided. Capital services have not been accounted for in establishing the cost equation. Capital costs seem unlikely to be a major part of the charge, but they may explain some part of the difference between the two modes of care.

Table 7-5
Charge per Week per Child for Custodial Care in 1974[a]

	In-Home	Unlicensed FDCH	Licensed FDCH
Seattle	7.63	16.22	18.86
(Black Provider)	(+3.70)	(+3.70)	(+3.70)
Denver	6.52	14.73	17.22
(Black Provider)	(−1.59)	(−1.59)	(−1.59)
(Chicano Provider)	(+.35)	(+.35)	(+.35)

[a]White provider, $R = 6$, *PCTCHLD* = 100.

Child Care Centers

Data were also collected from child care centers in the survey of providers in Seattle and Denver cited previously. The survey instrument used to collect data from child care centers differed from that used for the in-home providers and family day care homes in several respects. Because of the size of the centers, data were not collected on individual children. Although data were collected for individual providers, that information was useful only in aggregates because the provider information could not be identified with individual children. The center survey provided essentially a single observation for each center representing average values for the dependent and independent variables. Although all centers in both cities were surveyed, only 87 out of 124 center interviews provided enough data to estimate a cost equation. Even some of these were incomplete, but the missing variables were not vital ones and were therefore replaced with means from the complete observations. The form of the interview made it necessary to calculate the charge for a 40-hour week of care in a special way. The interview did not ask for charges for individual children but rather a charge schedule. The blank schedule in the interview allowed the charge to vary by the number of children per family and by the family income. A single average charge was produced from this schedule in two steps. First, for each category of number of children per family, I took a weighted average across income strata. For each city the weights were based upon the proportion of families in each stratum, as reported in the 1970 census. The next step was to average across the number of children per family, and the weights used were the proportions of families with that number of children in the two cities, taken from the 1970 census. The charge thus derived was then adjusted to a charge per 40-hour week.

The charge variable derived in this way is a mean charge for all children in the center. It was assumed for the centers as well as the family day care homes and the in-home providers that the charge for each child has an identical variance. The mean charge for a particular center therefore has a variance inversely proportional to the number of children in the center. Regressions using the charge as a dependent variable must be corrected or the error term will be heteroskedastic. The appropriate correction is to multiply the charge and all independent variables in the regression by the square root of the number of children at the center. Heteroskedasticity might also have resulted if the wrong form was chosen to estimate the regression. The form used in the regression for in-home providers and family day care homes was found to be inappropriate, and the regression was run directly on the charge rather than on the charge multiplied by the child/provider ratio.

There were several differences between the independent variables used in the center regression and those used in the in-home and family day care home regression. Dummies indicating whether providers had previously held a full-time job or provided other types of day care could not be produced from the center interviews. Also, none of the extra services sometimes provided by in-home providers or family day care homes were furnished by centers, so the variable counting the number of times the child stayed overnight with the provider and the dummies indicating that the provider cooked or did laundry were dropped. An attempt was made to construct a variable corresponding to *PCTCHLD* in the in-home provider, family day care home regression. Because the center questionnaire had no information on individual children, the variable was constructed using the number of full- and part-time children, with an imputed average attendance for part-time children. The variable had no predictive power in the preliminary regressions and was dropped.

Other variables specific to centers were added to the regression. The variable *CAPITAL* measured the market value of all capital equipment per child except buildings and grounds. Two proxies for facilities rental were tried, but neither contributed greatly to the regression. Poor quality of data may explain this result. Another variable was added to capture the effect of any direct subsidy to the center upon cost. The specific variable used was the amount of direct subsidy per child per week. Unfortunately, the subsidy information was for the previous year. Indirect subsidies were not considered. Subsidies to parents for day care should not have a direct effect upon costs. Dummies were also added to account for cost differences by center type. There are both public and private day care centers; and among private centers, there are both profit-making and nonprofit centers. The fact that centers usually have several providers led me to use means for variables measuring qualities of the providers. A mean age variable was tried for the centers. Although it was not useful in the in-home provider, family day care home regression, mean age proved to have some influence over cost for centers and was therefore retained in the final regression.

Combining Cities

Attempts were made to combine in the final regression the center data for Seattle and Denver, and little difference was found between the regressions for the two cities. Therefore, the data were combined, and only the constant term was allowed to vary between the two cities. The F test of the constraints implied by that particular combined regression was barely significant at the 2.5 percent level, within the 1 percent critical level previously set.

Cost Equations for Child Care Centers

The combined regression for Seattle and Denver, with the definitions of the variables, is given in Table 7–6. The most noticeable thing about this regression is the scarcity of variables that are significantly different from zero. Only *EDUC*

Table 7-6
Child Care Center Regression

Variable	Definition	Coefficient in Dollars (Standard Error)
C	The charge for a forty hour week of care	—
Constant		−15.24 (12.07)
1/R		−3.25 (3.16)
SEATTLE[a]	A dummy indicating a center in Seattle	.25 (1.20)
AGE[a]	The mean age of the providers in the center who responded to the survey	.22 (.13)
EDUC[a]	The mean number of years of education of the providers who responded to the survey	1.77* (.65)
EXPER[a]	The mean number of years of experience of the providers who responded to the survey	−.65 (.42)
PCTDEVL[a]	The average percent of time that providers who responded to the survey spent in developmental activities	.04 (.05)
PROFIT	A dummy indicating whether the center was operated for profit	2.86* (1.25)
PUBLIC	A dummy indicating that the center was run by a public agency	4.64 (2.54)
BLACK	The proportion of black providers employed in centers that responded to the survey	2.10 (2.50)
CHICANO	The proportion of Chicano providers employed in centers that responded to the survey	11.08 (9.97)
CAPITAL	The market value of all capital equipment used by the center except its buildings and grounds per child	.0004 (.003)
SUBSIDY	The value of direct subsidies to the center for the previous year per week per child	−.11 (.09)

Number of Observations: 87

$R^2 = .70$

Standard Error 31.75[b]

Asterisks indicate coefficients that are significantly different from zero at the 5 percent level.

Footnotes for Table 7–6

[a]The data from which the variables *AGE, EDUC, EXPER,* and *PCTDEVL* were calculated came from a questionnaire distributed to individual providers in the center. Not all questionnaires were returned, so these variables were averages based on sometimes partial information.

[b]The regression was weighted by the square root of the number of children in the center. Thus the standard error applies to the product of the charge and the square root of the number of children. Since the mean value of the square root is 6.63, this standard error is equivalent to a standard error of approximately $4.79 on the charge itself.

and *PROFIT* were significantly different from zero at the 5 percent level. The general, low-significance level is probably explained by the combination of a relatively small sample size and limited variation in the levels of variables that determine day care cost. While the final sample size was 87, the standard error of the unweighted dependent variable, the charge per child, was only 4.69 across centers. The small variation in the dependent variable suggested that the independent variables might be relatively constant, and further examination confirmed that few of the independent variables exhibit great variations across centers.

The small sample size and limited variability of independent variables in the regression have led to high standard errors of the coefficients, but the problem has not been so severe as to produce wild coefficient values. All the coefficients except those for average provider experience and the child/provider ratio have the expected signs. The variable *EXPER* measures the average experience of all providers in the center. Experience is a desirable quality and should have a positive effect upon cost. However, the regression predicts that each year of provider experience decreases the charge per child by 65 cents. Similarly, the coefficient of *R*, the child/provider ratio, measures the fixed cost per provider that must be divided among the children, and such a fixed charge is presumably positive. Neither coefficient is significantly different from zero at even the 10 percent level, and I conclude that the incorrect signs are a result of the variability of the parameter estimates caused by the small sample size and limited variation of the independent variables.

No other coefficients have signs different from what is to be expected and most have values in a range that seems reasonable. Two exceptions are the variables measuring capital per child and subsidy per child. The coefficient of the capital variable measures the charge per week per dollar of capital. When compounded, the coefficient implies a yearly return on capital of 2.3 percent. The coefficient is unreasonably low, but its large standard error indicates that it is very inaccurately measured. A 2 standard-error interval around the estimated coefficient more than covers all reasonable values of the coefficient. The coefficient of the subsidy variable measures the decrease in the weekly charge caused by a one dollar increase in the direct subsidy per child. As mentioned previously, the subsidy variable was based upon the previous year's subsidy, so conclusions about the effect of direct subsidies should be made cautiously. However, the interesting hypothesis for this coefficient is that the coefficient is one, implying a one for one tradeoff between subsidy and charge; and this hypothesis can clearly be rejected. The estimated coefficient is more than 10 standard errors away from one, so the hypothesis can be rejected despite the mismatching of the subsidy data. Direct subsidies do not seem to result in equivalent reductions in the charge per child.

The coefficients allow tests of other interesting hypotheses about the determinants of cost in child care centers. The coefficient of the dummy indicating a public center is nearly significant, and the coefficient of the dummy indicating centers operated for profit is significant at the 5 percent level. There are three types of centers: private, profit-making centers; private, nonprofit centers; and public centers. The *PROFIT* and *PUBLIC* dummies represent the differences in these three types of centers, and the significance of the coefficients indicates some differences between the charges of different types of centers. The significance or near significance of the coefficients of *PROFIT* and *PUBLIC* against zero imply that private, profit-making centers and public, nonprofit centers are each different in cost from private, nonprofit centers. The third hypothesis, that private, profit-making centers were equal in cost to public, nonprofit centers was also tested, and no significant difference in cost was found. Also, the coefficient of the variable indicating that a center was in Seattle was insignificant. This supports the hypothesis that there is little difference between the cost relationships for the two cities.

Custodial Care

Values for some of the independent variables in the regression that are appropriate for custodial care are given in Table 7-7. The values for the mean education level are taken, as for the in-home providers and family day care homes, from data from a sample of low-income families. The racial variables represent the racial composition of the group of providers with whom the average child came in contact. Note that as in the previous regression, the variable for Chicanos has been suppressed in Seattle. The custodial level of capital per child and the average age of providers are arbitrary numbers, substantially below the average for all centers. The custodial level of the child/ provider ratio was taken to be 6. It seems unlikely that the maximum level for the number of children per provider would differ greatly between provider types, and so the level for centers was chosen to be consistent with other provider types. Finally, a value of one year was chosen for the variable measuring the

Table 7-7
Values of Parameters for Custodial Care

Variable	Value for Seattle	Value for Denver
C	1	1
R	6	6
SEATTLE	1	0
AGE	25	25
EDUC	12	10
EXPER	1	1
PCTDEVL	0	0
PROFIT	—	—
PUBLIC	—	—
BLACK	.163	.193
CHICANO	—	.043
CAPITAL	150	150
SUBSIDY	0	0

average experience of providers as a practical lower limit for that variable. Table 7-8 presents charges for custodial care based upon the values in Table 7-7 for both cities and each of the three types of centers.

As for the other provider types, care in a child care center is more expensive in Seattle than in Denver. Unlike the in-home providers and family day care homes, the difference in cost between the cities arises directly from the different levels of education required rather than from differences in the cost relationship.

These estimates of the cost of custodial care place centers between in-home providers and family day care homes in both cities. For the reasons discussed previously, a comparison with the cost of custodial care for in-home providers is not justified. In-home providers have essentially a different service from the two other provider types. A comparison between centers and family day care homes is appropriate, however, and that comparison indicates that centers are somewhat less expensive than family day care homes. Since the greatest difference between the two modes is in the average size of their operations, this may indicate the presence of some economies of scale in child care. Centers may benefit from greater specialization or better organization than is possible in family day care homes. However, the difference in costs between the two types is not large enough to support any firm conclusions about their relative efficiency. Also, the superiority of private, nonprofit centers to the other types is even more striking when a comparison is made with family day care homes. Both of these results raise interesting questions for further research.

Table 7-8
Cost of Custodial Care in Child Care Centers

	Seattle	Denver
Private, Nonprofit Centers	10.98	7.37
Public, Nonprofit Centers	13.85	10.21
Private, For-Profit Centers	15.62	11.98

Notes

1. Abt Associates, Inc., "Costs and Quality Issues for Operators," *A Study in Child Care 1970–1971,* Vol. III, Boston, 1972; Westinghouse Learning Corporation and Westat Research, Inc., *Day Care Survey 1970: Summary Report and Basic Analysis,* April 1971.

2. It should be noted that although the child/provider ratio has the greatest effect upon cost, it is not necessarily the most important factor determining quality. The emphasis placed upon the child/provider ratio here should not be construed to be an assertion that other factors are not important influences on the quality of care.

3. Westinghouse and Westat, *Day Care Survey.*

4. This is not meant to imply that policymakers should only consider subsidization of custodial care, but that knowledge of the cost of custodial care provides a reliable minimum cost for day care that can aid in formulating policy.

5. The question of heteroskedasticity naturally arises in the estimation of a model like (7.4). There is no particular reason to suppose that C, the cost per child, has a constant variance for all providers. It seems just as reasonable that it is CR, the equivalent wage, and not C that has a constant variance for all providers. In order to find the correct form for the regressions presented below, I ordered their residuals by increasing value of R and plotted them. If the model estimated were heteroskedastic, the residuals would vary in absolute value systematically with R. Here a systematic relationship was found that was removed by multiplying all variables by R.

Appendix 7A

Capital Costs in Family Day Care Homes

Capital costs were left out of the cost equation for family day care homes because of the difficulty in determining how much of the services of household capital goods were used in child care. Another reason for ignoring these costs was that the use of household capital goods may not affect the cost of child care. If the capital goods were things that would be owned whether or not the home was used for child care, and if the children only use excess capacity that would not otherwise be used by the provider's family, then competition could be expected to drive the cost of these services toward zero. To test whether capital services increase the cost of family day care home service, it is necessary to measure these services. The only capital services that can clearly be attributed to child care are those of goods that are owned by family day care home providers and not by otherwise similar households. Thus a comparison of the household capital of family day care homes with a group of similar homes that do not provide child care offers the best test for the presence of capital as an element of cost in the provision of child care.

The Seattle and Denver Income Maintenance Experiments are a source of data on families that are suitable for this comparison. The control groups for these experiments differ from the family day care home families primarily in the fact that they do not provide child care. With this comparison in mind, half the family day care homes in each site were asked the same questions about durable goods as are regularly asked the SIME and DIME populations. Both SIME/DIME and FDCH families were also asked the number of rooms in their homes. Although the data are responses to the same questions, they do not represent the same time period for each group. While the Child Care Survey was conducted in May of 1974, the latest SIME data available are from February of 1973 and the latest DIME data from November of 1973. This difference in dates might invalidate comparisons between data from the two sources. To determine whether this is the case, comparisons were made within the SIME and DIME samples over an equivalent length of time.[1] These comparisons showed no systematic differences over time, thus supporting the use of the earlier SIME and DIME data for comparison with FDCH data from the Child Care Survey.

Another difficulty that arises in making a comparison between SIME/DIME and FDCH families is the definition of the variable or variables that are to be compared. The comparison might be made on total net worth of the family.

However, that quantity included the values of many assets other than buildings and equipment, and the presence of these other assets can only blur any comparison between the two groups. At the other extreme, comparisons might be made on individual items of equipment or aspects of buildings. This approach, too, has difficulties. One problem is that some items may be missing from many observations, complicating the comparison. Also, this method multiplies the number of comparisons, making it difficult to reach a single conclusion unless the true difference is very pronounced. The variables actually chosen for the comparison represent a compromise between these two extremes. They are:

1. The present value of all durable equipment in the home, excluding vehicles
2. The present value of all motor vehicles
3. The number of rooms in the house, excluding bathrooms and hallways.

These variables were computed in the same way from the raw interview data for both groups.[2]

These three variables can reasonably be expected to be influenced by many other factors besides the home's use as a child care facility. In comparing family day care homes to the SIME and DIME families, it is important to eliminate or at least minimize the effect of these other factors before the comparison is made. A straightforward way to do this involves the use of linear regressions. Regression models can be specified that explain the comparison (dependent) variables, including child care status. When these models have been estimated, values for the explanatory variables can be inserted to produce predictions. So long as reasonable values of the explanatory variables are used to calculate predictions, the differences between the predictions should reflect the true differences between family day care homes and SIME or DIME families.

This procedure was used to compare family day care homes to SIME and DIME families. Table 7A-1 lists the explanatory variables used in the models for each of the three comparison variables. Unfortunately, the list does not include some variables that seem likely to affect the comparison variables. Economic status as measured by family income and liquid assets should reasonably affect value of durables and value of vehicles. The number of rooms is also probably influenced by the number of children in the family. Data limitations prevented these and other possibly helpful explanatory variables from being included in the model. The absence of these variables may affect the comparison if there are systematic differences in the absent variables between the two populations.

The fact that there are three variables to be explained points to the use of multivariate regression for estimating the coefficients of the model. Multivariate regression is simply a generalization of the familiar regression model to the case in which there are several dependent variables. The technique produces the same estimates as would be produced by separate regressions on each dependent

Table 7A-1
Control Variables

1. Location	$\left\{\begin{array}{l} 0 \\ 1 \end{array}\right.$ Outside SIME or DIME area / Inside SIME or DIME area
2. Education	Years of schooling
3. Race	$\left\{\begin{array}{l} 0 \\ 1 \end{array}\right.$ White / Black
4. Age	Age of female head of family
5. Headship	$\left\{\begin{array}{l} 1 \\ 0 \end{array}\right.$ One-headed family / Two-headed family
6. Homeownership	$\left\{\begin{array}{l} 0 \\ 1 \end{array}\right.$ Does not own home / Owns home

variable. However, in hypothesis tests, the multivariate technique makes use of the covariances between dependent variables that would implicitly be assumed to be zero if tests were done using separate, single dependent variable regressions.

Models with the preceding dependent and independent variables were estimated for family day care homes in each city, as well as for SIME and DIME families in each city. Then predicted values of the comparison variables were calculated for each population using mean values of the independent variables from the SIME population for the Seattle comparison and from the DIME population for the Denver comparison. Hypothesis tests were done for each comparing the predicted values for SIME or DIME families against those for FDCH families. A simultaneous test for all three comparison variables was done first, and then a test for each comparison variable separately. The estimated models, the means of the explanatory variables, and results of the tests are presented in Tables 7A-2, 7A-3, 7A-4, and 7A-5. For each city, Tables 7A-2 and 7A-3 present regression coefficients for each group. The means of independent variables used to calculate predicted values and the mean differences between the predicted values for the FDCH and Income Maintenance families are presented in Table 7A-4. The results of the tests of the differences between the groups are given in Table 7A-5.

The differences in the predicted values of the comparison variables between Income Maintenance and FDCH families are consistent for Seattle and Denver. In both cities the predicted values of vehicles and durables are less for family day care homes, while the predicted number of rooms is greater. For both, the difference in the number of rooms is the most significant difference between the Income Maintenance and family day care homes. The only real difference

Table 7A-2
Seattle Regression Coefficients

| | Dependent Variables | | |
Independent Variables	Value of Vehicles	Value of Durables	Number of Rooms
SIME			
Education	65.7	8.9	−.020
Race	−116.0	−156.9	−.076
Age	−3.6	−5.9	−.006
Headship	−1141.0	−281.3	.178
Homeownership	367.7	214.0	.068
Constant	763.9	993.2	5.521
Seattle FDCH			
Education	−10.4	−23.0	−.032
Race	15.4	43.5	.525
Age	7.5	−5.8	.004
Headship	−779.8	−252.3	−.413
Homeownership	582.8	667.5	.944
Location[a]	23.5	−14.5	.472
Constant	632.26	918.07	6.740

[a]The location variable is not used for the SIME regression because all families were within the area.

between the cities is that the difference in value of durables is significant in Denver and not in Seattle.

The results strongly support the conclusion that family day care homes have more rooms on the average than similar homes that do not provide child care. The direction of the difference is reversed for the other two comparison variables, but this may reflect differences in the data rather than the differences between the two groups. While the data were responses to identical questions, they represent the first administration of the questionnaire to the FDCH families, while the SIME and DIME families had been asked the same questions several times before. This difference could be expected to lead to differences in reporting accuracy, especially since information collected in previous administrations of the questionnaires was used to prompt the SIME and DIME families. This difference in procedure must bias the durables and vehicles predicted values

Table 7A-3
Denver Regression Coefficients

Independent Variables	Dependent Varaibles		
	Value of Vehicles	Value of Durables	Number of Rooms
DIME			
Education	63.4	29.7	.086
Race	287.3	−14.8	.219
Age	−20.2	−10.9	.011
Headship	−466.2	−317.5	.160
Homeownership	281.6	622.8	.154
Constant	918.5	910.2	4.374
Denver FDCH			
Education	94.4	76.4	.022
Race	−574.1	70.3	.293
Age	−12.1	−10.1	−.002
Headship	−761.7	−143.3	.487
Homeownership	1118.2	548.1	1.311
Location[a]	129.9	70.7	−.441
Constant	423.8	85.32	5.81

[a]The location variable is not used for the DIME regression because all families were within the area.

upward for SIME and DIME families relative to that for the FDCH families. Such a bias seems the best explanation for the higher values of durables and vehicles exhibited by SIME and DIME families. If there is some extra quantity of durables or vehicles needed for the operation of a family day care home, it is obscured by the bias caused by the different administration of the interviews.

The fact that family day care homes had significantly more rooms than similar SIME or DIME homes suggests that capital does contribute to the cost of care in family day care homes. Unfortunately, this investigation may not have identified all sources of capital costs, and it has not measured the contribution of capital cost to the total charge. The nature of the family day care home enterprise makes the determination of the full effect of capital on cost very difficult. At the least, it would require a much more detailed survey instrument than has yet been used to produce the raw data from which capital costs could

Table 7A-4
Means of Independent Variables

	Seattle	Denver
Education	12.1	11.6
Race	.77	.74
Age	41.3	42.9
Headship	.44	.40
Homeownership	.17	.14
Location	1[a]	1[a]

Predicted Differences

	FDCH-SIME	FDCH-DIME
Value of Vehicles	−388.3	−514.9
Value of Durables	−216.5	−135.3
Number of Rooms	1.775	1.110

[a]Comparison was made within the SIME and DIME areas.

be calculated. For this study, it must be concluded that variation in amounts of capital among family day care homes has not been adequately accounted for in the model.

Notes

1. A paired comparison test was made for each variable. The value of the variable for a particular month was compared to the value for an earlier month for the same family. The number of months between the observations was the same as the number between the SIME or DIME observations and the FDCH observations.

2. These calculations are described in an unpublished memorandum "The Family Equity Longitudinal File" by Patricia Gwartney-Gibbs and Richard West, Stanford Research Institute, August 1975. Copies can be obtained from the author.

Table 7A-5
Seattle and Denver Test Results

Test 1: Comparison between SIME, DIME, and FDCH Families on All Three
Dependent Variables

Seattle		*Denver*	
Test Statistic:	8.184	Test Statistic:	8.367
Degrees of Freedom:	3,229	Degrees of Freedom:	3,224
Significance:	<.005	Significance:	<.005
(Highly Significant)		(Highly Significant)	

Test 2: Comparison on Value of Vehicles

Test Statistic:	2.071	Test Statistic:	4.903
Degrees of Freedom:	1,231	Degrees of Freedom:	1,226
Significance:	>.1	Significance:	<.05
(Not Significant)		(Significant)	

Test 3: Comparison on Value of Durables

Test Statistic:	3.047	Test Statistic:	.834
Degrees of Freedom:	1,231	Degrees of Freedom:	1,226
Significance:	>.05	Significance:	>.1
(Not Significant)		(Not Significant)	

Test 4: Comparison on the Number of Rooms

Test Statistic:	18.341	Test Statistic:	13.511
Degrees of Freedom:	1,231	Degrees of Freedom:	1,226
Significance:	<.005	Significance:	<.005
(Highly Significant)		(Highly Significant)	

8

Cost of Compliance with Federal Day Care Standards in Seattle and Denver
Samuel Weiner

Introduction

The federal day care standards currently in force are those published in 1968 ("Federal Interagency Day Care Requirements"), with amendments as given in the 1974 Title XX amendments to the Social Security Act. The Title XX amendments were put into effect on October 1, 1975, with the exception of the revised child/staff ratios for children under three.[1] The deadline for implementing the latter change was postponed until October 1, 1977.[2] However, the objections that arose from the attempt to sharply increase the number of staff required for children under three indicates that the requirements for that age group may be altered. In this chapter, the cost of compliance is calculated on two alternative assumptions:[3] first, that Congress will not put into effect the higher staff requirements for children under three, which means that the existing child/staff ratios applicable to three-year-olds will be used; second that Congress will put the standards as stated in Title XX into effect on or about October 1, 1977.

Moreover, since the federal standards apply only to licensed facilities this chapter will discuss the costs of compliance only for licensed family day care homes and day care centers. Unlicensed facilities do not receive federal funding and therefore are not subject to the federal guidelines. However, if it were considered useful, the approach used in estimating compliance costs for licensed FDCHs could also be used to estimate such costs for the unlicensed part of the FDCH sector.

Federal day care standards are arranged under nine headings: groupings of children, environmental standards, educational services, social services, health and nutrition services, training of staff, parent involvement, administration and coordination, and evaluation. The first category, grouping of children, relates to required child/staff ratios. This is the only standard for which I will use the survey data to estimate compliance cost.[4] In the other eight categories the standards are usually too ambiguous to determine specific and quantitative requirements and, consequently, to estimate compliance costs. Moreover, the survey data do not allow a quantitative estimate of how those eight ambiguous sets of standards are actually being met. In estimating day care cost functions, however, I found that the child/staff ratio was the overwhelmingly important cost element.

Originally released as Research Memorandum No. 40, Center for the Study of Welfare Policy, SRI International, May 1977.

Compliance Cost for Day Care Centers

Introduction

The data collected in the day care survey are not broken down in the manner needed to directly assess the extent to which child care centers in Seattle and Denver are complying with federal child/staff standards. Some assumptions must be made in using the data to determine the cost of compliance with such federal standards. The accuracy of the cost estimates depends directly on the validity of those assumptions.

Moreover, if public nonprofit centers are assumed to be just in full compliance with all the federal standards, we get a ballpark estimate of full-compliance costs by other centers.[5] Another, and probably more meaningful, way to use the public nonprofit centers as a yardstick is to say that the public centers provide a level of child care service that is an acceptable standard for all to aim for. These estimates are supportive of my conclusions and are presented in Appendix 8A.

The main concern, however, is with the child/staff ratios as a measure of compliance with the federal standards. The child/staff ratios effective as of October 1, 1975, including the Title XX changes that became effective on that date,[6] along with the proposed child/staff standards for October 1, 1977,[7] are given in Table 8-1.

The center data on age of children enrolled is broken down into three groups: children under two, children aged two to four, and children five and over. Therefore, to estimate the degree to which the Seattle and Denver centers conform to federal child/staff standards, the data must be placed into categories that can be compared with those in the guidelines. Table 8-2 places the survey data children into age groupings that provide both a minimum value and a maximum value for the number of staff needed, and it shows the child/staff

Table 8-1
Child/Staff Ratios Effective October 1, 1975

	Actual October 1, 1975	*Proposed for October 1, 1977*
For Children under 6 Weeks Old	NA	1:1
For Children 6 Weeks to 3 Years Old	NA	4:1
For Children 3 Years Old	5:1	5:1
For Children 4-5 Years Old	7:1	7:1
For Children 6-9 Years Old	15:1	15:1
For Children 10-14 Years Old	20:1	20:1

Table 8-2

Federal Child/Staff Standards by Age Groups and Age Groups Used for Seattle-Denver Day Care Survey Data

	Case 1[a]			Case 2[b]	
Survey Data Age Groups Used	Federal Child/Staff Standards Used			Survey Data Age Groups Used	Federal Child/Staff Standards Used
0-4 years	5:1	Minimum[c]		Less than 2 years old	4:1
5 years old and over	15:1			2-4 years old	5:1
				5 years old and over	15:1
		Maximum[c]		0-4 years old	4:1
				5 years old and over	7:1

[a]Case 1 refers to standards put into effect on October 1, 1975, with qualifications as stated in note 1.

[b]Case 2 uses the Case 1 standards for children three years old and over, but it assumes that the new Title XX standards for children under three years old will go into effect on October 1, 1977. There is also a ratio of 1:1 required for babies aged six weeks or under. That ratio, even if put into effect on October 1, 1977, is not relevant to the survey data.

[c]The minimum and maximum standards are presented for Case 2 only. The reason for not having a similar range for Case 1 is given in note 8.

ratios used. It must be remembered that minimum and maximum values will be estimated simply because the data do not allow us to precisely distribute users of center child care services in accordance with the age groupings found in the federal standards. *Minimum* means that the children from the survey are placed in categories that minimize the number of staff required; with the reverse being true for *maximum*. However, a minimum and maximum estimate will be made only for Case 2 requirements, i.e., only for the child/staff requirements due to be implemented on or about October 1, 1977.[8] It also, as stated previously, shows placement of the survey-data age groupings to obtain a minimum and a maximum value for staff requirements using the more stringent standards for children under three years of age.[9]

Using the standards in Table 8-2, three sets of compliance costs for centers will be presented. First, I will use data from individual centers to determine the extent of noncompliance for each center. The resulting distribution of centers by their level of noncompliance will provide the more realistic assessment of short-run costs of compliance with federal standards. These costs are based on the view that the existing market structure in the day care center sector is in an equilibrium that has some centers with less staff than needed for the children in attendance (according to federal standards), some centers with more staff than needed, and some centers just meeting the required staffing standards. Under this first estimate of compliance cost, I will determine how enforcement of the child/staff standards will affect only those centers that are not meeting the standards.

The second estimate of compliance cost (presented in Appendix 8A) will be based on the mean values of the child/staff ratios for all centers. This approach combines centers having staff deficiencies with those that have a surplus of staff, according to the staff needs implied in the federal guidelines. The rationale for this approach is that the market mechanism, and the subsidy policy followed by the federal government, will cause centers that have more staff than needed to meet federal standards to cut back on their staff or to increase the number of children cared for to be just in compliance with the federal requirements. The mean, or average, value for the additional staff needed to comply with the federal guidelines will, therefore, be the sum of those centers with deficiencies offset by those with staff surpluses.

The view that over time centers with a staff surplus, relative to the federal standards, would reduce staff or increase the number of children cared for in order to just conform to federal standards is not generally accepted. It is more likely that there will continue to be some differentiation of the centers' services according to the number of staff used in excess of federal requirements. However, there may also be some cutback of staff for centers with a surplus. The estimate of cost based on the mean value will, therefore, tell us the compliance cost if the federal subsidy policy is structured so that the incentive for all centers to just conform to the federal guidelines is very strong. At the extreme, where all surpluses as well as deficits are eliminated and all centers are just in conformance with the federal standards, the compliance costs estimated through use of the mean values would be appropriate.

The third estimate of compliance cost (presented in Appendix 8A) is based on the cost of public, nonprofit centers. The assumption is that those centers are in full compliance with all federal standards. In that case, the public, nonprofit centers can be used as a yardstick for determining the cost of compliance with all standards by nonpublic centers.

Center Compliance Cost Distribution Data

Table 8-3 shows the total number of staff needed for centers with a staff deficiency, given the child/staff ratios shown in Table 8-2 and the number of children, by age, who were enrolled in each center during the survey period.[10]

Table 8-3

Distribution of Staff Deficiencies for Day Care Centers in Seattle and Denver

	(1) Total Number of Centers	(2) Number of Centers with No Additional Staff Needed	(3) Total Number of Additional Staff Needed by Centers with Staff Deficiencies[a]	(4) Total Number of Regular Paid Staff in Centers with Staff Deficiencies	(5) Total Number of Regular Paid Staff in All Centers	(6) Ratio of Additional Staff Needed to Regular Paid Staff in Centers with Staff Deficiencies (3÷4)	(7) Ratio of Additional Staff Needed to Regular Paid Staff in All Centers (3÷5)
Seattle							
Nonprofit private	35						
Case 1		25	24.68	58	346	0.426	0.071
Case 2 minimum		25	25.06	58		0.432	0.072
Case 2 maximum		13	67.44	173		0.39	0.195
Nonprofit public	11						
Case 1		10	1.93	2	99	0.965	0.20
Case 2 minimum		10	1.93	2		0.965	0.20
Case 2 maximum		8	4.25	11		0.386	0.43
For profit private	21						
Case 1		12	9.60	71	158	0.135	0.061
Case 2 minimum		12	9.80	71		0.138	0.062
Case 2 maximum		7	39.17	106		0.370	0.248
Denver							
Nonprofit private	13						
Case 1		11	4.07	19	147	0.214	0.028
Case 2 minimum		11	4.07	19		0.214	0.028
Case 2 maximum		6	21.97	67		0.328	0.150
Nonprofit public	17						
Case 1		15	9.73	31	220	0.314	0.044
Case 2 minimum		15	11.68	31		0.377	0.053
Case 2 maximum		10	26.22	89		0.295	0.119
For profit private	17						
Case 1		8	35.47	79	158	0.449	0.224
Case 2 minimum		8	35.47	79		0.449	0.224
Case 2 maximum		3	80.01	131		0.611	0.506

[a]Staff deficiencies were computed by determining the number of staff required for each center to comply with the federal child/staff standards, given the number and age of enrolled children in each center. The deficiencies are calculated for the two cases listed in Table 8-2.

From Table 8-3 it is apparent that although a significant proportion of the centers had no staff deficiencies—i.e., they had at least the minimum number of regular paid staff needed to meet the federal child/staff requirements—there were a large number of centers with some staff deficiencies; a few deficient centers needed most of the additional staff shown in column 3 of Table 8-3.[11] Looking at changes in the number of children cared for over time leads to a hypothesis that adjustment lags may be a significant factor in producing the number of staff deficiencies shown. When the number of children in attendance increases, there is a lag in hiring new staff; similarly, when the number of children in attendance falls, staff layoffs may show a sizable time lag. In the distributional data, more of the former will show deficiencies; therefore, in the deficient group there tends to be a predominance of growing centers. However, there is no way that point-in-time data can be used to adjust for such dynamic changes.

Using the data from Table 8-3, we find in column 6 that in most cases the number of additional staff required is a substantial proportion of the number of staff already working at centers with staff deficiencies. For example, 42.6 percent more staff would be needed for the nonprofit, private centers in Seattle under the Case 1 standards, relative to the number of regular paid staff working in those centers as of the survey period. In Denver for the same case, an additional 21.4 percent of staff would be required. The percentage of additional staff needed for the nonprofit, public centers with staff deficiencies in Seattle is misleadingly large because of the very small base of regular paid staff employed in the few such centers that had any staff deficiencies.

Another way of looking at the effect of staff additions needed, or the percentage change implied, is to use the number of regular paid staff in all centers as the base. This would tell us what percentage increase in the total number of regular paid staff employed as of the survey date would be required to eliminate the staff deficiencies. The latter percentages are shown in column 7 of Table 8-3.[12]

Using the staff deficiencies shown in Table 8-3, along with average annual pay for regular employed staff in each of the three proprietary groups, the costs of compliance with federal standards can be calculated for all centers that are not in compliance with the child/staff requirements. These costs are presented in Table 8-4. Table 8-4 clearly shows that when data from individual centers is examined, every example would involve a significant cost in the enforcement of federal standards.[13] (This is in contrast to the results using average data,[14] which show a significant cost only for Case 2 maximum; even then, on the average, there would be no cost for the public, nonprofit centers.)

The Case 2 maximum standards are the most stringent; therefore, the overall costs of compliance for that example represent an upper limit to such costs. The size of that limit can be seen in Table 8-4 by examining line 9 for the Case 2 maximum standards. We find that in Seattle a 20 percent increase in the annual labor cost for all regular paid staff would be needed for the nonprofit, private centers to pay for the additional staff needed by deficient centers. For the

Table 8-4
Staff Needed for All Deficient Centers to Conform to Federal Child/Staff Standards and Costs of Compliance

	Seattle			Denver		
	Nonprofit		For-Profit Private	Nonprofit		For-Profit Private
	Private	Public		Private	Public	
Case 1						
1. Additional Staff Needed[a]	24.7	1.9	9.6	4.1	9.7	35.5
2. Annual Cost of Additional Staff[b]	$68,172	$9,196	$19,690	$11,345	$55,329	$91,626
3. Number of Regular Paid Staff in All Centers	346	99.0	158.0	147.0	220.0	158.0
4. Annual Cost of All Regular Paid Staff[c]	$954,960	$479,160	$324,058	$406,749	$1,254,880	$407,798
5. Annual Compliance Cost per Currently Enrolled Child in Deficient Centers[d]	$152.85	$367.84	$43.08	$85.95	$237.56	$134.94
6. Annual Compliance Cost per Currently Enrolled Child in All Centers[e]	$42.24	$28.21	$22.82	$16.07	$54.35	$83.45
7. Cost per Week per Child for Deficient Centers[f]	$2.94	$7.07	$0.83	$1.65	$4.57	$2.60
8. Cost per Week per Child for All Centers[g]	$0.81	$0.54	$0.44	$0.31	$1.04	$1.60
9. Ratio of Annual Cost of Additional Staff to Annual Cost of All Regular Staff[h]	0.07	0.02	0.06	0.03	0.04	0.22
10. Ratio of Annual Compliance Cost per Child in Deficient Centers to Total Cost per Child in Deficient Centers[i]	0.16	0.52	0.04	0.09	0.22	0.20

Table 8-4 — Continued

	Seattle			Denver		
	Nonprofit		For-Profit Private	Nonprofit		For-Profit Private
	Private	Public		Private	Public	
Case 2 Minimum						
1. Additional Staff Needed[a]	25.1	1.9	9.8	4.1	11.7	35.5
2. Annual Cost of Additional Staff[b]	$69,276	$9,196	$20,100	$11,345	$66,737	$91,626
3. Number of Regular Paid Staff in All Centers	346	99.0	158.0	147.0	220.0	158.0
4. Annual Cost of All Regular Paid Staff[c]	$954,960	$479,160	$324,058	$406,749	$1,254,880	$407,798
5. Annual Compliance Cost per Currently Enrolled Child in Deficient Centers[d]	$155.33	$367.84	$43.98	$85.95	$286.42	$134.94
6. Annual Compliance Cost per Currently Enrolled Child in All Centers[e]	$42.92	$28.21	$23.29	$16.07	$65.56	$83.45
7. Cost per Week per Child for Deficient Centers[f]	$2.99	$7.07	$0.85	$1.65	$5.51	$2.60
8. Cost per Week per Child for All Centers[g]	$0.82	$0.54	$0.45	$0.31	$1.26	$1.60
9. Ratio of Annual Cost of Additional Staff to Annual Cost of All Regular Staff[h]	0.07	0.02	0.06	0.03	0.05	0.22
10. Ratio of Annual Compliance Cost per Child in Deficient Centers to Total Cost per Child in Deficient Centers[i]	0.16	0.52	0.04	0.09	0.26	0.20

Table 8-4 – Continued

	Seattle			Denver		
	Nonprofit		For-Profit Private	Nonprofit		For-Profit Private
	Private	Public		Private	Public	
Case 2 Maximum						
1. Additional Staff Needed[a]	67.4	4.2	39.2	22.0	26.2	80.0
2. Annual Cost of Additional Staff[b]	$186,024	$20,328	$80,399	$60,874	$149,445	$206,480
3. Number of Regular Paid Staff in All Centers	346.0	99.0	158.0	147.0	220.0	158.0
4. Annual Cost of All Regular Paid Staff[c]	$954,960	$479,160	$324,058	$406,749	$1,254,880	$407,798
5. Annual Compliance Cost per Currently Enrolled Child in Deficient Centers[d]	$179.73	$278.47	$123.50	$148.84	$295.93	$210.69
6. Annual Compliance Cost per Currently Enrolled Child in All Centers[e]	$115.26	$62.36	$93.16	$86.22	$146.80	$188.05
7. Cost per Week per Child for Deficient Centers[f]	$3.56	$5.36	$2.38	$2.86	$5.69	$4.05
8. Cost per Week per Child for All Centers[g]	$2.22	$1.20	$1.79	$1.66	$2.82	$3.62
9. Ratio of Annual Cost of Additional Staff to Annual Cost of All Regular Paid Staff[h]	0.20	0.04	0.25	0.15	0.12	0.51
10. Ratio of Annual Compliance Cost per Child in Deficient Centers to Total Cost per Child in Deficient Centers[i]	0.14	0.21	0.12	0.13	0.21	0.27

aEquals staff needed minus staff employed summed over all centers where a deficiency exists, from Table 8-3.

bEquals additional staff needed in deficient centers times the average annual pay as of mid-1974 for all regular paid staff by proprietary type and city.

cEquals total regular paid staff in all centers times the average annual pay as of mid-1974 for all regular paid staff by proprietary type and city.

dEquals annual cost for additional staff needed divided by the total number of enrolled children in centers with staff deficiencies.

eEquals annual cost for additional staff needed divided by the total number of enrolled children in all centers.

fRow 5 divided by 52.

gRow 6 divided by 52.

hRow 2 divided by row 4.

iThe numerator is row 5. The denominator is constructed as follows: compute the annual rate of pay for all regular paid staff in deficient centers, using the mean hourly rate of pay and assuming 2080 hours of paid work per year. Assuming that labor cost is 75 percent of total costs, divide the annual rate of pay by 0.75, and divide that sum by the number of children enrolled in deficient centers.

nonprofit centers, an increase of only 4 percent would be needed; a 25 percent increase would be required in the for-profit sector. To eliminate staff deficiencies in Denver, comparable percentage increases in the labor cost for currently employed regular staff would be 15, 12, and 51 percent for the nonprofit private, public, and for-profit sectors, respectively.[15] The need to increase total labor cost by over 50 percent to bring the for-profit centers into compliance with federal child/staff standards is especially noteworthy. The ratio in line 9 for the other examples shows the proportionate increase in labor cost needed for compliance under less-stringent conditions than were used for Case 2 maximum.

On line 5 in Table 8-4, the compliance cost for deficient centers is divided by the number of enrolled children in those centers; in line 6 the same compliance cost is divided by the number of enrolled children in all centers. This tells us the compliance cost burden if it were prorated only among centers with some staff deficiency, as well as the burden if the cost were spread among children in all the centers. On line 10 of Table 8-4 the ratio of compliance cost per child to total cost per child for deficient centers is shown. That ratio is one indication of the financial burden that the deficient centers would be under if they were forced to comply with the standards given in Table 8-2. For example, in Case 1 we find that compliance cost amounts to 16 percent of total annual cost per child for nonprofit, private centers, 52 percent for the public centers, and 4 percent for the profit-oriented centers in Seattle.[16]

Using the mean value of the fees charged, for all centers according to proprietary type, for a standard 40-hour week, we can, using Table 8-4, get an estimate of the potential impact that enforcement of compliance with federal standards would have on these fees. The effect in terms of the percentage increase in fees implied by the costs in Table 8-4 is shown in Table 8-5.

The percentage increases in total fees to offset compliance costs, as shown in Table 8-5, indicate the increases in weekly fees for all children that would be required to pay for the cost of additional staff needed to comply with the federal child/staff standards. For example, if all for-profit, private centers in Seattle were to assume the burden of paying for the compliance cost incurred by deficient centers in that proprietary group, for Case 2 maximum costs, the fees per 40-hour week would be raised to $21.81 per child. In Denver for-profit centers, weekly fees would be raised to $27.65 per child.[17]

Compliance Cost for Licensed Family Day Care Homes

Estimates of the compliance cost for licensed family day care homes are subject to more serious reservations than similar estimates for centers.[18] Since there is no public, nonprofit sector that can be used as a yardstick, as was done for centers (Appendix 8A), we must concentrate on the required and actual child/staff ratios. That is, I will use data on the number of children cared for, by age,

Table 8-5
Fees per Standard 40-Hour Week of Child Care and Percentage Increase in Fees Implied by Compliance with Federal Standards

	Seattle			Denver		
	Nonprofit		For-Profit Private	Nonprofit		For-Profit Private
	Private	Public		Private	Public	
Fees per 40-Hour Week[a]	$18.79	$25.15	$20.01	$13.20	$19.40	$24.02
Percentage Increase in Total Fees to Offset Compliance Cost[b]						
Case 1	4.3%	2.2%	2.2%	2.3%	5.4%	6.7%
Case 2 minimum	4.4	2.2	2.2	2.3	6.4	6.7
Case 2 maximum	11.8	4.8	9.0	12.6	14.5	15.1

[a]Estimated from survey data. Averages for all centers within proprietary classes are shown.

[b]Compliance cost per week divided by total fees per week, multiplied by 100. Compliance cost per week equals line 2 of Table 8-4 divided by 52; and total fees per week equals fees per 40-hour week multiplied by the average number of children per center in each proprietary group, with that product multiplied by the number of centers in each proprietary group. These percentages can also be obtained by dividing line 8 of Table 8-4 by the fees per 40-hour week given above.

in the Seattle and Denver family day care homes surveyed, along with the known federal standards for family day care homes by age groupings.[19]

The federal child/staff standards for family day care homes are: (1) if children under two are being cared for, there can be no more than two children less than two years old and a total of no more than five children, including the caretaker's own children, who are under fourteen years of age; (2) if only children aged three to thirteen are cared for, a maximum of six children can be provided day care, including the provider's own children in that total if they are under fourteen years of age.[20]

Using these standards, I determined the excess number of children, if any, in the FDCHs surveyed. The excess children were divided into those under two and those from two through thirteen years old. For these excess children, I then computed the number of hours per week that they had been with an FDCH operator. This gave me the total number of hours of child care provided by child care operators who cared for children in excess of the federal standards.[21] Table 8-6 shows the excess hours for Seattle and Denver.

In Seattle the average number of hours that child care operators spent caring for children during the week before the interview was 46.1, in Denver it was 44.9. However, of the children cared for during any day, not all would be there for the full period. In fact, I found that on the average the capacity utilized in Seattle and Denver was 66 and 76 percent, respectively.[22] Deflating the average hours worked by these utilization rates, we find that the average number of hours per week that FDCH operators were available for child care was 30.4 in

Table 8-6
Weekly Hours of Care for All FDCH Children and for Children Who Were Excess According to Federal Child Staff Standards

	Seattle		Denver	
	Children under 2 Years of Age	Children Aged 2-13	Children under 2 Years of Age	Children Aged 2-13
Hours of Care for Excess Children[a]	550	2,402	668	935
Total Hours of Care for All FDCH Children[a]	5,871	26,482	5,964	19,268
Ratio of Excess Hours to Total Hours[b]	0.094	0.091	0.112	0.049

[a]Represents actual hours spent in day care during the week preceding the interview.

[b]Equals row 1 divided by row 2.

Seattle and 34.1 in Denver. These averages will be used as a measure of full-time care for any new FDCH operator that would be needed for the excess child-hours given in Table 8-6. Moreover, I assume that each child will receive care for the average number of hours given above.[23]

Finally, to determine the compliance cost I allocate the excess hours given in Table 8-6 among "new" FDCH operators, assuming that each of the "new" operators will take exactly the number of children required by the federal standards. Moreover, for these children, the "new" FDCH operators will provide the average (deflated) number of child-hours of care, as given in the preceding paragraph. Using the federal standards, the excess hours in Table 8-6, and the average hours of utilization previously given, we find that an additional 17.7 FDCHs would be needed in Seattle and 9.8 new FDCHs would be required in Denver for the excess hours in Table 8-6.[24]

It should be remembered, however, that the number of new FDCHs needed to provide care for the excess child hours in Table 8-6 is only for the sample of FDCHs interviewed. As described in Appendix 8C, 29 percent of the licensed FDCHs in Seattle and slightly over 44 percent in Denver were included in the sample. Since the sample selected was random from the total population, we can use the inverse of the proportion sampled as a weight to derive an estimate of the excess number of child-hours of care among all FDCH providers in Seattle and Denver; and we can therefore get an estimate, by using that weight, of the total number of new FDCHs that would be required to satisfy the federal child/ staff ratio. The inverse of the proportion sampled is 3.47 in Seattle and 2.25 in Denver; consequently, a total of 61.4 new FDCHs in Seattle and 22.1 in Denver would be needed to take care of the total excess child-hours. The increase in the total population of licensed FDCHs implied by these figures is 8.3 percent in Seattle and 5.9 percent in Denver.

To obtain the compliance cost, we need to estimate the cost of establishing the required new family day care homes. Estimates will be given based on the number of new FDCHs implied by using the hours of excess care from Table 8-6. The estimate weighted by the inverse of the sampling proportions will be used to obtain the cost estimate for all excess child care hours in each city. The essential element of these estimates is the labor cost involved. I will use three measures for the opportunity cost needed to recruit new providers into the business of providing family day care home services. The alternative measures are:

1. The average expected wage[25] of current FDCH providers, along with the actual hours worked as a day care provider during the week preceding the interview, as well as nonlabor variable cost.
2. The same as item 1, but using the minimum wage as of May 1, 1974, in place of the average expected wage of current providers.[26]
3. Adjusted annual gross earnings of current providers plus nonlabor variable cost.

Table 8-7 presents the data needed, as well as providing estimates of compliance costs for licensed FDCHs.

The compliance costs as given for Measures 1 and 2 in line 4 of Table 8-8 probably represent upper limits, because the wage actually received by day care providers, as derived from earnings and hours data, is considerably below wages used in Measures 1 and 2. However, if expansion of the system is proposed, the opportunity costs suggested may be more relevant as an estimate of costs. The compliance cost given for Measure 3 in line 4 of Table 8-8 may be a more accurate reflection of those opportunity costs as seen in actual day care market conditions. Moreover, the hourly costs chosen for Measures 2 and 3 are fairly close to fees per hour estimated from the survey data for currently enrolled children.[27]

Finally, as shown on lines 5 through 7 of Table 8-7, substantial cost would be involved if public funds were to subsidize expansion of the FDCH sector. Even in the lowest cost measure (3), it would require approximately a third of a million dollars in either city to provide FDCH child care for 500 to 600 additional children needing such care.

Table 8-7
Estimated Costs per Family Day Care Home

		Seattle	Denver
1.	Mean Expected[a] Hourly Rate of Pay for Current Family Day Care Home Providers	$2.85	$2.61
2.	Mean Hours Worked as Child Care Provider during Survey Week	46.1	44.9
3.	Mean Gross Earnings of Current Provider (Adjusted as an Annual Rate)	$2,568	$2,260
4.	Mean Nonlabor Variable Cost per Year	$1,338	$993
5.	Measure 1 Total Cost per Family Day Care Home[b]	$8,170	$7,087
6.	Measure 2 Total Cost per Family Day Care Home[c]	$5,893	$5,429
7.	Measure 3 Total Cost per Family Day Care Home[d]	$3,906	$3,253

[a]If seeking non-day care market employment.

[b]Line 1 times line 2 times 52, plus line 4.

[c]1.90 times line 2 times 52, plus line 4.

[d]Line 3 plus line 4.

Table 8-8
Measures of Compliance Costs for Family Day Care Homes[a]

	Seattle (N = 61.4)[b]	Denver (N = 22.1)[b]
1. Measure 1 Annual Costs for New FDCHs Required	$501,638	$156,622
2. Measure 2 Annual Costs for New FDCHs Required	361,830	119,981
3. Measure 3 Annual Costs for New FDCHs Required	239,828	71,891
4. Costs per Hour of Child Care[c]		
Using Measure 1 Costs	$0.89	$0.72
Using Measure 2 Costs	0.64	0.55
Using Measure 3 Costs	0.42	0.33
5. Annual Additional Costs per 100 Existing FDCHs[d]		
For Measure 1 Costs	$67,811	$41,813
For Measure 2 Costs	48,912	32,031
For Measure 3 Costs	32,420	19,193

[a]Using the number of additional FDCHs implied by the hours of excess child care from Table 8-6, which is then weighted by the inverse of the sampling proportion.

[b]Total number of new FDCHs required to meet federal child/staff standards in all of Seattle and Denver.

[c]The numerator is the annual cost given in 1-3 above divided by 52. The denominator is constructed as follows: first determine the number of new FDCHs that could, according to the federal standards, have five and those that could have six children. This is done by multiplying the number of new FDCHs needed by the proportion of excess hours for children under two years of age to the total number of excess child care hours. That gives the number that could have five children, and the residual is the number that could have six children. Second, multiply the number of children allowed by the number of new FDCHs with that number of children, and then multiply the product by the average weekly hours of care provided to each child, which are 30.4 in Seattle and 34.1 in Denver. For example, in Seattle the weighted number of total excess child-hours is 10,243. Approximately 18.6 percent of those hours are for children under two years of age. The number of new FDCHs required to take care of these excess hours is 61.4. The computation, therefore, is as follows: $501,638 ÷ 52 = $9,647; 0.186 × 61.4 = 11.4; 61.4 − 11.4 = 50.0; therefore, 50.0 new FDCHs could have six children, for a total of 300 children, and 11.4 FDCHs could have five children, for a total of 57 children. These 357 children are cared for an average of 30.4 hours, for 10,853 total hours of care. Therefore, the cost per hour of child care is $9,647 ÷ 10,853 = $0.89 for Seattle.

[d]Derived by multiplying the total cost per 100 existing FDCHs by the percentage increase in FDCHs needed to accommodate the excess child-hours of care (8.3 percent in Seattle and 5.9 percent in Denver). The intuitive reasoning behind this calculation is that if, for example, 8.3 percent more FDCHs were needed for each 100 existing FDCHs, the cost would be equal to the total cost for 100 FDCHs *plus* an additional cost amounting to 8.3 percent of that total.

Moreover, as shown in the three measures on line 5 of Table 8-8, the annual additional cost per 100 existing FDCHs for compliance with federal child/staff standards would be significant. Even for the lowest cost measure (3), the added cost would mean an increase of 6 to 8 percent over the current costs of operating licensed family day care homes.[28]

Summary and Conclusions

Based on a 1974 survey of child care providers in Seattle and Denver conducted for the Seattle and Denver Income Maintenance Experiments, I was able to provide estimates of the cost to the child care industry in those cities of meeting the federal standard for the provision of licensed child care services. Although the survey was designed for a different purpose, I believe it provides a reasonable basis for estimation of compliance costs, especially with regard to changes in the child/staff ratio requirements. The estimates are provided separately for day care centers and family day care homes.

Day Care Centers

The principal conclusions with regard to the cost of compliance for centers are shown in Table 8-9, which analyzes cost for two cases: Case 1 is the cost of compliance for federal standards put into effect in October 1975 with regard to the child/staff ratios; Case 2 represents the cost of compliance to meet the more stringent requirements that were originally expected to go into effect in February 1976 and have now been temporarily postponed. The standards for Case 2 are similar to those put into effect in October 1975, except for more stringent child/staff ratios for children under three years of age.

Table 8-9 shows, for each case and each center type, the annual cost per currently enrolled child and the added cost per child if the deficient centers were brought up to standard. These costs are averaged over all centers of each type, but clearly not all centers are deficient. Columns 4 and 7 of Table 8-9 show the percentage of centers not in compliance. As can be seen, compliance cost is most significant for private, for-profit centers, in which required cost increases range from about 5 percent in Seattle under Case 1 to 27 percent in Denver under Case 2. About half of these centers are not in compliance, indicating a widespread problem of compliance.

The percentages of increase in cost for nonprofit, private centers are lower, ranging from 2 percent for centers in Denver under Case 1 to 13 percent for centers in Seattle under Case 2. The compliance problem is widespread for nonprofit, private centers under Case 2 but is concentrated among fewer centers under Case 1. The compliance cost problem for the public centers is significant only for the centers in Denver under Case 2, in which costs would increase about 8 percent on the average, and in which almost 40 percent of the centers have compliance problems.[29]

Table 8-10 shows the estimated total number of children in each center category in each city and the overall magnitude of compliance costs. Note that the distribution of children among center types is different in Seattle and Denver. The private, nonprofit centers are the most important in Seattle, whereas private, for-profit centers dominate in Denver. According to the estimates in Table 8-10, compliance under Case 1 would increase center costs by 4.2 percent

Table 8-9
Change in Costs Due to Compliance with Child/Staff Requirements by Centers

	Total Annual Cost per Currently Enrolled Child[a] (1)	Annual Compliance Cost per Currently Enrolled Child (2)	Case 1		Annual Compliance Cost per Currently Enrolled Child (5)	Case 2[b]	
			Percent Change in Total Cost Due to Compliance Cost (3)	Proportion of All Centers Not in Compliance (4)		Percent Change in Total Cost Due to Compliance Cost (6)	Proportion of All Centers Not in Compliance (7)
Seattle							
For-profit, private	$501	$23	4.6%	0.429	$75	15.0%	0.540
Nonprofit, private	789	42	5.3	0.286	100	12.7	0.547
Nonprofit, public	1,960[c]	28	1.4	0.091	61	3.1	0.268
Denver							
For-profit, private	495	83	16.8	0.529	134	27.1	0.585
Nonprofit, private	768	16	2.1	0.154	76	9.9	0.475
Nonprofit, public	1,644[c]	54	3.3	0.118	137	8.3	0.383

[a]See footnote b to Table 8-10. The total annual cost from Table 8-10 was divided by the total number of currently enrolled children in all cities.

[b]For Case 2, minimum and maximum estimates are provided in Table 8-4, line 6. Those estimates are based on the age breakdown of children in the survey. For the summary, a weighted best estimate is provided, based on the age distribution of children using day care centers, taken from a national survey conducted by Unco, Inc.

[c]The discrepancy between the public and private cost per child is due to three factors: a much higher average hourly pay received by public center employees, a somewhat higher average number of hours worked per week by public center employees, and a lower average ratio of children to staff in public centers. For example, the first two factors made the average annual estimated pay for public center employees almost two-and-one-half times that of the paid staff in private, for-profit centers.

Table 8-10
Total Annual Compliance Cost and Estimated Total Annual Cost for Centers

	Number of Currently Enrolled Children in Centers 1974[a]	Percentage of Total Enrollment	Total Annual Cost (not including Cost of Compliance)[b]	Annual Compliance Cost[c]	
				Case 1	Case 2
Seattle					
For-profit, private	862	30.8%	$432,077	$19,851	$64,725
Nonprofit, private	1,614	57.6	1,273,280	67,767	161,400
Nonprofit, public	326	11.6	638,880	9,117	19,886
Total	2,802	100.0%	$2,344,237	$96,735	$246,011
Denver					
For-profit, private	1,098	38.9%	$543,731	$91,151	$147,132
Nonprofit, private	706	25.0	542,332	11,294	53,656
Nonprofit, public	1,018	36.1	1,673,173	54,988	139,466
Total	2,822	100.0%	$2,759,236	$157,433	$340,254

[a]Taken from data collected in the survey.

[b]It has been estimated that personnel costs are approximately 75 percent of total costs. (See Abt Associates, Inc., "Costs and Quality Issues for Operators," from *A Study in Child Care, 1970-1971,* Vol. III; and Gilbert Steiner, *The State of Welfare,* The Brookings Institution, p. 69.) Using that estimate I multiplied the annual cost of all regular paid staff, line 4 of Table 8-4, by 1.333 to obtain estimates of annual total costs. For Case 2 the minimum-maximum figures were adjusted to derive one best estimate. That adjustment was based on the age distribution of children using day care centers, taken from a preliminary draft of a national survey conducted by Unco Inc. Using $1.90 per hour, the minimum wage for newly covered workers that went into effect on May 1, 1974, rather than the actual rate of pay received by regular paid staff would not increase the compliance costs since the mean hourly rate of pay for regularly paid center staff was greater than that minimum for all proprietary types in both cities.

[c]This was computed by multiplying the compliance cost per child from Table 8-4, line 6, by the total number of currently enrolled children in day care centers surveyed in Seattle and Denver.

in Seattle and 5.7 percent in Denver. Compliance under Case 2 would increase costs by 10.5 percent in Seattle and 12.3 percent in Denver.

To demonstrate the possible national implications of compliance with the federal day care standards, I have extrapolated the Seattle and Denver center cost estimates to a national total, as shown in Table 8-11. These estimates are based on the assumption that nationally approximately 910,000 children use child care centers.[30]

Table 8-11

Estimated National Cost of Compliance for Centers Projected from Seattle and Denver Experience[a]

	Case 1	Case 2
National Cost–Seattle Distribution	$31.2 million	$79.4 million
National Cost–Denver Distribution	$50.8 million	$109.7 million

[a]Compliance cost total from Table 8-10 divided by the ratio of the number of children in centers in Seattle or Denver to the number of children in centers nationally. For example, for Case 1 in Seattle, we have ($96,735 ÷ 2802/ 910,000 = $96,735 ÷ 0.0031 = $31.2 million.

Table 8-11 indicates that compliance cost nationally would run from a minimum of $31 million for Case 1, if the Seattle experience is representative of the nation, to a maximum of $110 million for Case 2, if the Denver experience is representative.

An alternative view of compliance cost assumes that all centers would move toward the compliance criteria; that is, that centers above the compliance level, for which the number of staff was larger than necessary, would eventually reduce their staff or increase the number of children enrolled. Estimates under this less likely assumption are presented in Appendix 8A. An estimate of the cost of compliance for centers to meet all the federal standards in addition to those dealing with the child/staff ratio is also presented in Appendix 8A. These costs are based on a hypothesis that the public, nonprofit centers comply—and just comply—with these standards.

Licensed Family Day Care Homes

Licensed family day care homes (FDCHs) provide a significant proportion of licensed care in both Seattle and Denver. In Seattle an estimated 58 percent of the children enrolled in licensed facilities are in FDCHs; in Denver FDCHs care for 38 percent of such children. Extrapolating the survey results leads to an estimated 3840 children in FDCHs in Seattle in 1974 and 1714 children in FDCHs in Denver.

The cost of compliance is estimated in terms of the additional FDCHs needed to provide for all those children now in such homes, if the existing homes were required to reduce the number of children to comply with the federal child/staff standards. According to my estimates, the 735 FDCHs in Seattle would have to be increased by 61; in Denver the existing 373 homes would have to be increased by 22. These additions to the stock of homes imply cost increases averaging 8.3 percent in Seattle and 5.9 percent in Denver, as shown in Table 8-12. These estimates are rough approximations, because the

Table 8-12

Total Annual Compliance Cost and Estimated Total Annual Cost for Licensed Family Day Care Homes

	Total Annual Compliance Cost[a]	*Total Annual Cost*[b] *(For Existing FDCHs)*	*Compliance Cost as a Percentage of Total Cost*
Seattle	$361,830	$4,378,499	8.3%
Denver	119,981	2,041,304	5.9

[a]Based on the $1.90 per hour minimum wage used from line 2 of Table 8-8. That wage rate was used because it went into effect for newly covered workers on May 1, 1974.

[b]The estimate presented is the product of line 6 of Table 8-7 and the total number of licensed FDCHs in each city. Line 6 was used because it is based on the minimum wage as used for the compliance cost figures.

true cost for additional homes depends on the salary or wage levels assumed for family day care home operators; and the costs per home could range from $4000 to $8000, depending on the assumptions used.

In conclusion, this chapter shows that a significant proportion of licensed child care operators in Seattle and Denver are not in compliance with existing and proposed federal standards. Especially heavy costs would have to be incurred by the private, for-profit centers who are not in compliance. On the average, the increases needed in the number of FDCHs or staffs of day care centers are significant, but not overwhelming.

Notes

1. With the exception of the 1:1 child/staff ratio for children under six weeks of age, the Title XX amendments with regard to child/staff ratios were put into effect on October 1, 1975. However, Congress enacted Public Law 94-120, which provided that no penalty for noncompliance with the child/staff ratio requirements for preschool children could be invoked before February 1, 1976. During that four-month interlude, the existing state standards for children under six were to provide a minimum standard. For Washington and Colorado, the 1968 federal interagency day care requirement (FIDCR) was used as the base for setting state standards, although both states differed somewhat from the FIDCR standards. In estimating the compliance costs for the four-month interim period, I have used standards from the 1968 FIDCR for preschool children and the Title XX standards for children six and over.

2. As of the publication date of this book, a further postponement to October 1, 1978, is being considered and appears likely.

3. Designated as Case 1 and Case 2 in Table 8-2.

4. Except where I use public centers as a yardstick for compliance with other standards. In addition, in calculating the child/staff ratios from the survey data, I have made no adjustment for the fact that in both centers and FDCHs some children are in attendance part time. I assume that each enrolled child has equal weight in calculating the numerator of the child/staff ratio. If I were to adjust the number of children to a full-time equivalent status, the number of additional staff needed to meet federal standards would be lower than the numbers given in this chapter. The compliance costs would therefore also be lower. Overall, about 75 percent of the currently enrolled center children in each city were in attendance full time (about 8.5 hours per day); the part-time children attended the centers an average of 4 hours per day in Seattle and almost 5 hours per day in Denver. Using those percentages, along with the average hours of care for full-time and part-time children, I can estimate the upward bias in the compliance costs as being about 15 percent in Seattle and 11.5 percent in Denver. As presented below, other problems in the data impart some offsetting biases in the cost estimates.

5. That is, with regard to all nine sets of standards.

6. See note 1 for relevant qualification with regard to applicable standards.

7. May be extended to October 1, 1978.

8. The reason for not presenting minimum and maximum child/staff standards for Case 1 in Table 8-2 is based on the age distribution of children who use child care centers, as determined in a national survey recently completed by Unco, Inc. These data were used to weight the specific age categories used in our survey. Unco found that 26.5 percent of the children using at least 1 hour of day care per week in centers were zero to three years old, 23.9 percent were four years old, 17.8 percent were five years old, and 31.6 percent were six or over. What this means is that the standard as presented in Case 1 for the zero-to-four-year-old group overstates the staff needed, since the four-year-olds actually require a ratio of 7:1; while the standard for the five-year-olds and over understates the staff needed, since the five-year-olds also require a ratio of 7:1. However, as seen from the Unco distributions, these two ages (four and five years old) represent roughly comparable percentages of total use, and it can be assumed that the overestimate of staff needs for four-year-olds is roughly offset by the underestimate for five-year-olds.

9. See footnotes to Table 8-2 for details of these assumptions and groupings.

10. See Appendix 8B for discussions of bias introduced by not accounting for volunteer help in determining compliance, and by assuming full utilization of additional staff.

11. The distribution of deficient centers according to the number of additional staff needed is not presented in Table 8-3. What I found, essentially, is that a relatively small number of deficient centers were grossly deficient and needed most of the additional staff. This was especially true for the nonprofit, private centers in Seattle and the private, for-profit centers in Denver.

12. In all cases, the proportion shown should be multiplied by 100 to obtain the relevant percentage.

13. For a more accurate assessment of the cost implications, one would have to take account of volunteer help and hours spent at the centers for both children and staff.

14. See Table 8A–2 of Appendix 8A.

15. As of the survey period.

16. The rates for public centers are high because the costs for the few public centers that are not in compliance are relatively high (because of the much larger average annual pay for staff in public centers).

17. Equals $20.01 × 1.09 for Seattle and $24.02 × 1.151 for Denver.

18. The estimates for FDCH compliance cost are based on the number of new homes that will be needed to ensure compliance with federal child/staff standards; for the centers, however, compliance cost was based on the number of additional staff that the existing centers would have had to hire.

19. The data on the number of children cared for by age are much more useful in determining compliance with federal child/staff standards for the FDCH sample than were the corresponding data for centers. The age of children in FDCHs is given by actual months for each child.

20. The federal interagency day care requirements with regard to child/staff standards for family day care homes are actually written a bit differently than stated here, but the requirements amount to my description regarding the allowable number of children per caretaker. However, there is some ambiguity in the regulations concerning two-year-olds. It is not clear whether they were meant to be put into the *under-two* class. I have, however, made a literal interpretation of the regulations, so that two-year-olds are put into the older age group. This leads to a very small understatement of the compliance cost.

21. When any given FDCH operator was found to have excess children, according to the federal standards, the problem arose as to which children were to be considered in excess of the standards. Selection of particular children is important since different children could be in attendance for different numbers of hours per day. Therefore, the actual number of excess hours could be affected significantly by the children chosen to be in excess. My criterion for selection was to pick the children with the smallest number of hours of paid care, and their hours of paid care are the excess hours in Table 8–6. This approach provides a minimum amount of excess hours and therefore biases the compliance cost downward. My rationale for using children with the lowest number of paid hours of child care was that it was appropriate for determining the short-run impact of the federal standards; if the federal standards were imposed today, given the number of children cared for from the survey data, what would be the result tomorrow? I assume that for the short run, to be in compliance, providers would release those children contributing the least to their child care revenue. Some adjustment, in fact, might be needed to account for personal preferences

of FDCH operators; however, the criterion is generally appropriate if the policy-maker wants to determine short-term impacts. However, if we are concerned with the long-run cost of compliance, after adjustment to a new market equilibrium, the average child hours would be an appropriate criterion for selection of excess children. My compliance cost figures, then, understate the long-run compliance costs, assuming that a new equilibrium position after imposition of federal standards presents a distribution of child hours comparable to that found in the survey.

22. Capacity utilized was constructed as follows: (1) I formed the maximum number of children taken care of for pay during any day of the week; (2) for each day of the week, I multiplied that number by the maximum number of hours that the provider took care of children for pay during that day, which is the measure of capacity; (3) the sum of item 2 for the week was then divided into the actual total hours of paid care that the FDCH operator reported providing for all children during the week. The result was my measure of capacity utilized.

23. If we wanted to obtain a lower bound for the cost needed to maintain federal child/staff ratios in FDCHs, we could use the larger, undeflated average number of hours for each child; that is, if each child were to spend 46.1 hours in care in Seattle, the cost of setting up the needed number of new FDCHs to take care of the excess child hours for Seattle would be a lower bound for such compliance costs. However, it is important that in estimating the costs for new FDCHs we use the mean hours that providers actually worked during the survey week, i.e., 46.1 in Seattle and 44.9 in Denver.

24. To show how these figures were obtained, I will use the Seattle excess hours from Table 8-6. There were 550 excess hours for children under two and 2402 for children two through thirteen. Since children under two is the constraint, in the sense that no more than two can be cared for in any FDCH, we find that 9.05 FDCHs would be required to provide the needed 550 hours of care, at 30.4 hours per child for two children. Those 9.05 FDCHs could also take care of three additional children aged two through thirteen. Therefore, they could provide 825 child-hours of care for the older group. That leaves 1577 child-hours of care needed. Since six children two through thirteen can be cared for, each for 30.4 hours, it would require an additional 8.65 FDCHs for the other 1577 child-hours. Therefore a total of 17.7 new FDCHs would be needed, as reported previously.

25. In seeking non-day care full-time employment.

26. I use the rate for newly covered workers, $1.90 per hour.

27. The mean fee per hour per child was $0.58 in Seattle and $0.47 in Denver.

28. This is calculated by dividing Measure 3, line 5, Table 8-8 by 100 X line 7, Table 8-7.

29. To estimate the cost per child, or the percentage increase in cost for noncomplying centers only, divide the numbers in columns 2, 3, 5, or 6 by the numbers in column 4 or 7; e.g., the cost per child for the noncomplying private, profit centers in Seattle under Case 1 is $53.61 ($23 ÷ 0.429).

30. In March 1972 a national estimate of day care center capacity was given as 805,361. The average rate of growth of capacity since 1967 was 15.4 percent per year. Using that percentage, I estimate center capacity in mid-1974 to be 1,072,500 children. Assuming that 85 percent of capacity is utilized, on the average, I estimate that the number of children enrolled in centers nationally would be 911,625. The original data were obtained from *Child Care: Data and Materials*, Table 21, pp. 58-59, U.S. Senate Committee on Finance, 93rd Congress, Second Session, October 1974.

Appendix 8A
Alternative Compliance Cost
Estimates for Centers

Mean Value (Average) Data

Compliance cost for centers based on distributional data as presented in the text is perhaps the most policy-relevant measure to use, especially for determining the short-run effect of enforcing the federal day care standards. However, as stated previously, another estimate of compliance cost, based on the mean (average) values of child/staff ratios for all centers, may also be of importance for policy choice. The extent of its importance is related to how one views the market mechanism operating in the day care sector, as discussed in the chapter.

Table 8A-1 compares the number of staff needed and employed per center, given the ratios shown in Table 8-2 and the average number of children by age who were enrolled as of the survey period.

From Table 8A-1 it is apparent that for Seattle, under all but the most stringent standards (Case 2 maximum), centers on the average have enough regular paid staff to comply with the required federal child/staff ratios. Even in the most stringent case, it is only the private, for-profit centers that have any sizable difference between the staff needed and the number employed.[1] In Denver, on the average, more staff is needed in the private, for-profit sector for every alternative child/staff standard used; this is even true on the average for the nonprofit centers when the standards of Case 2 maximum are used. To obtain an estimate of the cost for compliance with federal standards in those instances where a staff deficiency is shown in Table 8A-1, I will use the average annual rate of pay for regular paid staff members for the three proprietary groups.

As can be seen from Table 8A-1, only for Case 2 maximum are significant staffing deficiencies indicated by the average data.[2] As stated previously, that situation provides the most stringent standards and can be viewed as the upper bound of compliance costs. Table 8A-2 shows the costs of compliance in accordance with Case 2 maximum standards for each type of center in Seattle and Denver. To achieve these standards, costs per center, based on the average values for the centers in the sample, would have to be increased substantially. In Denver those standards imply an average increase in total costs per child per year of $184 for the profit-making centers. In Denver even the public, nonprofit centers would have an increase in their total cost of $48 per child per year under the new standards. Although the absolute number of additional staff needed by the public, nonprofit centers is fairly low, the higher annual wages of their staff,

213

Table 8A-1
Staff Needed and Staff Employed per Center

| | Nonprofit | | | | For-Profit Private | |
| | Private | | Public | | | |
	Minimum	Maximum	Minimum	Maximum	Minimum	Maximum
Seattle						
Case 1–Staff Needed[a]	7.7	7.7	4.8	4.8	6.7	6.7
Case 2–Staff Needed[a]	7.8	10.2	5.0	6.4	6.8	9.0
Staff Employed[b]	9.9	9.9	9.0	9.0	7.5	7.5
Denver						
Case 1–Staff Needed[a]	8.7	8.7	10.1	10.1	10.1	10.1
Case 2–Staff Needed[a]	8.8	11.9	10.2	13.4	10.1	13.9
Staff Employed[b]	11.3	11.3	12.9	12.9	9.3	9.3

[a]This represents the number of staff required for the centers to comply with federal child/staff standards, given the number and age of the enrolled children. These values are given for the two cases and two alternatives shown in Table 8-2.

[b]Refers to regular paid staff employed as of the survey date.

Table 8A-2

Maximum Staff Needed per Center to Conform to Federal Child/Staff Standards[a] and Cost of Complying with These Standards[b]

	Seattle			Denver		
	Nonprofit		For-Profit Private	Nonprofit		For-Profit Private
	Private	Public		Private	Public	
Case 2 Maximum						
Additional Staff Needed[c]	0.3	—	1.5	0.6	0.5	4.6
Annual Cost of Additional Staff[d]	$828	—	$3,076	$1,660	$2,852	$11,873
Annual Compliance Cost per Currently Enrolled Child	$17.96	—	$74.84	$30.57	$47.61	$183.79
Annual Compliance Cost per Week per Currently Enrolled Child[e]	$0.34	—	$1.44	$0.59	$0.92	$3.53

[a]Where staff needed minus staff employed > 0 (see Table 8A-1).

[b]Since the costs given are averages for all centers, to find the aggregate cost of compliance we would have to multiply the costs in this table by the number of centers in the different proprietary groups.

[c]Equals staff needed minus staff employed, assuming a deficiency exists (see Table 8A-1).

[d]Equals additional staff needed times annual pay for regular employed staff.

[e]Equals annual compliance cost per child divided by 52.

relative to other proprietary types, leads to higher total annual costs of compliance for the public centers.[3]

Under the most stringent standards, compliance would result in a significant increase in fees for users of private, profit-oriented centers if the costs were passed along to the user. In Seattle the weekly fee for a standard 40-hour week per child was $20.01 in profit-making centers, and $24.02 for similar centers in Denver. The additional cost for profit-oriented centers comes to $1.44 per week per child in Seattle and $3.53 per week per child in Denver.[4] These costs represent increases of about 7 percent in Seattle and almost 15 percent in Denver.

Comparing the staff deficiencies and the compliance costs shown in Tables 8-3 and 8-4, where data from each center were used, with those from Tables 8A-1 and 8A-2, where mean values were used, shows how the use of averages hides the extreme values in staffing deficiencies and compliance cost. In the results using average values, some of the deficiencies are offset by the excess staff in conforming centers. In Seattle, for example, the aggregate data showed staff deficiencies only for the nonprofit, private and for-profit centers for Case 2 maximum (see Table 8A-1), whereas in Table 8-3 we find that there are some deficiencies for all cases and alternatives for each proprietary type. Even for the nonprofit, public centers, some staff deficiencies were observed, although the total number of additional staff needed was small. More important, some larger deficiencies in individual centers were averaged out in Table 8A-1. For example, in Table 8A-2 the private, nonprofit centers in Seattle showed an average deficiency of 0.3 staff in Case 2 maximum. Since 35 private, nonprofit centers were surveyed, the total number of additional staff needed, given the average deficiency, was 10.5. From Table 8-3, however, we find, using Case 2 maximum, that 22 of the 25 private, nonprofit centers needed an additional 67.4 staff to make up for their deficiencies, while the remaining 13 private, nonprofit centers had at least the minimum number of staff needed for the number of children enrolled, given the required child/staff standards.

Public Centers as a Yardstick

The methods used above provide only a very rough approximation to the costs of compliance with regard to all federal standards concerning day care centers. If we assume that public, nonprofit centers are just in full compliance,[5] we can obtain an alternative estimate of compliance costs for private centers.[6] This estimate tells us the compliance cost if all centers conformed to the standards involved in public, nonprofit centers. The estimate will be derived in Table 8A-3. It should, however, be taken as a ballpark estimate of the compliance costs needed for meeting all requirements, including those implied in the child/staff standards.

The additional cost per week per child shown in line 8 of Table 8A-3 is very large in comparison with the current fee per child for a standard 40-hour week of care. If the additional cost implied in line 8 were levied against users, the weekly cost per child would rise over 75% for the private, nonprofit centers and by over 120 percent for the private, profit-making centers in Seattle; the comparable increases in weekly fees in Denver would be 157 and 90 percent for the private, nonprofit and profit-oriented centers.[7]

Notes

1. The offsetting adjustments with regard to volunteer help and capacity utilization discussed in Appendix 8B are also relevant here.

2. Moreover, about one-fourth of the currently enrolled children attend the centers part time in both Seattle and Denver. These are generally the school-age children. The average hours per day that they attend centers is 4.8 in Seattle and 4.6 in Denver, whereas full-time children are at the center an average of 8.4 and 8.5 hours per day in Seattle and Denver. Therefore, if the child/staff deficiencies were adjusted for part-time involvement, there would be an even lower degree of noncompliance. However, this may be offset by the fact that, on the average, regular paid employees worked 29.2 hours per week in Seattle and 32.8 hours per week in Denver.

3. It is also true that the compliance costs are underestimated by the extent to which labor costs are less than 100 percent of the operating costs. However, only the nonstaff operating costs that are a function of the total number of staff members employed should be included. A priori I feel that most of the nonstaff operating costs are related to the number of children enrolled and not to the number of staff employed.

4. Assuming a full 52 weeks per year use of center services (see Table 8A-2).

5. The point that public centers do not exceed requirements is critical here.

6. As mentioned previously, a more meaningful way to look at the use of public centers as a yardstick is to say that the public centers provide a level of child care that would be an acceptable standard for all centers to achieve under the federal guidelines.

7. This would still not include the cost of such expenses as health tests provided and paid for by public, nonprofit centers.

Table 8A-3
Estimates of Cost for Compliance with Standards Found in the Average Public Center

	Seattle				Denver			
	Nonprofit		Public	For-Profit Private	Total	Nonprofit	Public	For-Profit Private
	Total	Private				Private		
1. Ratio of Currently Enrolled Children to Regular Paid Staff	4.6:1	4.6:1	3.3:1	5.5:1	5.4:1	4.8:1	4.6:1	6.9:1
2. Additional Staff Needed to Reach Ratio for Public, Nonprofit Centers[a]	3.7	3.8	—	4.9	1.9	0.5	—	4.7
3. Average Annual Variable Cost per Regular Paid Employee (Includes Current Market Value of Equipment)	$5,751	$6,159	$6,910	$4,453	$7,228	$4,513	$9,268	$6,122
4. Amount Needed per Employee to Equal Costs for Public, Nonprofit Centers[b]	$1,159	$851	—	$2,457	$2,040	$4,755	—	$3,146
5. Annual Variable Costs for Additional Staff Needed at the Rate Applicable to Public, Nonprofit Center[c]	$25,567	$26,258	—	$33,859	$17,609	$4,634	—	$43,560
6. Additional Variable Cost Needed per Regular Paid Employee to Bring Variable Cost to Public, Nonprofit Center Level for Currently Employed Staff[d]	$10,431	$8,425	—	$18,428	$22,848	$53,732	—	$29,258
7. Sum of Lines 5 and 6	$35,998	$34,683	—	$52,287	$40,457	$58,366	—	$72,818
8. Additional Cost for Compliance with All Standards per Currently Enrolled Child per Week[e]	$16.52	$14.46	—	$24.46	$12.94	$20.67	—	$21.67

[a]This is computed by determining the number of paid staff needed by each of the other centers to reach the child/staff ratio for public, nonprofit centers. Then the actual number of paid staff employed is subtracted from that derived staff requirement.

[b]Equals the difference between the average annual variable cost for public, nonprofit centers (in line 3) and the similar cost for the other proprietary types (in line 3).

[c]Equals the public, nonprofit variable cost in line 3 times the additional staff required in line 2.

[d]Equals line 4 times the number of regular paid staff members currently employed.

[e]Equals line 7 divided by the number of currently enrolled children.

Appendix 8B
Estimates of Bias

Volunteer Staff in Centers

Since I do not include volunteer help in determining compliance of centers with federal child/staff standards, and since volunteers are acceptable in meeting federal standards, compliance costs, where staffing is deficient, are higher than would be necessary. Using the limited data collected on volunteers, I estimate the extent of that bias to be between 5 and 18 percent in Seattle and 1 to 6 percent in Denver. These estimates are based on the ratio of volunteers to paid staff and the ratio of average hours of child care work provided by volunteers to the hours provided by regular paid staff. Table 8B-1 sets out the data used.

The data collected from volunteers were very limited: only 33 out of 372 volunteers returned their staff supplement questionnaires. Therefore, the data used in Table 8B-1 are not reliable, especially because the returned questionnaires were not a random selection from the total population. However, it is the only information on the use of volunteers that I could get from the survey. I was told by respondents involved in local child care activities that the percentage of volunteer involvement appeared "reasonable." The estimated bias can be used as a rough deflator of the compliance costs estimated in Chapter 8.

Table 8B-1
Estimated Extent of Bias from Excluding Volunteers

	(a) Ratio of Volunteers to Regular Paid Staff		(b) Ratio of Average Hours of Work for Volunteers to Average Hours for Regular Paid Staff		(c) Estimated Bias in Compliance Cost by Not Including Volunteers as Staff [percent (a × b × 100)]	
	Seattle	Denver	Seattle	Denver	Seattle	Denver
Nonprofit						
Private	0.626	0.133	0.284	0.253	17.8	3.4
Public	0.289	0.248	0.284	0.253	8.2	6.3
For-Profit						
Private	0.173	0.032	0.284	0.253	4.9	0.8

Staff Utilization Assumptions

The figures on center staff deficiencies in Table 8–2 are biased downward because of the assumption that additional staff are fully utilized in accordance with the federal child/staff requirements; that is, I assume that the additional staff are in attendance for the total time that the center cares for full-time children. Moreover, the converse is also assumed to be true, that is, that the full-time children are in attendance for the time that the staff are there. This means child care capacity for new staff is fully utilized. However, from the data we know that there is some underutilization of capacity. As in industrial activities, there may be some "normal" level of capacity utilization that is below the theoretical 100 percent level. If that is true for the child care industry, it means that we have to inflate the additional staff needed to take into account this "normal" level of underutilization. To obtain some idea of the possible extent of that inflation, the following capacity utilization rates for centers computed from the survey data are provided:

	Percent of Capacity Utilized	
	Seattle	*Denver*
Nonprofit, private	74.9%	81.4%
Nonprofit, public	73.1	84.9
For-profit, private	78.4	83.7

This implies that the number of additional staff needed might have to be increased by 15 to 27 percent to take into account capacity utilization. However, this could be considered as an offset to the deflation implied by not including volunteer staff and by assuming that all children are to be treated equally in computing child/staff ratios (see note 4 of Chapter 8).

Another source of downward bias in the number of additional staff needed is my use of all staff members in calculating staffing deficiencies; that is, I had to include some staff that do not work with children, such as cooks. These staff members are not allowed to be used in determining compliance with federal child/staff standards. The number of such staff included in the enumeration of regular paid staff from the survey is approximately 6 percent of the total in both Seattle and Denver. That percentage indicates the order of magnitude by which the additional staff needed is underestimated because of the inability to exclude staff that do not interact directly with children. If I could properly exclude that group, compliance costs would be slightly higher than those presented in Table 8–4.

Appendix 8C
Day Care Survey

Introduction

In a survey operation one rarely has the resources to undertake both an extensive and an intensive investigation.[1] The Abt study was an indepth, intensive look into a handful of high-quality child care center operations;[2] whereas the Westinghouse-Westat study provided a broad, extensive review of a large number of child care operations.[3] In the former, you can get at details, such as the provision of in-kind services or the relationship between day care operations and tax writeoffs. Such detailed data can rarely be obtained in the survey attempting to obtain a broader coverage. Given a budget restriction, what is chosen depends on the research design and the questions that design elicits.[4]

I attempted to go more in depth than the Westinghouse-Westat survey yet include a larger sample for coverage than the Abt survey. Therefore, the survey was not as extensive as the former and not nearly as intensive as the latter. My compromise did, however, provide detailed data on a sufficiently large sample to enable reliable estimates of the supply relationships in the Seattle and Denver child care industry to be obtained.

My preliminary review of the child care industry indicated that it is composed of three main sectors: centers, family day care homes (licensed and unlicensed), and in-home providers. Three basic survey instruments were designed to obtain the needed data from each of the three child care sectors. Following is a discussion of the sample selected for the survey and of some problems that arose in the data collection process. However, this discussion will be concerned only with compliance costs for centers and licensed family day care homes. Therefore, issues and problems associated with unlicensed family day care homes and in-home providers will not be discussed.

Sample Selection

The size of the sample was based on estimates of the total population size in the two relevant sectors of the industry, along with the budget limitation for the survey. Estimates of the population of centers and licensed family day care homes (FDCHs) in both Seattle and Denver are very reliable, although there is a significant turnover in the latter sector.

There were 74 eligible centers within the city limits of Seattle and 50 in Denver. All centers were to be included in the survey. There were seven refusals (about 9.5 percent) in Seattle and three refusals (about 6 percent) in Denver. Consequently, I was able to obtain 67 completed interviews in Seattle[5] and 47 completions in Denver.

The SIME/DIME state liaison people gave me current lists of licensed FDCHs in Seattle and Denver. From these lists I selected a random sample for the survey consisting of 29 percent of the Seattle and about 44 percent of the Denver FDCH population. The refusal rate in this sector was almost 10 percent in Seattle and 1 percent in Denver. The total of licensed FDCH questionnaires completed was 214 in Seattle and 167 in Denver.

Problems in Data Collection

Interviewing began on May 2, 1974 and ended, with the exception of a few hard-to-reach cases, by June 7, 1974.[6] In almost all instances, this meant that the interviews were done during the regular school year. However, May 30 (Memorial Day) was included in the survey period, and some adjustments were needed to account for the fact that most users did not have their children in day care facilities on Memorial Day. The adjustment was mainly concerned with using the mean number of children cared for during other days of the Memorial Day week to estimate the number of children who would have been cared for during the missing day if it had been a regular work day.

The list of licensed FDCHs in Denver is not complete because anyone who does not want her name used in a referral is not placed on the list compiled by referral agencies. Since I used that list to determine the total population of licensed FDCHs in Denver, the FDCH count is not accurate. Fortunately, only a small number of licensed FDCHs refuse to be listed.

Of the sample of unlicensed FDCHs selected, 17 were later found to be licensed. This usually came to my attention during the interview, when the unlicensed FDCH respondent would answer "yes" to question 501 (Are you licensed by an agency of the city or state as a family day care home operator?). For those who were later confirmed to be licensed, I changed their ID number to reflect their actual condition, thereby placing them in the licensed FDCH sample. The same problem did not exist in Seattle, since all licensees are on the list supplied by the Department of Social and Health Services.

A supplemental questionnaire was left behind at each center interview for distribution to each center employee. After completion of her individual supplement, the staff member was asked to seal the form in an enclosed envelope and return it to the center director, who was to forward all the staff supplements to the Urban Opinion Survey office. Although a large number of these staff questionnaires were returned, a significant number were not. For the regular paid staff, of 1128 questionnaires distributed in both cities, 612 (54.3 percent) were returned; for volunteers, only 8.9 percent of 372 questionnaires were returned.

Notes

1. This discussion will be concerned only with licensed facilities because, as pointed out in the chapter, these are the only facilities for which I will estimate the costs of compliance with federal standards.

2. Abt Associates, Inc., *A Study in Child Care 1970-1971,* Volumes I-III.

3. Westinghouse Learning Corp. and Westat Research, Inc., *Day Care Survey—1970,* April 1971.

4. See, for example, Paul A. Samuelson, "Parable and Realism in Capital Theory: The Surrogate Production Function," *The Review of Economic Studies* (June 1962): 193-194.

5. Two were partially completed. However, the data needed for estimation of compliance cost were obtained.

6. I will point out only problems that are relevant to the estimation of compliance costs.

Index

Index

About the Contributors

Arden Hall is an economist at the Center for the Study of Welfare Policy, SRI International. He received the Masters degree in statistics and the doctorate in economics from the University of California. His research interests include the economics of education and job search behavior as well as child care.

Meredith A. Larson, a policy analyst in the Educational Policy Research Center at SRI International, is currently on leave serving with the staff of the Subcommittee on Elementary, Secondary and Vocational Education of the U.S. House of Representatives. Ms. Larson has carried out research in several areas of federal policy including adolescent compensatory education, educational administration, and day care. She has authored numerous reports including: "Survey of Basic Skills Program for Adolescents in Seven States," "Better Basic Skills for Youth: Four Proposals for Federal Policy," "Federal Policy for Preschool Services: Assumptions and Evidence," and "Adolescence: Alternative Strategies for Compensatory Education."

James D. Marver is a policy analyst in the Educational Policy Research Center, SRI International, and a lecturer at California State University, San Jose. His articles and reviews have appeared in a number of educational and political science journals, and he has consulted to the National Academy of Sciences and American Public Health Association. He is a doctoral candidate at the Graduate School of Public Policy at the University of California, Berkeley.

Robert G. Spiegelman is director of the Center for the Study of Welfare Policy at SRI International. Dr. Spiegelman received the Ph.D. in economics from Columbia University. He has been involved in economic analysis of government programs at SRI International for the past 18 years. During the past 7 years, he has served as project leader and principal investigator of the Seattle and Denver Income Maintenance Experiments. Dr. Spiegelman has had numerous publications on the design and evaluation of social experiments.

Jane Stallings is manager of Classroom Process Studies at SRI International She received the B.A. from Ball State and the Ph.D. from Stanford University. She is the author of *Learning to Look,* a handbook on classroom observation and teaching models.

Susan Stoddard, M.C.P., is senior analyst, Berkeley Planning Associates. She is a candidate for the Ph.D. in planning at the University of California, Berkeley. In her dissertation research, she was a participant-observer in the planning, design, and implementation of the Santa Clara Child Care Pilot Study, conducted by the

Califoinia State Department of Education. Previously she was, for two years, chairperson of the Marin County, California, Child Care Planning and Advisory Council. Ms. Stoddard serves on the faculties of the University of California Extension/Berkeley and Antioch College/West, where she teaches courses in planning and economic analysis.

Mary Wilcox is a senior education researcher at SRI International. She received the B.A. from the University of California, Berkeley, and the Ph.D. from Stanford University. She has experience as a classroom teacher and an elementary school principal.

About the Editors

Philip K. Robins is a senior economist in the Center for the Study of Welfare Policy, SRI International. He received the Ph.D. degree in economics from the University of Wisconsin. For the past several years he has been associated with the Seattle and Denver Income Maintenance Experiments as a principal researcher. He has authored numerous articles in the fields of child care, labor supply, and housing.

Samuel Weiner is an economist in the Center for the Study of Welfare Policy, SRI International. He has been a research economist with a large labor union, a research and teaching assistant at Stanford University, and a Research Associate at the Brookings Institution. He received the B.A. from the University of Illinois and the M.A. from Stanford University in economics. He has authored numerous articles and reports on child care, drug abuse, and economic aspects of medical education, as well as a book on the federal reserve system and the supply of money.